THE ABCs
OF COOKING

THE ABCs
OF COOKING

by Charlotte Adams

DRAWINGS BY MONA MARK

DOUBLEDAY & COMPANY, INC.
Garden City, New York

Library of Congress Cataloging in Publication Data

Adams, Charlotte, 1899–
The ABCs of cooking.

Includes index.
1. Cookery. I. Title.
TX651.A33 1983 641
ISBN 0-385-18512-X
Library of Congress Catalog Card Number 82-45139

FOR

SUSAN BINGER

*With admiration, respect
and great affection*

Contents

Introduction

Cooking is one of the most satisfying and creative experiences anyone can have. In my opinion, every boy and every girl who's born into this world should learn to cook. Too many people today never have that sort of training. When they are faced with providing food for themselves and guests and, eventually, for a family, the pickings are unhappily pretty slim and also pretty dull. Be assured that it's a great thrill to produce a delectable dish, and an even greater thrill to present it to an appreciative family and/or friends. The purpose of this book is to give you the answers to questions that arise in the minds of every cook—experienced or not. It is intended to be used for reference by the novice who wants to avoid pitfalls or to rescue herself or himself from disasters, by the food writer who wants to make sure of a fact, by the knowing cook who wants to check the authenticity of one dish or the basic proportions involved in another.

It is taken for granted that you will own at least one basic cookbook and, I hope, as many specialized ones as you want or can afford. There is only one complete recipe in this book, and it is used for a reason other than that you might want to make it!

You will find here a minimum of material on nutrition. This is not the result of indifference or oversight, and I should like to explain why it is so. Nutrition is a rapidly and marvelously growing science. The best of the nutritionists are the first to tell you that we have learned a great deal in the past few decades—and have probably barely scratched the surface of what we shall one day know. As research goes on, nutrition information changes constantly. In my opinion, the best way to keep up with its findings is through newspapers, government pamphlets, the Journal of the American Medical Association, and similar current publications. It is also my opinion that one reads such material with care and interest, being sure to discover, if possible, whether findings are definite, controversial, or frankly "iffy," as they sometimes are. One waits for the absolute before changing the whole family's pattern of eating. So! Read, weigh, and be calm. Often some warning regarding the dangers inherent in eating certain foods is totally reversed in a couple of years. Often the first alarming reports are only possibilities, not proven.

Avoid fad diets and fad foods. Often their use is a sure sign of hypochondria. These fads are not only foolish, but may be downright dangerous to health. The American public, unhappily, contains entirely too many people who are ready to jump at the first quack diet or pill purporting to thin them down or make them young and vigorous—or whatever may be their ambition of the moment. A lot of illness and even hospitalization, due to malnutrition, results from such jumping at magic cure-alls.

Above all, I wish you joy in your cooking, and hope that this book may be a help in achieving that happy state of mind.

C.A.

THE ABCs
OF COOKING

1. How to Make a Food Budget

If you've never had a good food budget because you hate the thought, be of good cheer: You are one of many so minded. However, be assured that if you once make such a budget, find it suitable for your family's needs, and stick to it, a complicated problem will be solved and you will be much happier and more comfortable about life in general.

How do you start this project? Well, it is a gradual process and can be taken in easy stages. First, decide about how much you'd like to spend for food. Such a decision can be only tentative. After you've tried it for at least a month, review the situation and revise your budget if necessary—either up or (good luck!) down. Keep careful records of everything you buy and just what it cost. It will be an enlightening experience.

No set percentage of income to be spent on food can be suggested in times of inflation. The proportion you spend in that area is a very individual matter. Time was when we were told to spend about 20 percent to 33⅓ percent of our total income, but with prices fluctuating wildly (and mostly upward), it is impossible to lay down such rules. In the end, the larger the income, the lower the percentage spent on food, which is cold comfort for those on the lower end of the scale. Nevertheless, we all must eat and will do it better if we plan carefully, rather than take the haphazard route.

Keep good track of special sales in the food markets. This is often a great help in cutting or holding down food costs. Try to buy fresh foods in season and, insofar as possible, locally grown. For example, I love avocados. A few months ago I decided that I would buy one only if it cost less than a dollar; I was able to buy very few under that limitation. However, a couple of days ago, as I wandered through a market, I found them for thirty-five cents apiece! It was like receiving a present!

Most people do not realize that a food budget *must* include the cost of meals eaten in restaurants or clubs. Following this rule, you may find it impossible to eat outside the home with any frequency. Sad as that may seem to you, you will probably be able, on the same basic budget, to afford better food at home because you're not spending cash on labor (which is often the major portion of the cost of food eaten "out") and other frills.

Do *not* include in your record of food expenditures such non-food items as paper towels, cleaning materials, polishes, garbage bags, and the like. They are household expenditures, to be sure, but you can't eat them, though you buy them in the same place as you do food.

Shop in person as much as you possibly can. It enables you to do some comparison shopping, which is an absolute *must* if you're serious about saving money on food. Try "house brands" which you will find in the big supermarket chains. They are always less expensive than the big-name brands we all know about. On the other hand, buy only one sample of any food you haven't yet tried in the house brand in question. You may not like it—food you waste is no bargain.

If your aim is to work out a food budget that will save you as much money as possible, think about the large economy size in canned and sometimes frozen foods. Whether it's a real bargain for you depends largely on two things: the size of your family and the extent of your storage space. If there are sales on such items and yours is a large family, chances are you can find a place to store a case or whatever quantity you want to buy. If you are a single person, your refrigerator space may not serve to keep the food in question fit for consumption until you use it all. In that case, it wouldn't constitute a bargain.

If you grow some of your own food and either preserve or freeze some of it, you will probably not only save money but will certainly eat better. If you live in a situation where you can do this, you will also probably be well equipped to store as much as you can prepare of such foods.

2. Planning Menus

First, check your refrigerator to see what leftover foods might be incorporated into your plans. Then decide what else is needed to make them into tasty dishes. Check your newspapers and radio reports for plentiful foods. Read your cookbooks for inspiration. As you do all these things, make lists of foods needed. When you decide to make a specific recipe, list every ingredient required to prepare it. Then check your staple shelves and refrigerator to be sure you have all the items required. Now make your market list, including every staple and fresh food you require.

It's a good idea to plan menus for a week in advance if you have leeway for changes due to unexpected factors, such as bargains in the market, last-minute guests, or last-minute invitations for yourself. It is perhaps easiest for a housewife with a large family to plan meals for a whole week ahead because the number of people to be fed is relatively constant in her setup. In reverse, the woman or man who lives alone, unless a misanthrope, is likely to be invited out to dinner frequently. Therefore, for her or for him, planning and marketing far ahead is likely to waste food.

It is necessary to plan all three meals for each day, not just dinner —that is, if you expect your family to eat them. Breakfast is, for instance, an exceedingly important meal. It gives you the impetus for the morning's work, a right start for the day. Therefore, variety is important, to offer the essential appetite appeal. Although you may proceed with breakfast on the conventional plan of fruit, cereal or eggs, toast and coffee, the meal can be varied by serving different kinds of fruit in season, sometimes cold cereals, sometimes hot; cooking the eggs in different ways; serving them sometimes with bacon or sausage or scrapple; and offering muffins or coffee cake occasionally, instead of toast, which can be varied itself if you provide different kinds of bread and a variety of jams or marmalades to go with it. Planning for lunch is equally important. To be sure, lunch offers a fine opportunity to use up leftovers, which make some of the best dishes in the world if combined and cooked properly. But you cannot always count on having leftovers, so you must be prepared at least with canned or frozen foods which you can produce for lunch at a moment's notice.

To Avoid Running Out of Staples

The best way I know is to keep a pad, fastened somewhere in the kitchen, on which you write down every staple you use, when you find it is dwindling. Only you can know whether, in your house, you should buy more flour if you have only five pounds left, or if you have only a cup (in some houses a cup might last weeks). But if you do keep this running list and check it every time you are making a market list, you should never run out of anything.

3. How to Make a Market List

No one should ever go to market without a well-planned market list. It may surprise you to know that many people don't make such a list. If that's the case, it shows that you do, so you've got a head start already. People who do not make market lists inevitably forget some things they need and have to go back to get them. They also wander around the market looking at food items, in an effort to remember what it was they needed and in the process do at least a little of that "impulse buying" which is the prime wrecker of any food budget. Impulse buying is what happens most often when the master of the house goes to the food market. If he was given a good list, he may bring home everything on it. If he has no list, he may forget practically everything he was told to buy. *But,* in either case, impulse buying will lead him to throw the food budget completely askew, and he will come home with smoked oysters, fancy biscuits, too many kinds of beautiful cheeses, black or tree-ripened olives, instead of the stuffed ones on the list, and so on and on! There are women who behave this way, too, but men are best at it and are therefore the darlings of food merchants.

After you've planned your menu or menus, look up the recipes you propose to use and make a list of ingredients needed. Now check all the staple foods required (milk, sugar, salt, flour, etc.) to make sure you have an adequate supply. You now put together the list on your kitchen pad and the one you've made for the menu or menus you've planned. Here's how to do it to save yourself time and money.

Make a habit of writing your final shopping list as nearly as possible in divisions which will fit the layout of your market. If you know your market well (which you should take time to do), this is quite possible. Be it said, however, that some markets have no signs at all to designate what's to be found in the various aisles, and others have signs which are so vague that it's very difficult to find what you need. If you are confronted with either of these situations, think seriously of changing to a market where sections are well marked. In fact, plan a search to uncover one.

Here's a possible division of sections into which you might divide your list:

Meat

Eggs, butter or margarine, milk, cheese

Fresh fruits and vegetables

Canned goods

Frozen products

Dried foods (rice, pastas, beans, etc.)

Cereals

Baked goods and baking mixes

Coffee and tea

Staples (flour, salt, sugar, oils, vinegar, baking powder, etc.)

Seasonings (herbs and spices, condiments like catsup, chocolate, and cocoa)

Non-food items (paper products, mops, brushes, scouring cloths and powders)

In case you are troubled by the fact that you're not quite sure how much of certain foods you should buy for your purposes, here is a list which will help you with some of the basics. If you or your family have appetites which are either colossal or tiny, adjust for that.

Meats, Poultry, and Fish

Without bone (chopped beef, liver, sausage, veal cutlet, etc.): ¼ to ½ pound per person

With moderate amount of bone (steak, roasts, chops): ½ to ¾ pound per person

With much bone (neck, breast, spareribs, short ribs): 1 pound per person

Broiler-fryers: ¼ to ½ bird per person
Roasters: ¾ to 1 pound per person
Stewing Chicken: ½ pound per person
Duck: 1 to 1¼ pound per person
Turkey: ¾ to 1 pound per person
Solid-meat fish: (salmon, halibut, etc.) ¼ to ⅓ pound per person
Fish with bones in (trout, mackerel, blue, etc.): ½ pound per person

Dairy Foods

Eggs: 1 per person per day
Butter or Margarine: Buy a week's supply at a time, not more.
Milk: Children: 3 to 4 cups daily; teenagers: 1 quart or more daily; adults: 2 or more cups daily; pregnant women: 1 quart or more daily; nursing mothers: 1½ quarts or more.
Cheese: Buy ½ to 1 pound at a time, depending upon frequency of use.

Fresh Vegetables

Leafy: ⅓ to ½ pound per person
In shell (peas, beans): ½ pound per person
Stalk types (broccoli, asparagus): ⅓ to ½ pound per person
Root types (beets, carrots, turnips, potatoes): ¼ to ⅓ pound per person
Corn: 1 to 3 ears per person
Eggplant (medium): Serves 3–4
Tomatoes: ⅓ pound or 1 medium per person

Fruits

Quantities of fruit to buy are fairly obvious—half a grapefruit or cantaloupe per person; an apple or banana per person. The amount to buy at one time varies greatly with eating habits, so the decision on quantity rests largely on the family's likes and dislikes.

Frozen Vegetables

One package serves two big appetites, three average appetites, or four bird-like ones.

Cans

Weight	Cups	Servings
8-ounce	1	1–2
10½-ounce	1¾	3
16–17-ounce	2	3–4
1 pound, 4-ounce	2½	4–5
1 pound, 13-ounce	3½	6–7

4. Shopping for Food

If you have taken seriously our advice on making a market list, you are well on your way to doing an expeditious job on shopping. Armed with that list, you will sally forth to market, knowing that you will be able to cover your needs with reasonable speed, which is a matter of importance to anyone who is a cook and bottle-washer.

A full-time housekeeper should not have to go to market every day. If you plan your meals for a week ahead, you should be able to do the bulk of your marketing on one day. Perishable foods and forgotten items (everybody has some of those) will have to be picked up at more frequent intervals, but daily visits to the market should not be necessary if you plan well. The best time of day for the full-time type to go to the market is either as early in the morning as possible, or between twelve and two, when many people are having lunch. In either case, you avoid crowds and can accomplish your job in a reasonable length of time without having to hurry. You also help the working people who cannot shop at those times, by not adding to the crowds that appear at the end of the day or in the evening.

People who live alone and have jobs as well do better to shop for food daily. They are more free than families to accept (and give) last-minute invitations. Thus, sometimes they have to get in food for several people unexpectedly—and on the other hand, can skip marketing if they've accepted an invitation for dinner that very night.

This whole matter is somewhat determined by what freezing-compartment space is available. One who has plenty of that can always keep on hand the makings of a meal for one or two. You can do approximately the same thing with canned goods. Perishables are best bought at the last possible moment, no matter how you live.

There's no one answer to the question of whether it's better to shop in supermarkets or in small independent stores. If you find it possible to keep careful track of where bargains are to be had, you will probably find them in both types of store. Often you can get standard foods at exactly the same price in a small independent store as in a supermarket—sometimes even for less. Both types have special sales. Some relatively expensive stores are worth using for special items. Some are expensive and not always to be relied upon. Some stores where merchandise is cheap offer goods of poor quality. However, if you shop in them carefully and in person, you may find real bargains.

Some people claim that shopping in supermarkets is necessarily confusing. This is only true if either you or the store management is basically disorganized. Either can happen. If you know your supermarket as you should, and thus are aware of approximately where each of the items you want is to be found, all should go smoothly. No matter where they are situated, however, the refrigerated items should be picked up next to last and the frozen, last of all.

It is really best to buy food in person if you possibly can. However, if you must save time rather than money, you will frequently have to order food by telephone. If that is the case with you, at least appear in your market often enough at the start so that you get to know the personnel—and they, you. You will thus establish the standard you require, and they will, by and large, do well by your telephone orders.

Stores that provide delivery service usually have prices slightly higher than stores that do not. The reason is that such service requires more personnel, takes more time, and sometimes involves the expense of operating a truck. All this, naturally, has to be paid for by the consumer. There are also some stores (usually small chains) which will send your food at a specific cost per delivery. This is the only instance in which you can tell exactly how much extra it costs you not to collect your food yourself.

It undoubtedly costs at least a little more to shop in stores where you can have a charge account than in those where you cannot. Such stores have to pay bookkeeping costs and cover occasional losses from bad accounts. For some people, however, it is worth the extra cost. People with children can send them to the store without involving them in the business of taking money and returning change. Working people can order and have foods delivered when they are in their offices, if they have someone at home to pay for them.

It is pleasant, and in many ways advisable, to shop in stores where you become known. However, it is very foolish not to explore as many food stores as you can so that you do not miss new items and bargains. There is never *one* store which has all of them.

Although not everyone will agree with me, I think it is very definitely best, *if* you can find one, to buy meat from an independent butcher. Some butchers in supermarkets will cut meat for you, but I have an absolute horror of the pre-packaged meats in refrigerated chests. Chops turn out not to be of the same size and thickness. The weight or number of items in a package is never exactly what I want. Besides, being friendly with one's butcher is one of the great pleasures in life! Dealing with an independent butcher does not at all necessarily mean that you will pay more for your meat. This is again something worth exploring. Find a good butcher who is not expensive, if you can—they are a disappearing breed. Although it would be fine if everyone knew all about cuts and grades of meat, it will be a long, cold day before that's true, if ever. The butcher knows. He also learns quite quickly exactly the sort of thing you want. Furthermore, if you would really like to learn about meat and what to buy, your butcher, if you make a good friend of him, is the best teacher.

5. How to Store Food

The way you store food is of great importance, perhaps most of all because if it is not properly done, a great deal will be wasted, and in days like these, wasting food is an inexcusable action. Following is a guide for storing certain important foods.

Butter

Butter can be stored in the refrigerator for up to two weeks. It should be tightly wrapped or put into a covered container in the coldest part of the refrigerator. Keep only as much butter in the butter keeper as is needed for immediate use.

Do not let butter stand around at room temperature, so it will spread easily, for any great length of time, because exposure to heat and light hastens rancidity.

Canned Foods

Preferably, canned foods should be stored in a cool, dry place. Rust does not damage canned foods unless it is sufficient to penetrate the cans. However, if your cellar is damp, it is best to store canned foods in a tight cupboard or closet. High temperatures for stored canned foods may impair the color and flavor of some of them, though not their wholesomeness.

It is entirely safe to leave unused canned foods in their cans after the cans have been opened if you cover and refrigerate the can, just as you would store any other cooked food for future use.

Cheese

Cheese should be kept in the refrigerator, since few of us have places to keep cheese at 60 degrees, which is best for the moldy cheese, such as Blue, Roquefort, and Gorgonzola. However, any cheese should be removed from the refrigerator and brought to room temperature at least an hour before it is to be served, in order that it may return to the full flavor which refrigeration dulls.

Cheese stored in the refrigerator should be tightly wrapped to keep out air (Saran Wrap is especially good for this). Most ripened cheese will keep several weeks thus. Hard cheese will keep indefinitely. Cheeses with strong odor, such as Limburger, should be stored tightly covered. Soft cheeses such as cottage, cream, and Camembert should be stored, tightly covered, in the coldest part of the refrigerator and used within five days of purchase.

Meat

Cured and smoked meats may be stored in their original packages. Fresh meats should be in the coldest part of the refrigerator, loosely wrapped, so that the meat may benefit from some circulation of air in the refrigerator. Ground meat should be used within one or two days of purchase. Roasts, chops, steaks, and cold cuts may be held three to five days. Leftover cooked meats and meat dishes should be used within one or two days. Pork should be stored in the refrigerator, loosely wrapped, for not more than a few days. Ground pork is perishable and should be eaten promptly, as should sausage. Uncooked cured pork may be stored longer than fresh pork, but the fat will become rancid if the meat is held too long. Cooked pork should be stored in the refrigerator and used promptly.

Milk

As soon as possible after fresh fluid milk is purchased or delivered, the bottle or carton should be refrigerated. The ideal temperature for storing milk is 40 degrees, which is about that in most mechanical refrigerators.

Evaporated and condensed milk may be stored at room temperature until the container is opened. Then it should be refrigerated in the same way as fresh fluid milk.

Dry milks will keep for several months at room temperatures of 75 degrees or lower, or they may be kept in the refrigerator. They should be stored in tightly covered containers to prevent moisture absorption, which causes off-flavors and makes reconstitution difficult.

6. Making Wise Use of a Small Freezing Compartment

We concentrate in this book on the freezing compartment because there are many more people whose only "freezer" space consists of a compartment in the refrigerator than there are people who own (or have space for) a full-size freezer. The compartment is thus indeed the ABC of freezing food.

If your freezing compartment is relatively small, be very sure to use it for important foods, such as meat, cooked vegetables, ice cream, leftover foods, commercially frozen foods, some frozen egg whites (saved every time you use only a yolk in a sauce or whatever). My pet "always present" frozen necessity is a small plastic bag each of frozen minced parsley and one of minced chives. This is especially important for small households because, no matter how you try, it is relatively difficult to buy a *small* bunch of parsley or of chives. They freeze beautifully, however.

When you're going away and have butter on hand, freeze it. Butter also keeps long and well in the drawer under the freezing compartment, if you have one of those.

There are some foods that don't freeze well. They are not many, but it is well to know which they are: lettuce and other greens, raw vegetables, and fresh fruits of any kind. When most of them are used as ingredients in a mixed dish, however, they may be frozen without damage to texture or flavor. Cooked egg whites become tough when frozen, but if they are grated and then frozen, they're fine. Custard and cream pies do not freeze well. Mayonnaise, by itself, separates when frozen, but can be frozen in combination with other foods. People who have big freezers can freeze bread in them and save a lot of time and trouble in the process, but the owner of a mere freezing compartment cannot afford to waste space that way.

Keep in mind that foods frozen commercially or in a home freezer are done at 0 degrees or lower. Your freezing compartment is never at such a low temperature, so what you freeze in it should be eaten within a week or two for best flavor and texture—and for safety.

It is safe to refreeze food which you have partially defrosted because you wanted to use only part of it, if there are still some ice crystals present or if the foods are still cold. You can judge a good deal by smelling the food you are about to refreeze. If it has any off odor or off color, throw it away.

It is easiest to make sure that you consume the foods in your compartment within safe time limits if you label them on freezer tape or other labels, telling what is in each container and the date it was frozen. You may also keep a running list of what's inside attached to the freezer compartment door with a magnet.

Use space-saving containers for any home-cooked foods you wish to freeze. Round containers waste space. Square or rectangular ones can be stored much more efficiently and thus use every bit of the available space economically. Containers should be rigid, and I find plastic best, though one can freeze certain foods in glass with success. It is important that the tops be airtight. To ensure this for some containers, seal them with freezer tape. As with a home freezer, foods frozen in the freezer compartment must be placed directly on the freezer surface until they are frozen, after which they may be stacked.

You will probably have to keep two ice-cube trays in your freezing compartment all the time to meet your ordinary needs. Store them one on top of the other, always putting the newly filled one underneath, if you have emptied only one. For a party, keep emptying the trays as soon as they are frozen, either into a good ice bucket, with a lid, or into the drawer under the freezing compartment, where they will keep very nicely. If your party is going to be very large, buy extra ice cubes.

7. How to Store Wines

Although the term "wine cellar" implies lots of space, you can take proper care of your wines in a small apartment, if you go about it properly—on a small scale, of course. The main requirements for a wine cellar are good ventilation, a temperature that doesn't go over 60 degrees (up to 70 degrees will do no harm if it doesn't last too long and the change is gradual), and the absence of hot pipes or other heating apparatus nearby.

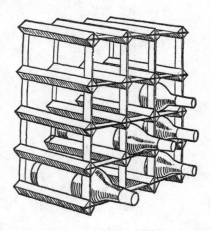

Wines should be stored lying on their sides. Readily available wine racks of wood or metal can take care of this. The reason for laying wine on its side is that it comes in contact with the cork, which thus doesn't dry out. If it were stored standing up, the way fortified wines, liqueurs, and spirits are kept, air would get into the bottle and spoil the wine.

White and sparkling wines should be kept in the coolest part of the storage space, which is the lowest part. Red wines go above them —and on top, spirits, liqueurs, and fortified wines (like sherry).

If your storage possibilities are limited (as most people's are), take care not to overbuy or you will waste a lot, despite the fact that wine, like spirits, is cheaper by the case than the bottle. It isn't cheap if it spoils and is undrinkable. How much wine is consumed in your house in any given length of time, plus the amount of space available, should be your guide to how much you buy at one time.

8. How to Read and Use Recipes

There is a group of people to whom all food writers owe deepest thanks—namely, the ones who say, "I love to read cookbooks, especially when I go to bed at night." Usually, this is followed by, "I don't cook." Although one writes recipes with high hopes that they will be of help to cooks, it's delightful to know that there is another, more or less unsuspected, group of enthusiasts. Without them, it might be rather hard to make a living at one's trade.

There's a great deal of importance in how you read a recipe. First, you should go through the list of ingredients; then, read the instructions with care. Decide whether it's too complicated or time-consuming for you, at the moment or forever. To most good cooks, the matter of time is less important than the result to be attained. However, if one is a working person, there is sometimes just not that much time available and one must concentrate on simple, more or less short-order dishes.

If you do this already, I'm sure you will agree that one most important part of reading a recipe is being able to taste it in your head and decide whether you like the taste. Once you have been able to do this, you will seldom be disappointed in your choices.

If you decide to make a dish that is new to you, the next move is to make a full menu to set it off. Then you go through the list of ingredients, particularly to check on your staple stocks. If you have kept lists as suggested in other sections of this book, that will be a quick process. Make your market list and lay in your supplies. Let's just make a sample menu here to illustrate:

Saturday Dinner

Artichokes Vinaigrette

*

Roast Lamb, Roman Style
Potatoes Anna
Frenched Green Beans, Amandine
Melba Toast

*

Crème Brulée

Market List

6 artichokes
2 10-oz. packages frenched green beans
Melba toast
1 quart cream
1 8-pound leg of lamb

Staples to be checked

Olive oil
Vinegar
Salt and pepper
Rosemary leaves
Sage leaves
Garlic cloves
Flour
Wine vinegar
Anchovy fillets (need 4)
Kitchen bouquet
Potatoes (need 8)

1¼ cups butter (2½ sticks) for potatoes
Slivered almonds
Sugar
8 egg yolks (freeze whites)
Vanilla
Light brown sugar

Roast Lamb Roman Style

1 8-pound leg of lamb
1½ teaspoons salt
¾ teaspoon freshly ground
   black pepper
1 teaspoon rosemary leaves
¼ teaspoon sage leaves
1 small clove garlic, mashed

4 tablespoons flour
¾ cup hot water
¾ cup wine vinegar
2 tablespoons water
4 anchovy fillets, minced
1 teaspoon kitchen bouquet

Place lamb on rack in a roasting pan. Mix salt, pepper, rosemary, sage, garlic and 2 tablespoons of the flour. Rub over lamb and let stand about an hour. Pour hot water and vinegar into the pan. Place in 325-degree oven and roast about 1½ hours (145–150 degrees on meat thermometer) for pink lamb, which this should be, basting occasionally. Remove meat to a hot serving platter. Strain pan drippings. Mix remaining 2 tablespoons flour with the 2 tablespoons water and add to pan drippings. Stir and cook 1 minute to thicken. Add anchovy fillets and kitchen bouquet. Serve sauce with lamb. Serves 6 to 8.

When you get back from market with all the ingredients you need, you're ready to start cooking. Keep the cookbook or clipping or card upon which your recipe appears in front of you on the counter so that you can check each step as you do it. The time may come when you know some recipes so well that you can do them without looking at them, but that's never true the first time. As you continue to reuse various recipes, you may think of ways to improve them and that's just great, but you will have no way of knowing whether the dish is really good if you don't follow instructions to the letter the first time around. A rack for holding the cookbook in comfortable reading position as you work is a great help, though I caution about the clear plastic ones which are so handsome but so fragile that it's practically impossible to work with them and not break them.

A last word about getting to know your sources for good cooking, just as you would insist on knowing your sources for doing a piece of research. It won't take you long to find out which cookbooks are reliable and which are hopelessly unclear—alas, there are both kinds! The same is true of magazine and newspaper food material. There are, of course, reviews written about all these, but in the end the only person to judge what works for you is you. At the start of a cooking career, you'll have to make a few mistakes to find out what works best for you.

9. Cooking Terms and What They Mean

Bake: To cook in the oven (when referring to meats, this is called roasting). Also, occasionally applied to top-of-the-range cooking, as in "baking" pancakes or waffles.

Barbecue: To cook meats over an open fire, indoors or out. Many very complete modern kitchens contain charcoal broilers for such cooking. Meats are sometimes marinated in a sauce before barbecuing.

Baste: To pour or brush melted fat, water, wine, or other liquid over food. This is sometimes done before cooking, to inject flavor and to tenderize meat. It is often done during the cooking process, to keep foods moist and to add flavor.

Beat: To mix briskly with a spoon, rotary beater, or electric beater. A good beating thoroughly mixes all ingredients involved.

Beat Lightly: A term usually applied to eggs, involving sufficient light beating with a fork to mix yolks and whites completely.

Beat Stiff: This is applied to egg whites. Beat with electric or rotary beater until almost dry and until peaks will hold their shape when the beater is lifted up through the whites. It cannot be done with a blender.

Also applied to whipping cream. Beat until cream holds definite peaks, but *be very careful* not to overbeat or you will have the beginnings of butter. In beating cream with a blender, turn it on and off pretty constantly to avoid such a contingency. With an electric beater or rotary beater, cream takes longer to reach the desired consistency, but should be checked frequently after it begins to thicken.

Beat Until Peaks Are Formed: This is applied to egg whites. Beat with electric or rotary beater until soft peaks are formed when the beater is lifted up through the whites. At this point the beaten whites will still be moist and shiny. This cannot be done with a blender because its action is too severe to beat egg whites.

Bind: To hold foods together with a sauce so that they form a cohesive mass.

Blanch: To immerse foods briefly in boiling water. In preparing many fresh vegetables for freezing, for instance, they are first blanched to hold the color and flavor by stopping or slowing the action of enzymes. Nuts, tomatoes, and other fruits are blanched by being plunged into boiling water for from one to three minutes to loosen their skins. They are then drained and rinsed in cold water so that the skins slip off easily.

Blaze: To pour warmed liquor over food and set it aflame.

Blend: To incorporate several ingredients completely into one another with a spoon. Or to whirl in an electric blender or processor to achieve the same result.

Boil: To cook in boiling water (212 degrees F. at sea level). So long as bubbles rise to the top and break, the water is boiling. The fastest is a "full, rolling boil." Slowest is a low boil, which is just above a simmer.

Braise: To brown meat or vegetables in hot fat. A small amount of liquid is then added, and the food is cooked covered, long and slow.

Bread: To roll in crumbs. Often food is first dipped in beaten egg, then rolled in crumbs.

Broil: To cook under (range broiler or portable electric broiler) or over (open fire or grill) direct heat.

Brush: To coat food with melted fat or liquid. A pastry brush is most satisfactory for accomplishing this job.

Candy: To cook fruit in a heavy syrup, drain, and dry it, as for orange or grapefruit peel. Applied to vegetables, it means to cook them with fat and sugar or corn syrup until they are glazed, as with sweet potatoes or carrots.

Caramelize: To melt sugar over low heat, stirring constantly with a wooden spoon, until it turns liquid and browns to the degree desired.

Chop: To cut into fine or coarse pieces, as required by the recipe, with a knife or special chopper or a food processor. Chopped food is never as finely cut as that which is ground.

Clarify: To clarify stock, broth, or consommé, add egg white and egg shell and bring to a rolling boil. Strain. Bits of food involved in the original making stick to the egg, and the resultant liquid is entirely clear. To clarify butter, melt it over moderate heat. Skim off foam and pour the melted butter into a bowl, leaving the milky residue in the bottom of the pan. This residue may be stirred into sauces to enrich them.

Coat: To cover food thoroughly with seasoned flour or with crumbs. Also, boiled custard is cooked "when the mixture 'coats' the spoon," that is, a film has formed on it.

Coddle: To cook gently below the boiling point, as for fruit or eggs.

Cream: To mix fat and sugar together with the back of a spoon until they are smooth and creamy.

Crisp: To place in ice water until crisp and well chilled, as for vegetables. Also, to place in a low oven until brown and crisp, as for making thinly sliced bread into Melba toast.

Cube: To cut into small, equal squares.

Cut: 1. To divide food into pieces with a knife or kitchen shears. 2. To mix fat into dry ingredients with two knives or a pastry blender, as for making piecrust.

Degrease: To remove accumulated fat from the surface of hot liquid (from the French "degraisser"). This can be done with a slotted spoon or with paper towels. In the case of fat drippings from a roast, the fat can be removed with a bulb baster.

Devil: To prepare food with hot seasonings, or to serve cooked food with a hotly spiced (deviled) sauce.

Dice: To cut food into very small cubes.

Disjoint: To cut a chicken, turkey, or other bird into pieces at the joints. Easiest with poultry shears—or, even better, have your butcher do it for you.

Dot: To scatter small bits of fat (usually butter) over food before cooking.

Dredge: To cover food completely with a dry ingredient, such as flour or crumbs. It can be done by shaking the food to be dredged in a paper bag with the dry ingredients (and seasonings, if desired), or by using a shaker designed for the purpose (some containers are made with shaker tops).

Dust: To sprinkle food lightly with a dry ingredient.

Flake: To break food into (not necessarily even) flat pieces, usually with a fork.

Flambé: The French equivalent of blaze.

Fold: The gentle combining of two or more ingredients with a spoon, a spatula, or the hand. This process usually involves a mixture which would be flattened and ruined by hard beating. Whatever instrument you use, put it down through the mixture to the bottom of the bowl, across, and up to the top. This is continued until the ingredients are well mixed, but still retain air.

Fricassee: A stew, or stewing. The main ingredient of the dish is browned or not, as desired, then cooked long and slow in liquid.

Fry: To cook, partly or wholly immersed in fat, either in a skillet containing one to two inches of fat or in a deep-fat fryer with lots of fat. These can be top-of-the-range, or electrically controlled utensils.

Garnish: To decorate, usually with other foods.

Glaze: To give food a shiny finish, as: vegetables, in butter and sugar; meat, with a sauce, usually containing some sugar; or cold foods by covering with aspic.

Grate: To pulverize food by rubbing it against a rough surface (grater). The same result can be achieved with many foods by whirling them in the food processor or blender.

Grill: To broil—referring to the rack on which food is cooked.

Julienne: To cut food into match-like strips.

Knead: To fold, turn, and press down on a dough with the hands until it becomes smooth and elastic. There are dough-hook attachments for some electric mixers which accomplish the task of kneading without much use of muscle.

Lard: To place broad or narrow strips of fat (usually salt pork or bacon) over the top of meat or birds, or insert them into the meat with a larding needle or skewer. This is usually done to very lean meat which needs fat added in order that it may not dry out in cooking.

Marinate: To soak food in a marinade.

Mask: To cover food completely with mayonnaise, a thick sauce, or aspic.

Mince: To cut or chop into very small pieces.

Pan-fry: To cook, uncovered, in a hot skillet using very little grease.

Parboil: To cook food in boiling water until partially done. The cooking is usually finished by putting the parboiled food into a casserole, by frying or sautéing it, or by some other means of cooking.

Pare: To remove an outer skin. To peel.

Poach: To simmer food gently in a hot liquid.

Puree: To force food through a sieve, or whirl it in the processor or blender until it is completely smooth.

Reduce: To boil a liquid until it reaches the quantity required in a recipe, thus concentrating the flavor.

Render: To melt fat down so that any connective tissue may be removed.

Roast: To cook in an oven. The term is usually applied to meat. (*See* Bake.)

Roux: A mixture of flour and butter cooked together for a few minutes before any liquid is added. For a white sauce, this is done over low heat so that it will not brown. For a brown sauce, the mixture is browned before liquid is added.

Sauté: To cook food on top of the range in a small amount of fat, for whatever time the recipe requires. Sometimes the food is sautéed to brown it, sometimes not.

Scald: To heat liquid (such as milk) to the boiling point, but not let it boil. A few tiny bubbles will appear on top when the right point is reached.

Score: To make slashes in food with a sharp knife. This can apply to meat and to bread or cakes before baking.

Sear: To brown fast over high heat or in the oven. Usually refers to meat. The process seals in the juices and adds to flavor.

Shuck: To remove a natural outer covering from food, such as shells from oysters or husks from corn.

Sift: To put dry ingredients through a sieve or a sifter.

Simmer: To cook gently in liquid below the boiling point. There should be only barely observable bubbles coming to the top of the liquid. Used in long, slow cooking as a rule.

Skewer: To put meat and/or other foods on thin metal or wooden pins for broiling (or, occasionally, for sautéing). Also, to hold meat together with short metal pins.

Skim: To remove scum, fat, or other floating substances from a liquid. It is usually done with a spoon, or a slotted spoon known as a "skimmer." For removing fat, it is often best to lay a paper towel over the surface. Also, to take cream from the top of milk.

Sliver: To cut food into thin pieces, as for nuts.

Steam: To cook food over boiling water, which does not touch it. There are special pots for steaming, also racks to put into any pot which will lift the food above the water. Sometimes used also with reference to food cooked in a very little liquid or fat, as with onions to get them "soft, but not brown."

Steep: To extract the essence from a food by soaking in hot liquid. Most commonly used in reference to tea, but applicable to many leaves, such as saffron and other herbs.

Stew: To cook long and slow in liquid.

Stir: To blend ingredients with a circular motion. Less vigorous than beating.

Truss: To tie the wings and legs of a bird to the body so that the shape is not lost in cooking. A ball of white string in the kitchen for such purposes is indispensable.

Try Out: To remove fat from such meats as salt pork and bacon. The liquid fat is then usually used for frying and the solid pieces for toppings and the like. (*See* Render.)

Whip: To beat rapidly in order to incorporate air and expand the ingredients, such as eggs, cream, and gelatin dishes.

10. How to Time Food Preparation

It is possible to either waste or save a lot of time in the preparation of food. Much depends upon the degree of planning you put into the work you do in your kitchen. First, your kitchen should be efficiently arranged—for *you*, not according to any rules laid down by "experts." One reason it's so hard (and it really is) to cook in other people's kitchens is that one can never find anything one badly needs. That's because no two cooks operate in exactly the same way—at least one can say we're not robots! So, hang most of your pots and pans on pegboard on your kitchen walls as I do, or if the very thought makes you shudder, do it your way—whatever that may be. My brief for the hanging pots and pans is that they're so easy to spot at once and easy to take down from their places to use where you want them. There are other matters of kitchen arrangement which can be vital to the cook's peace of mind and efficiency. Only you know what yours are, but do pamper yourself and have them.

A problem common to all cooks, experienced as well as novice, is how to make each part of a dinner come out on time. It ought not to be so hard, but it is complained about most frequently. What you should do, as soon as you've planned your menu, is to write down how long each dish takes to cook and following that, the time at which it should go into the oven or the skillet or whatever. Your cookbooks will tell you cooking time, if they're any good at all. If you have any that don't, discard them at once; there are plenty that don't let you down that way.

For example, take the menu to be found in the chapter on How to Read and Use Recipes. Here is a schedule that will fit it like a glove and, I certainly hope, will solve all problems.

Day before the dinner: Cook artichokes, cool, and refrigerate. Make Crème Brûlée.

Morning before dinner: Finish topping of Crème Brûlée.

If dinner is to be served at 7:30

5:20	Preheat oven
5:30	Put lamb in oven
5:45	Make vinaigrette sauce
6:00	Baste lamb
6:15	Prepare beans and potatoes
6:30	Baste lamb
6:35	Put potatoes on to cook. (This will take 45 minutes, or longer; when they're done, keep them warm.)
7:00	Remove lamb from oven
7:05	Cook beans
	Sauté slivered almonds
7:20	Drain beans and mix with almonds. Keep warm.
	Make sauce for lamb. Keep warm.
7:30	Serve artichokes
	Put dinner plates into turned-off oven to warm
7:45	Serve main course
	When ready, serve dessert
	Coffee in the living room.

You may well ask how you're expected to remember, or know, after the guests arrive and are having cocktails, what time it is or what you're supposed to do. The answer is to use one of the greatest boons to efficient cooking that's ever been invented—the timer. All good new ranges either have electric timers as part of standard equipment or they can be had as an extra. But hand-operated ones, just like the timers used in hair-dressing shops, are to be had with ease. When you start your lamb, you simply set the timer to go off thirty minutes later, to remind you to baste it—and if you've forgotten what it was reminding you of, you've got your "little list" to refer to.

By the way, I cross each item on *my* little list off as soon as I've accomplished it. For me, this works well, though I'm sure it wouldn't for everybody, but I hope you'll at least try it.

The matter of keeping foods warm in case guests are late, which is unfortunately a thing to be expected, can be taken care of in several ways. Double boilers are fine for holding meat or fish dishes that have sauces. Drain any cooked vegetable well and place the colander over hot water with a lid that fits down over the vegetable. Rice or noodles can be well drained and put into a double boiler with butter or whatever else you'd put on them. You can also try making a "steam table" with a baking pan or pans, into which you've put water, brought it to the boil, and then turned it way down. Put the pans in which you've cooked your dinner into this and cover the foods well. Some of their freshness will be lost, but the result will be reasonably good.

11. Leftovers

Party Food

Sometimes it makes sense to plan food for a party so that there will be leftovers. For instance, if you're having steak, what better dish to look forward to for another day than a steak-and-kidney pie? Order more steak than you need and later cook the beef kidney to go with it. In any event, after any party, you will have leftovers.

Occasionally you will find that you have leftover food which can't be used for anything. In my opinion, leftover green salad is in this category. On the other hand, too many hostesses are inclined to look at dribs and drabs of leftovers and throw them out because there isn't enough "to do anything with." This is a grave mistake. A couple of tablespoonsful of Hollandaise sauce, for example, will improve the flavor of any gravy or sauce. The same is true of other tiny bits of food. Hang on to them. Experiment with them. They can often improve or stretch a dish.

In making the following charts for uses of leftover foods, I have taken it for granted there is not quite enough of any one food for your family. It is obvious that cold meats are delicious and that the stew type of dish tastes better warmed over. Such uses are not suggested in these charts. Foods listed are to be combined with other foods, with sauces and the like.

It is presumed that you are willing to be adventurous, to try combinations suggested here that you have never heard of before, and to make up dishes of your own. If you don't know it already, you will shortly discover that some of the world's best dishes are concocted from leftover ingredients.

At the risk of some repetition, I should like to point out that some rules for leftovers hold true in general.

1. Leftovers make wonderful casseroles. Always add sauces. You can change the basic flavors by the addition of herbs and spices, tomatoes (which combine well with almost anything), egg yolks, milk, cream, sour cream, cheese, and leftover homemade or canned soups.

2. Soufflés, omelets, and croquettes make wonderful eating and can be made from all sorts of leftover meats and vegetables and fish.

3. Thin pancakes (crêpes), stuffed with minced meats, fish, or vegetables, rolled up, covered with sauce, and browned under the broiler are interesting, unusual, and delicious.

4. Hashes can be made out of any leftover meat, liver, or chicken. Put them into a béchamel or other sauce in a fireproof dish or a copper-bottomed skillet and brown them under the broiler just before serving.

LEFTOVERS CHART

Breads

Type	Combine with	Make into	Seasonings that blend well
Bread, Rolls (Dry out thoroughly)	Milk; eggs; etc.	Bread crumbs; bread pudding	Vanilla; coffee; chocolate
Muffins, Biscuits, Rolls		Split, toast, and butter	

Type	Combine with	Make into	Seasonings that blend well
Sandwiches with sweet fillings (like jelly)	Milk; eggs; butter	Sandwich pudding	

Desserts

Type	Combine with	Make into	Seasonings that blend well
Cake	Sherry; whipped cream; ice cream and sauce	Tipsy pudding; ice-cream cake	
Fruit	Prepared vanilla pudding; Jell-O; sugar-and-water base	Fruit pudding; sauce for pudding or cake	Vanilla; sherry; kirsch
Pies	Ice cream	Pie à la mode	
Puddings	Cake, as a filling; whipped cream and lady fingers	Cake filling; charlottes	

Eggs

Type	Combine with	Make into	Seasonings that blend well
Egg yolks	Milk; whole egg; etc. Butter; lemon juice; cream sauce; flour; sugar; etc.	Custards; Hollandaise; rich sauce; gold cake	Vanilla; almond
Egg whites	Flour; sugar; corn syrup	Angel cake; meringues; white cake; cake icing	Vanilla; almond
Hard-cooked Eggs	Grate	Decoration for canapés, spinach, etc.	

Type	Combine with	Make into	Seasonings that blend well
Fish and Shellfish			
Lobster, Oysters, Shrimp, Clams	Newburg or cream sauce; mushrooms	Sauce for fish pudding, fillet of sole, etc.; sauce for chicken	Dill; thyme; parsley; celery
Solid-meat fish (sole, halibut, swordfish, etc.)	Egg whites and seasonings; cream sauce; shellfish; tomato sauce; white wine sauce; mayonnaise	Fish pudding; creamed fish on toast; casseroles; salads; soufflés	Chives; basil; thyme; parsley; tarragon; chervil
Meats			
Beefsteak	Kidneys and gravy; potatoes; brown sauce; tomato sauce; sour cream; red wine	Beef and kidney pie; hash; sliced beef in sauce	Garlic; onion; celery
Chicken	Rice; almonds; cream sauce; mushrooms; macaroni; vegetables; sour cream; chopped clams; béchamel sauce; white wine; aspic and vegetables; celery; green and red peppers	Hash; casseroles; creamed chicken on toast; soufflés; croquettes; salads; curry; pie; stuffed pancakes; chow mein	Rosemary; Summer savory; parsley; paprika; curry; garlic; tarragon

Type	Combine with	Make into	Seasonings that blend well
Duck	Mushrooms; stuffing; gravy; brown sauce; sherry and olives; tomato sauce; rice; orange-and-currant-jelly sauce	Salmi; casseroles; soup; in sauce over toast or rice; ragout	Poultry seasoning; parsley; onion
Frankfurters	Noodles; tomato sauce; cheese; potato salad; hot boiled potatoes; baked beans	Casseroles; salads	Mustard; garlic; onion
Ham	Eggs; macaroni and cheese; pork; lima beans; barbecue sauce; spinach; wine sauce	Soufflés; omelets; casseroles; eggs Benedict; meatloaf; timbales	Marjoram; clove; basil; parsley; onion
Hamburger or Meat Loaf	Cornmeal mush; corn; celery; chili beans; rice; gravy; barbecue sauce	Tamale pie; chili con carne; Spanish rice; casserole with vegetables	Onion; green pepper; savory; chili
Kidneys	Beefsteak; gravy; white wine; red wine; sherry; cream	Beef-and-kidney pie; ragout; in cream on toast	Parsley; mace; onion
Lamb	Peas and carrots; cream sauce;	Shepherd's pie; hash; lamb	Mint; rosemary; curry

Type	Combine with	Make into	Seasonings that blend well
	mushrooms; apricots; white wine; curry sauce	curry; croquettes; casserole with vegetables; stew	
Liver	Cream sauce; mayonnaise and chopped egg; rice; vegetables; white wine; sherry; tomato sauce	Hash; canapés; dumplings; casseroles	Onion; garlic; thyme; basil
Pork	Gravy; rice; apples; sweet potatoes; bean sprouts; mushrooms; sauerkraut; cornmeal mush	Casseroles; chop suey; polenta	Poultry seasoning; onion; cumin
Roast Beef, Pot Roast, or Beef Stew	Vegetables; curry sauce; potatoes; gravy; red wine; rice; barbecue sauce	Stew; hash; beef curry; beef-and-vegetable casserole	Bay leaf; marjoram; garlic; onion; curry; parsley
Sausage	Baked beans; rice; tomato sauce; corn	Casseroles; sausage-and-vegetable fritters	
Sweetbreads or Brains	Eggs; vegetables; chicken; oysters; cream sauce; Newburg sauce; velouté sauce; mushrooms	Scrambled eggs and sweetbreads or brains; casseroles; salad; timbales	Lemon juice; parsley; mace; onion

Type	Combine with	Make into	Seasonings that blend well
Tongue	Greens; chicken; Swiss cheese; wine sauce; macaroni; mushrooms; béchamel sauce	Chef's salad; casseroles; in sauce on rice croquettes	Cloves; bay leaf; onion; horseradish
Turkey	Rice; stuffing; gravy; cream sauce; crisp bacon; currant sauce; vegetables; mushrooms; green pepper, onion, and celery; oysters; noodles	Hash; casseroles; creamed on toast; soufflé; croquettes; curry; pie; stuffed pancakes; shortcake	Rosemary; curry; paprika; onion
Veal	Sour cream; cream sauce; white wine; vegetables; aspic and vegetables; mushrooms	Croquettes; hash; salad; curry; casseroles; soufflé	Paprika; anchovies; curry; chives; celery seed; garlic

Sauces

Type	Combine with	Make into	Seasonings that blend well
Bearnaise	Cream sauce; Hollandaise; gravy; casseroles	Flavor agent for another sauce	Nothing—it carries its own
Béchamel	Any other sauce; gravy; casseroles	Base for a sauce of different flavor	Parsley; celery seed; curry

Type	Combine with	Make into	Seasonings that blend well
Cheese	Cream sauce; gravy; tomato sauce; casseroles	Added flavor for another sauce	Onion; curry; chili
Cream	Any other sauce; gravy; cream soup; casseroles	Good extender of other sauce	Onion; curry; cayenne; paprika
Curry	Cream sauce; tomato sauce; gravy; casseroles	Flavor agent for another sauce	Nothing—it carries its own
Gravy	Any other sauce; casseroles	Added richness for other sauces	
Hollandaise	Cream sauce; béchamel; gravy; Bearnaise; white-wine sauce; casseroles	Added richness for other sauces	
Red Wine	Gravy; tomato sauce; fish or meat; casseroles	Flavor change for another sauce	Thyme; onion; garlic
Sour Cream	Any sauce; gravy; casseroles	Added richness for a sauce	Chives; garlic; onion; paprika; cayenne
White Wine	Cream sauce; Hollandaise; béchamel; gravy; casseroles	Delicate flavor for another sauce	Thyme; dill; tarragon

Type	Combine with	Make into	Seasonings that blend well

Soups

Type	Combine with	Make into	Seasonings that blend well
Chowders	Fish; other soups; cheese; eggs	Casseroles; another soup	Thyme; cayenne; curry
Consommé or Bouillon	Raw meat or vegetables, to cook them; flour and butter	Stock; sauce	Almost any herb or spice
Cream	Gravy; cream sauce; other cream soups	Sauces; base for vegetable or meat casseroles	Curry; chili; cayenne; paprika

Vegetables

Type	Combine with	Make into	Seasonings that blend well
Asparagus	Water in which cooked; cream; cream sauce; other vegetables; eggs; mayonnaise or French dressing	Cream or vegetable soup; casseroles; omelet; salad; vinaigrette	Thyme; marjoram
Beans Baked	Cold with mayonnaise; catsup	Sandwiches	Onion
Beans Chili	Rice, hamburger, and chili sauce; cold with chili sauce	Casserole; sandwiches	Chili powder to taste
Beans Lima	Other vegetables; mayonnaise; water in which cooked; cream; corn	Salad; vegetable soup; succotash; casseroles	Cayenne; chives; onion

Type	Combine with	Make into	Seasonings that blend well
Beans Snap or Wax	Other vegetables; mayonnaise; French dressing; gravy; cream sauce; cheese	Salad; vegetable soup; casseroles	Onion; basil; rosemary
Beets	Greens and French dressing; liquid in which cooked; sour cream	Salad; borscht *Never* in cas- seroles (colors whole dish)	Tarragon
Broccoli	Water in which cooked; cream sauce; chicken or turkey; French dressing	Cream soup; casseroles; salad	Lemon juice; garlic; chervil
Cabbage, Raw	Apples, greens, and mayonnaise	Salad	Onion; celery seed; cara- way seed
Cabbage, Cooked	Cream sauce; cheese; beets and sour cream	Au gratin cas- serole; borscht	Onion
Carrots	Other vegetables; peas; mayonnaise	Vegetable salad; vege- table soup	Mint
Cauliflower	Cream sauce and cheese; water in which cooked; cream; celery	Au gratin cas- serole; cream soup; salad	Poppy seed; chives; onion; thyme; parsley
Corn	Lima beans; eggs; milk; green pep- per; cornmeal; hamburger	Succotash; fritters; corn pudding; tamale pie	Onion; pa- prika; chili

Type	Combine with	Make into	Seasonings that blend well
Macaroni	Butter and a little milk	Fried macaroni au gratin	
Mushrooms	Cream sauce; gravy; meat; other vegetables; water in which cooked; sour cream; cream	Sauces; casseroles; gravies; spaghetti sauce	Tarragon; basil
Noodles	Meats; vegetables; tomato sauce; gravy; cream sauce; cheese; consommé; crumbs	Casseroles; soup	Onion; garlic; chives; parsley
Peas	Carrots; other vegetables; onions; cream sauce	Vegetables; salads; casseroles	Mint; basil; onion
Potatoes Baked	Onion; hot milk; butter; cheese	Fried; au gratin casserole; soup	Parsley; dill; paprika
Potatoes Boiled	Mayonnaise; green pepper; celery; hard-cooked egg; cream sauce; cheese	Salad; creamed; au gratin; fried	Parsley; paprika; onion
Potatoes Mashed	Milk and butter; cheese	Topping for casseroles; au gratin; bordure for steak or fish; pancakes	Parsley; chives; onion

Type	Combine with	Make into	Seasonings that blend well
Rice	Tomato sauce; green pepper; meat; gravy; eggs and milk; cheese	Spanish rice; casseroles; fritters or croquettes	Saffron; onion

12. How to Avoid or Correct Cooking "Disasters"

Too Much Salt: There is no help for this disaster, so be chary with the use of salt in your cooking. This is an easy habit to get into, and a good one, when so many people today are on low-salt diets. Salt can be added at the table by the individual diner, but you cannot get it out once it's added.

Cracked Hollandaise Sauce: If your Hollandaise Sauce cracks, beat in a tablespoonful of boiling water with a wire whisk. If this does not bring it together, add one more tablespoonful of the boiling water, beating it in as before. If this does not work (though it practically always does), give up!

Watery Baked Custard: Baked custards will "weep" if they are cooked too long or at too-high temperatures. Almost any baked custard served warm will "weep," but a good cold baked custard will be firm and smooth. Custard baked in a large dish should be done in a 350-degree oven for thirty to forty minutes. Individual custards take less time. The best way to test for doneness is to insert a flat knife into the center of the custard. If the knife comes out clean, the custard is done.

Curdled "Boiled" Custard: "Boiled" custard should be stirred continuously while it is cooking and, as soon as it thickens and coats the spoon, removed at once from the heat. Be very careful never to let a "boiled" custard boil, or it will surely curdle.

Removing Food from a Mold: If it is a pudding or a gelatin dish, the best method is to put the serving dish on top of the open part of the mold, invert it, and then place a hot, damp cloth on the mold itself, long enough to loosen the contents and not melt them. Let us admit at once that this takes practice. Sometimes it helps to run a blunt-edged knife or a spatula between the food and the mold before applying the hot cloth. This must be done with care not to break the contents and thus make the unmolded dish less attractive.

Burned Butter: When you are going to sauté or fry any food in butter, add a dash of peanut or other oil (not olive) so that the frying fat will not burn.

Odor from Cooking Cabbage: This goes for brussels sprouts and cauliflower as well as cabbage. Put a piece of bread into the cooking water at the start. The result is not perfect, but it is some help.

Moldy Cheese: If you enclose cheese carefully and tightly in plastic wrap, it should not develop mold. But if you find you have moldy cheese, just scrape off the mold and you will find the cheese perfectly good to eat.

Soft-Cooked Eggs: When soft-cooked eggs break in cooking, add salt to the water to keep the whites from seeping out.

Poached Eggs: To keep poached eggs in shape, hunt for "muffin rings," which are hard to find and old-fashioned, but perfect for keeping eggs in manageable and agreeable shape. The "poaching" pans do not turn out as good a tasting egg as the "muffin" rings.

Soft Scrambled Eggs: It is a sin to overcook any egg, but some people always seem to cook scrambled eggs until they're dry. To avoid this—and have much tastier eggs—melt butter in a skillet. Break eggs into this and, over low heat, start scrambling at once with a fork. When just coagulated and *not dry* at all, serve immediately.

Mayonnaise—to Insure Against Cracking: Beat one or two tablespoons of boiling water into the mayonnaise when you have finished making it.

Cracked Mayonnaise: Put one egg yolk into a warmed bowl, beat it briefly, then beat in the mayonnaise very gradually until it thickens again satisfactorily.

OR: Place a teaspoonful of prepared mustard in a warmed bowl. Add a tablespoonful of the cracked mayonnaise and beat with a wire whisk until they are smoothly combined. Add the rest of the mayonnaise, a teaspoonful at a time, until all is incorporated smoothly.

To Remove the Peel and Zest from Oranges: Cover the fruit with boiling water and let stand 5 minutes. Not only the peel, but the zest comes off easily.

Onions Without Tears: Hold onions under cold running water while slicing.

To Keep Pasta from Sticking or Boiling Over: Always add a dollop of oil to the water in which you cook pasta—this will prevent both of the above disasters.

Fruit Breads or Cakes: If the fruit always sinks to the bottom when you make these delicacies, you must have forgotten to flour it (with part of the flour required in the recipe). This makes the fruit stay suspended throughout the whole muffin, cake, or whatever.

Lumps in Sauce or Gravy: If you pay close attention to what you're doing in making sauce or gravy—melting the butter, adding the flour, stirring constantly until there isn't a lump in sight, adding the required liquid, and, again, stirring constantly until thickened, all should be as smooth as silk. This means that you never take your eyes off what you're cooking and never stop stirring. It all takes a very short time and is worth the effort.

OR: Use "instantized" flour (for which, in my opinion, there is no other thinkable use).

OR: You can whirl the gravy in the food processor or blender.

OR: You can try forcing the lumpy gravy through a fine sieve, which doesn't always do the trick.

Paying attention in the first place is the simplest solution.

If Syrup Crystallizes: Stand container in a bowl of hot water and the crystals will disappear.

How Not to Make Butter: When you want to whip cream, the cream, bowl, and beater should be chilled. The other important thing to remember is to watch the product carefully and *don't overbeat,* unless you're interested in making sweet butter.

To Prevent Food from Burning: If you don't want to stand around and watch the pot boiling, use your kitchen timer to remind yourself to check on how the dish you're cooking is coming along. This frees your mind for thinking of less pedestrian matters.

To keep food warm and prevent it from burning after it is cooked, buy yourself a Flame Tamer—a marvelous gadget which you place on one of your top-of-stove burners, set on lowest heat. You can put the food in a pan, covered, on top and keep it warm practically indefinitely. The Flame Tamer works on both gas and electric ranges.

How to Deal with a Burned Pot: If you discover that the contents of a pot is burning, remove the pot at once from the range and stand it in cold water to stop the cooking. *Never* add water to the contents, which simply spreads the burned flavor throughout the whole. Now, with a big spoon or a ladle, remove the top portion of the food and place it in a clean pot, being very careful not to include any of the burned part. Add more liquid, if needed, to complete the cooking. If there are onions in whatever you're cooking, add some now. This will help eliminate any burned flavor which may remain. If the food still has a burned flavor, discard it. The case is hopeless!

Dried-Out Bread: If you have a small amount, make bread crumbs in the processor or blender. If you have bought French or Italian bread (which, if it is properly made, becomes rock-hard in a day) and have the best part of a loaf remaining, wrap it in a damp cloth and store it in the refrigerator for 24 hours. Cut off only what you want for one meal and continue to store the rest, dampening the cloth when necessary.

The Buckling Pastry Shell: To avoid this disaster, butter lightweight foil and line the shell with it before baking, pressing it well against the pastry, then fill it with dried beans. Or prick the bottom well with a fork. You can also place another pan or mold like the one in which you are baking your shell, buttered on the bottom, inside the shell and weight it down with a few dried beans.

Causes of Uncooked Spots on the Bottom of a Pie: They are usually caused by one of these factors: inadequate blending of fat and flour; insufficient mixing after the water is added so that the dough is unevenly moistened, especially if too much water is used; combining warm dough with cold dough; or drops of water in the pie pan when the dough is put into it.

Cause of Shrinkage of a Baked Pie Crust: Some shrinkage is normal in a baked pie crust. Too much shrinkage may be caused by the use of too much water or by overhandling.

Tough Pie Dough: This happens when too little fat or too much water is used or when the fat is not mixed properly. Overmixing pastry after the water is added will also make it tough.

Cause of Crumbling Pastry Dough: Too little water or too much fat will cause pastry dough to crumble.

Raw Pared Potatoes: To keep them from turning dark, place them in cold water for a short time. Do not pare them so far ahead that they must soak in water for a long period.

Waffles Sticking or Breaking in Electric Baker: This can be caused by opening the baker before the waffle is done. Always wait for the light to go out before opening the baker. If you use a packaged mix or a recipe which does not call for shortening, add at least ¼ cup of melted shortening or oil to prevent sticking. Use unsalted shortening to season grids. Do not wash the grids. Brush out crumbs, then wipe with a dry soft cloth or paper towel. Then let the baker cool with the top up.

To Keep Apple Slices from Turning Brown: Cover them with water mixed with a small amount of lemon or lime juice. Drain and pat dry before using.

Poor Texture in Quick Breads Made with Baking Powder: Overmixing is often the cause of this disaster. A batter, such as muffin batter, which contains about twice as much flour as liquid, should be mixed only enough to moisten the dry ingredients, as recipes often instruct you. Too much stirring or beating develops the gluten in the flour, and as a result, tunnels are formed. Too high baking temperatures also may cause poor texture in quick breads.

Tough Baking-Powder Biscuits: This probably happens because the dough is overhandled. Biscuits must be made quickly, with a delicate touch, if they are to be tender. They are kneaded, of course, but only for a few seconds.

Biscuits That Are Dry and Small: Biscuits may be dry and have poor volume because too little liquid or baking powder was used, or they may have been mixed too much or baked at too low a temperature.

Coarse Texture in Homemade Yeast Bread: The most common cause of such texture is allowing the loaf to rise too much before baking.

Sour Flavor in Yeast Bread: A sour flavor will develop in bread if a poor yeast is used, or if the dough has been allowed to rise too long or at too high a temperature. Insufficient baking or baking at too low a temperature will also affect the flavor of yeast bread.

Lack of Volume in Homemade Bread: If your bread lacks volume, you may have used too little yeast, allowed too little time for rising, or held the dough at too low a temperature. Or you may have added the yeast to liquid that was too hot or let the dough rise at too high a temperature. Under the right conditions, yeast produces carbon dioxide gas, which leavens the bread. Warmth is needed for the process, but too much heat kills the yeast cells. A temperature of about 80 degrees is best. Overkneading the dough, which may injure the baking quality of the gluten in the flour, is another possible cause of poor volume in bread.

Soggy Muffins: Muffins may be soggy if their dough contains too much liquid or if they were baked at too low a heat.

Falling Cakes: A cake is likely to fall if too much sugar or fat or baking powder or liquid is used. Undermixing or insufficient baking, too low an oven temperature, or moving a cake during baking before it has "set" also may cause a cake to fall and be soggy.

Cake with Peaked or Cracked Top: If the batter is low in shortening or has been overmixed, the cake may form a peak while baking. Too little leavening (baking powder or soda) or too much flour may also cause a peaked top. Cracking of the top crust may result from baking the cake in too hot an oven.

Sponge and Angel Cakes Smaller Than They Should Be: They will probably also be tough. This is usually because the cake has been baked in too hot an oven. They should be baked in a 325-degree oven. If you are getting such results at that heat, have your oven regulator checked.

Shrinking: This may result from too much liquid or too much fat in the recipe or from too much batter in the pan. Also, a cake may shrink if the pan is too heavily greased. Baking in a too-hot or too-cool oven may result in poor volume in a cake.

13. Cooking Equipment—
Large and Small

For the average kitchen (having one oven, a broiler, and four top-of-the-range units), I offer the following complete list, which is my own. Let me point out that no two cooks would make exactly the same requirements, so I may list some things you would have no use in the world for, and leave out something without which you cannot live. Please leave out mine and get yours, by all means!

Things You Can Cook In or On

Boilers, double, 1 or 2
Bowls
  mixing, in graduated sizes
  wooden one for chopping
Canister set for flour, sugar,
  coffee, tea
Casseroles
  1 or 2 large ones with covers
  4–6 individual ones
Colander
Cookie sheets, 2
Cups, 6 for custard

Dutch oven
Frying basket
Griddle
Pans
  angel food cake
  cheesecake
  crêpes
  layer cake, 2
  loaf, 1 or 2
  muffins, 2
  omelets
  pie, 2

Pans
  roasting, shallow
  saucepans, 2 or 3 in grad-
    uated sizes, with lids
Pitcher, quart
Plates, 4–6

Platters, 1 or 2
Skillets
  large one with lid; 2 or 3
    smaller ones with lids
Soufflé dish

Pie Pan

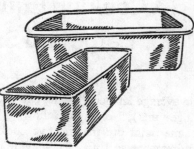

Loaf Pans

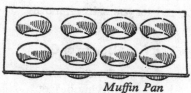

Muffin Pan

Angel Food Cake

Layer Cake

Shallow Roasting Pan

Omelet Pan

Sauce Pans

Utensils and Small Kitchen Tools

Bottle opener
Brush, vegetable
Bulb baster
Chopper
Cleaver, small
Corer, apple
Corkscrew
Cutters
  biscuit
  cookie
Flatware, stainless steel for
    kitchen use
Fork, long-handled
Funnel, small
Garlic press
Grater, cheese
Knives
  French cook's
  grapefruit
  paring, 2 or 3
  slicing
  utility
Ladle
Lid lifter

Measuring cups, 2 1-cup and 1
  2-cup
Meat thermometer
Pastry blender
Pastry brush
Peeler, vegetable
Rolling pin
Scissors, game
Sharpener, knife
Shears, kitchen
Spatulas
  metal
  rubber, 3 (narrow and
    broad)
Spoons
  basting
  measuring, 2 sets
  slotted
  wooden, in different sizes
Strainers, 2 or 3 in different
  sizes
Tongs
Turner, pancake
Whisks, wire (small and large)

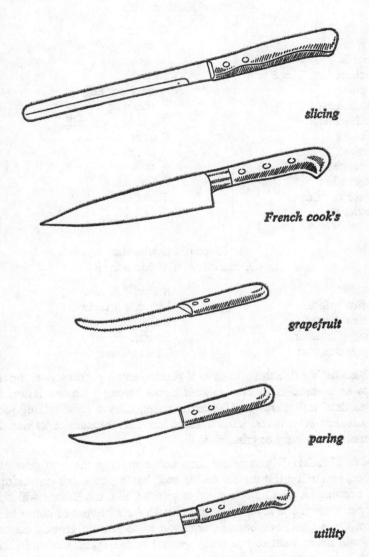

slicing

French cook's

grapefruit

paring

utility

General Kitchen Aids

Beater
  rotary
Boards
  chopping, 2 or 3
  pastry
Cloth, pastry
Coffee maker
Grinder
  meat
  pepper
Ice crusher
Juicer or reamer
Kettle, tea

Opener
  can
  jar-top
Rack
  cake-cooling
  roasting
Ricer or food mill
Shaker
  flour
  salt
Sifter, flour
Timer

Small Electrical Equipment
(as you can afford it, if you want it)

Blender
Coffee grinder
Coffee maker
Food processor
Fryer, deep-fat

Mixer, full-size
Mixer, portable
Rotisserie
Toaster
Toaster-oven

A Blender is a fine thing to have if you haven't a processor—and perhaps as a stand-in in case anything goes wrong with the latter. It saves time and energy and, in many cases, does a good mixing job. Its use, however, is restricted in some instances because of its size. It cannot make pastry or grind meat.

Coffee Grinder: If you really care about making the best possible coffee, you will grind the coffee for each batch you make just before the brewing. A small electric coffee grinder, like the Braun, which I happen to own and love, can grind enough for a big pot of coffee in a trice. Once you have become accustomed to freshly ground coffee, you will never want to use ready-ground coffee again. Coffee in the bean keeps much longer than ground coffee, however you store it. Many people keep the beans in the refrigerator or freezer, but it really isn't necessary unless you want to buy a huge amount at a time. It is fun, too, to experiment with various blends of beans. Mocha-

and-Java is fairly standard and very good. For a good many years, I have been buying Arabica beans, which make a delectable brew. In any case, I'm pretty sure that once you have embarked upon grinding coffee from the bean, you will never be content with another way of making it.

Coffee Maker: I did not put this on the initial list of small electrical appliances, as I do not really like the coffee it makes as well as that made in a glass filter pot. Just the same, if you have the urge to buy one, it should have balanced construction and be comfortable to hold and pour from. There should be a brew selector for making mild, medium, or strong coffee. The maker should keep the coffee at serving temperature when it is made. It should be easy to clean. The cup markings should be clearly visible. It should have the safety feature of a cutoff, in case the coffee maker runs dry.

The Food Processor is, to my mind, the most wonderful electrical appliance that has come along so far for the cook. It can do anything a blender can do and a whole lot more. It saves an unbelievable amount of time. It can take the place of a lot of the cooking utensils listed at the start of this section, like the cheese grater, ice crusher, pastry blender, chopper, meat grinder, and ricer or food mill. One of its most delightfully magical operations is in the making of pastry. You put in the flour, salt, and butter, start the machine going, add ice

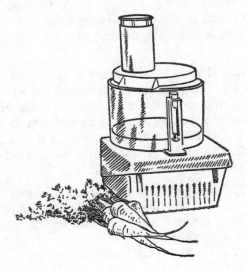

water in the right amount, through the feed tube, and in a minute or less you will see before you a ball of pastry dough. Remove this, refrigerate it for an hour or so, and proceed with rolling it out and shaping it to suit your needs of the moment. A good processor is expensive, but well worth the money if you can get it together. Since new ones come out all the time, consult some authority like Consumer's Union to see what is the best one at the time when you want to buy.

Some women have told me that their husbands would not let them use the processor when they got it because they feared it must be dangerous to do so. I have had mine for several years and have come to the conclusion that all the warnings on the safe use of these machines were put there to be overcautious, as it would be impossible to get one's hand caught in the blades, whatever one did. I live alone and, whether I am having guests or not, use my processor at least twice a day and often more. They are very easy to clean and dry—so why not?

Fryer, Deep-Fat: If you do a lot of deep-fat frying, this piece of equipment is almost indispensable. The controlled heat is most important, and this is the easiest way to be sure it's correct.

Mixer, Full-size: If you have space and do a lot of cooking for large numbers of people, it will be well worth your while to own a counter-type mixer. If you don't want to keep it on the counter all the time, be sure to figure out, before you buy it, where you're going to store it.

Mixer, Portable: If you are very limited in space and cannot store a full-size one, a portable hand mixer is exceedingly useful. It is much easier to use than even the best rotary beater. It can be hung on the wall. In buying one, be sure that it is comfortable to hold and well balanced. It should have a steady heel rest. It should have fingertip speed control. The beater ejector should be conveniently located. The motor should be permanently lubricated.

Rotisserie: If you have space to store it and you cook a lot of roast meat, a rotisserie is a fine thing to own. Meat and poultry roasted this way are about the best. Rotisseries take up a lot of room and are heavy, though, so yours should really stay in the place where you use it, if possible. You can also broil in most rotisseries.

The Toaster is perhaps the most essential piece of electrical equipment. If you have a large family, get one that toasts four slices of bread at once. For most people, the two-slice type is fine. If you have a toaster-oven, of course, the need for a toaster is eliminated.

A Toaster-Oven is especially good for a single person—or even for a couple without children, as one can bake two individual casserole dishes in it at once. It is also useful as a supplement to the range for heating rolls, for instance, when the rest of the dinner is all being cooked on top of the range and you do not want to turn on the oven. You should try to have such an oven calibrated occasionally, as they are likely to slip a bit in the temperature department.

Non-Electrical Equipment

Before going further into some of the suggested non-electrical equipment, be it said that for *any* equipment you use a lot, it is a sound investment to buy the best you can afford. Cheap equipment which is used infrequently for easy tasks may be adequate, though even cookie cutters, for instance, work better if they are sturdy and won't bend, for which asset you have to pay extra.

Aluminum Cookware: Wrought aluminum is better than cast aluminum because it is more highly purified than cast aluminum and resists corrosion better. The old saw that says aluminum cookware can contaminate food is wrong. Aluminum used in cookware is in no way injurious to health. Most of the propaganda against it has come from manufacturers of competing types of utensils.

Dark stains on aluminum pans come from the alkalies in boiling water, vegetables, and melting soap. These stains can be removed by cooking highly acid foods in them, like tomatoes or rhubarb; or cook a weak solution of vinegar and water in them. Applesauce cooked in an aluminum pan that is stained will make the pan clean and shiny, but this in no way contaminates the applesauce. It is an acid food, which is why it causes the pan to shine.

Bulb Baster: It is a tube of glass or metal with a rubber bulb on the end of it which is used to draw up juices from a pan and pour them back over the meat or whatever is cooking.

Can Opener: I used to think that an electric can opener was a rather large investment for the amount of use it gets—unless you eat entirely out of cans. However, now I have one and I love it and can't imagine why I continued to struggle with even the wall variety when such ease was to be had.

Cleaver: Even the small home-kitchen type will cut through bones of poultry or meat as no other knife can. It is also useful for pounding meat to make it thinner (with the flat) and for crushing a clove of garlic or a slice of ginger so that the flavor will be sure to be brought out when it is cooked and yet the item can be easily identified and removed from a dish, if desired.

Colander and Strainer: The colander has large, coarse holes in it. The strainer has a fine mesh. The colander also has legs so that it can stand on its own while foods drain. The strainer must, of course, be set over a pan or bowl to drain.

Cookie Sheets: The best are made of stainless steel. Tin ones bend and dent and thus do a bad job of browning the cookies or whatever you put on the sheets.

Copper Cooking Utensils: These conduct heat and are handsome to behold *if* they are kept polished—otherwise they should be kept out of sight. Also, since they are lined with tin, it is necessary to have them relined periodically, and in these days it is sometimes quite a chore to find anyone who knows how to do this job. So, unless you love to polish copper, or have someone to do it for you, I suggest that you buy pots and pans of other, far less expensive, materials.

Corkscrew: Buy the kind that has a pair of "wings" which go up as you turn the screw down into the cork. You then push down on the "wings" and the cork is smoothly lifted from the bottle. I will say, in all frankness, however, that I have never had, or heard of, a corkscrew that did not eventually get out of whack and have to be replaced. You may, in the process of such replacements, have found, or be about to find, one which will suit you far better than the one described suits me.

Dutch Oven: A deep, heavy pot with a lid, used for making stews and such dishes. Dutch ovens come in many materials, but the best one is still the heavy iron. If you can find it, get one lined with stainless steel, which will not rust and is much easier to clean. An enameled Dutch oven is perhaps even better.

Enamel-Covered Iron Cookware: The best of this is the white enameled ware, lined with a baked-on Teflon lining, which comes from Waterford, Ireland. It is absolutely great. By and large, I have no use for Teflon linings. When they first arrived on the scene, everyone was interested in their non-stick qualities. But the attendant do's and don'ts turned out to be more trouble than the pans were worth. The Irish ones, however, may be treated like any other pan—scrubbed with steel wool, if desired, without scratching—and may be cleaned in a twinkling. For omelets, they have turned out to be a sheer blessing. They are also very handsome; the casseroles come from oven to table as decorations, as well as containers.

The greatest advantage of enamelware—the more usual kind than that just described—is that it is so easy to clean. It is not dangerous to cook in chipped enamelware, because the possibility of swallowing enough small chips to do harm is so remote that it is not regarded as a hazard. On the other hand, enamelware that has been chipped so that the iron underneath is exposed may unpleasantly affect the flavor and color of certain foods.

Flan Ring: This is a French pastry ring with no bottom, used for making tart shells. The ring is set on a baking sheet, the pastry molded into it and baked. When the tart shell is done, the ring is removed and the shell slid from the baking sheet to a rack or a serving dish.

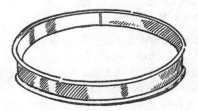

Flour Sifter: The type through which you sift flour by squeezing the handle is the easiest to use. There is a small one of this kind, through which you sift flour into a cup—a great convenience.

Food Chopper: If you have a food processor, you do not need a food chopper. But if you haven't that kitchen wizard, I suggest that you buy the kind with three blades, the center one controlled by a spring.

Whatever kind you buy, be sure that it has stainless steel blades, so they will not rust.

Game Shears: Game shears are exceedingly handy as an aid in carving a duck, for one thing, as they will cut through bone and gristle easily. They are also useful in cutting up poultry or game birds before cooking them.

Garlic Press: If you are smart and care about your hands, you will put an unpeeled clove of garlic into the press, squeeze it, and discover that the crushed garlic comes through, leaving the skin inside. It is easy to remove the skin with the point of a knife.

Glass Cookware is good, but I am most attached to glass ovenware, such as pie and loaf pans. Of course, a glass double boiler has the advantage of letting you see (if you keep looking) whether there is still water in the bottom, but I do not think it is compensated for by the fact that the utensil is so much more easily broken than a metal one. The only top-of-the-range glass utensil I really like is a coffee maker, which is easy to keep absolutely clean—an essential for coffee makers—which is difficult to achieve with metal, and even earthenware ones.

Grater: If you have a food processor, you do not need a grater. However, if you haven't, the best kind is a Mouli. It eliminates grated fingers and nails and does a splendid job. It is also very easy to clean. Also, do not forget that you can "grate" hard substances like cheese and nuts with a blender.

Ice Crusher: You can crush ice in a food processor, though it always makes me feel as though I were asking too much of it—it's such a noisy process! If you haven't one, the best invention for crushing just a little ice is a long-handled, flexible gadget with a round, spoon-like arrangement at the end. When you whack a cube of ice with this, it is crushed in no time. Another possible arrangement is a sturdy canvas bag and a mallet for pounding the ice. *Never* let anyone crush ice in your tea towels. They will be destroyed in no time.

Jar-Top Opener: A metal gadget with grips that can be opened or closed by means of a wooden handle on top, to grip the top of a jar and then turn it. For people whose fingers are not as strong as steel, it is indispensable in the kitchen.

Kitchen Scissors: While any ordinary scissors will do, I am particularly devoted to the type, specifically made for the kitchen, which come apart completely into two pieces for washing. This is especially handy when you have been cutting foods with these scissors. They are also perfectly good for cutting kitchen string and for other uses.

Layer-Cake Pans: I like the kind with false bottoms, as they make it possible to get the cake out neatly. They should be sturdy pans of heavy aluminum or steel.

Meat Grinder: If you have a food processor, a meat grinder is totally unnecessary. The processor can do anything the grinder can do, better and faster. If you haven't, you will certainly need a meat grinder if you want to be an adequate cook. One sad thing about modern kitchens is that there is never any place to screw on the meat grinder, because all counters are so flush with their cupboards. An attempt to solve this problem has been made by constructing a meat grinder with suction cups to hold it to the counter. So far, I am unhappy to report, this has not worked out very well. The grinder inevitably "walks" about on the counter after a few grinds.

Omelet Pans: *See* Enamel-Covered Iron Cookware on page 63.

Pans: It is very important that the bottoms of pans be flat, because if they are uneven the heat will be unevenly distributed and the foods may burn in places yet remain undercooked in others. Discard pans with dented or otherwise uneven bottoms. If you buy good, sturdy cookware, it is unlikely to get into such a condition.

Parsley Mincers: They are not a good tool, because they crush the parsley rather than mince it. A French knife minces parsley both fast and well.

Pressure Cookers: They are one of my pet hates. It is impossible to get consistent results with them. For instance, if you buy peas in the market, it is quite difficult to know how old they are, how long they have been in transit, and other factors bearing on the length of time they should be cooked. If you cook them in a pan, with or without a lid, in which you can test them periodically to see whether they are done, all is well. Doing them in a pressure cooker, however, you cannot be sure whether you will get little bullets or what is practically a puree. Stews made in a pressure cooker save a great deal of time but do not turn out as well by this method as they do when cooked long and slow with loving care in a Dutch oven.

The Reamer: I am often asked, "Do you really think a reamer is a necessary kitchen tool?" This seems to mean that since the advent of frozen and pasturized fruit juices, no reamer is necessary. However, lemon and lime juice are called for in many recipes and must be squeezed fresh if the dishes are to have the proper flavor. If you try to do this by just squeezing the fruit with your hand, you will be very wasteful. So, a reamer is really needed for cooking, as well as for making fresh fruit juice, if you go to that trouble—and can afford it. My favorite kind is the metal one, set on a wooden base, into which you put a piece of cut citrus fruit, then pull down a handle which squeezes it beautifully and keeps the seeds and rind inside.

Rotary Beater: It pays to buy a good rotary beater. This is a tool you may use a great deal, especially if you don't own an electric one. A cheap, wobbly one with tin beaters that rust is an abomination. The more expensive ones are far easier to use, since the best have ball bearings and practically work themselves. Their beaters are made of stainless steel and thus are very easy to clean.

Spatulas: Buy a narrow metal one with a flexible blade, either square or rounded at the end, for taking cookies off a cookie sheet, spreading icing on cakes, etc., and rubber ones of varying size for mixing, scraping food from the sides of a beating bowl, and such operations. There are other metal spatulas of various sizes and shapes which, if you become a devotee, you may wish to buy.

Spring-Form Pan: This is a baking pan that has a fastener on the side, which permits the side to be removed when the cake is done, without touching the cake, which is left on the bottom of the pan. Sometimes these pans have just a plain flat bottom; sometimes they come with a plain bottom, a fluted one, and a tube one. They are indispensable for making cheesecake.

Stainless Steel with Copper Bottoms: These are some of my favorite pans. Again, the bottom should be kept polished, or else out of sight, as tarnished copper is not very attractive. There are those who say that unpolished copper-bottomed pans hold the heat better than polished ones. I have used them in both conditions and must say that I see very little difference in their effectiveness.

Stainless Steel Knives: Though some people cling to old knives that are not stainless because they think it is possible to keep a better edge on them, this is really a superstition. Stainless steel is easiest to clean, will not rust, and retains its edge beautifully. In any case, buy good knives. Cheap ones are useless and a waste of money.

Good knives retain an edge by being given proper care. Never throw good knives into a drawer in a jumble with each other and with other utensils. They should be kept on a rack: either one of the glass-fronted wooden variety with slits for knives of varying sizes, or a magnetic rack to which they cling, or a wooden wall rack in which they rest on their handles with the blades protected in slots. Knives should be sharpened before they show signs of dullness. A dull kitchen knife is a disgrace and a great handicap to the cook.

If you have been taught to sharpen knives properly with a hone, you will think that is the best way to do the job—and you will be right, but few people have this skill. I like a small wall-mounted sharpener, through which a knife is drawn down between two little round wheels. Mine is attached to the side of my glass-fronted knife rack, and I draw each knife gently through every time I put it away. Electric knife-sharpeners can do an excellent job, but the novice must be careful not to wear the knives away with it.

Tin Cookware: The greatest disadvantage of this ware is that it bends and dents too easily. Foods baked in it brown well, so it is good for muffin tins and cake pans. But aluminum is much more substantial, as is stainless steel—and, in the long run, more satisfactory. Anyone who owns them knows that tin pans have a tendency to rust. The solution is to be absolutely sure that they are always thoroughly dried after washing.

Wire Whisk: This is a hand beater made of thin wires, with a sturdy handle, and is wonderful for beating sauces and the like. Some people refuse to use anything else for beating egg whites, but I think that is making life unnecessarily hard when they can be beaten without effort in jig time with a rotary or an electric beater.

14. Glossary of Foods

A

Aioli: A very garlicky mayonnaise which comes from Provence in France. Garlic cloves are peeled and crushed and mixed to a paste with egg yolk and seasonings to taste. Then olive oil is added gradually, as in mayonnaise, and beaten in well with a wire whisk until the mixture reaches the consistency of a thick, smooth mayonnaise. Some recipes instruct the thinning of this with a bit of fish stock or vinegar. It is usually served with hot or cold boiled or poached fish, but may also be served with meats or mixed with vegetables to make a salad.

Antipasto: An Italian appetizer or first course, literally translated as "before the pasta." Great attention is, and should be, paid to preparing food which is varied and appetizing in its use of color. Red roasted pimientos (from a can) are often used; prosciutto and other cold meats; stuffed artichokes; clams; mussels; mushrooms, stuffed or plain; onions; eggplant in various guises; broccoli; tomatoes—almost what you will can be used. Cooked or raw, the antipasti are best served cold.

Apples: When shopping for apples, remember that two large, three medium, or four small apples make a pound.

There are many varieties of apples. Those best for eating raw are Delicious, McIntosh, Stayman, Jonathan, Winesap, and Golden Delicious. Many of these are also good for cooking.

Tart or slightly acid varieties like Yellow Transparent, Gravenstein, Lodi, and Newton are especially good for pies and other apple desserts.

Rome Beauty, Rhode Island Greening, Northern Spy, and some of the varieties eaten raw are excellent for baking. Large or medium-size apples are best for this purpose.

Apples grown in Western states are usually packed to meet state grades. Those from states east of the Rocky Mountains are usually graded on the basis of U.S. grades.

Since apples keep longer than most fruits, you can buy them in quantity and keep them for reasonable periods at cool temperatures. Some varieties have better keeping qualities than others, and you should try to familiarize yourself with which are best for your purposes. Whatever apples you buy should be firm, crisp, bright, clean, and well colored, which should mean that they will have good flavor. Immature apples lack color and have little flavor. They sometimes are shriveled in appearance from having been held too long in storage.

Apricots: Apricots are usually picked when "mature," but in a hard stage, in order that they may reach market in firm condition. The best quality and flavor are found only in apricots that have been ripened on the trees to not less than a firm-ripe stage. Such fruit cannot be shipped well, as it is very perishable. For that reason, you are likely to find them only in markets adjacent to where they are grown. The largest producing areas are California, Oregon, and Washington.

Artichoke (Globe): The globe artichoke is a member of the daisy family, originally grown in southern Europe and North Africa. This delicious vegetable is most plentiful here in the spring. When buying them, be sure to pick those with uniform leaves, tightly packed and of good, bright-green color. Avoid those with withered leaves or brown spots. Medium-size ones are usually the best, as the huge ones are too much to eat and not as flavorful.

To prepare artichokes, cut off the stems near the bottom (so that the cooked product will stand evenly on a plate) and cut the prickly tips off the leaves with kitchen scissors. Boil in salted water with a dash of olive oil in it for about forty minutes, or until the bottom can be easily pricked with a fork. Drain upside down in a colander. Then serve at once, if to be eaten hot, or cool and chill if to be eaten cold as a first course or after the entrée in place of a salad. Hot ones should be served with Hollandaise sauce or melted butter. Cold artichokes are served with a vinaigrette sauce or with mayonnaise. It is always better to serve artichokes as a separate course, providing small plates to hold the leaves as they are eaten, and the choke, when one reaches it and is ready for the best part of all—the bottom (*fond* in French).

Artichokes may be stuffed in various ways, but it is a nuisance to prepare them and, in my opinion, a matter of gilding an already beautiful lily.

Artichoke Bottoms (Fonds d'Artichauts): These are the most delicious part of the vegetable, having more of the distinctive flavor than any other part. As one eats the leaves, one is looking forward to arriving at the prickly "choke," which is easily scraped from the bottom and discarded. Eating the bottom is the crowning touch.

Fonds d'Artichauts also come in tins, imported from France. They are quite expensive and perfectly delicious. One sautés them gently in butter to warm, never to brown them. They can be filled with a pureed vegetable (peas are especially handsome used in this way). Pureed mushrooms (duxelles) are also delectable used as a filling. Add a little cream to them and let it heat through before spooning them into the hollows in the *fonds*.

Asparagus: Asparagus is a member of the lily family and a native of Europe, where it is sometimes grown white, a variety which I dearly love, but which is too much trouble for our mass-producing food growers to bother with. We can buy white asparagus in cans imported from Europe at vast expense. If you're in a humor to treat yourself, and able to do so, even the canned is exceedingly good.

The preparation of asparagus for cooking is easy. Simply cut off any tough, woody bottoms of the stalks, seeing that all you cook are of uniform size, then remove the scales with a vegetable peeler (makes the vegetable more attractive, as well as tender). Tie the stems into a bunch, or bunches, with kitchen twine and cook them, covered, standing them up so that the stems are in water and the tips out. (This is easily accomplished by standing the stalks in the bottom of a double boiler and using the top for a lid.) Cook the asparagus until it is done to your taste, but do not cook it until it is soft and flabby. The stems should be at least a little crisp.

Asparagus is probably at its best served hot with lemon butter or cold with a vinaigrette sauce. However, it takes kindly to Hollandaise, Maltaise (an orangy version of Hollandaise), and any others you can dream up and find you like. Cold, it takes well to mayonnaise (mustard mayonnaise if you want to give it a little snap).

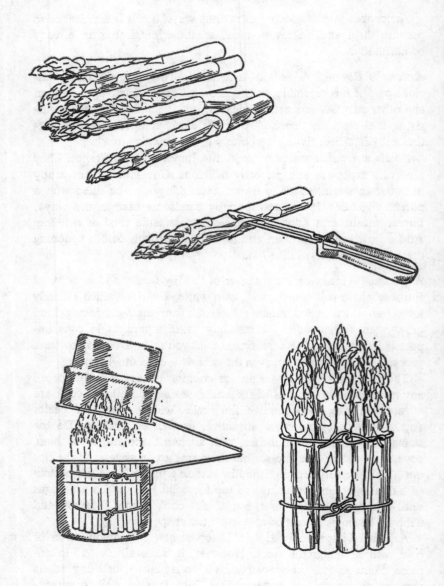

Asparagus Milanese is a wonderful luncheon dish. Place stalks of cooked asparagus in shallow individual oven-proof dishes. Break an egg carefully over the asparagus in each dish. Top with a bit of butter. Bake 10–12 minutes in a 350-degree oven, or until egg is done to your taste. Sprinkle with salt, pepper, nutmeg, and grated Parmesan cheese. Serve at once.

Asparagus is very good as the main ingredient in a quiche. Cold, it is an addition to almost any salad, combining well with any other ingredients you may choose to use.

Aspic: There are two definitions of aspic. First, it is a jelly (in French, *gelée*) made from stock (chicken, beef, or fish) and unflavored gelatin. For jellied soups, add one envelope of gelatin to three cups of stock. Second, an aspic is a dish, made with stock, gelatin, and a solid, such as minced meat or fish, to form a mold, an arrangement which makes many delicious summer dishes. For this, one envelope of gelatin is used with two cups of stock. Use the same proportion in making aspic to use, chopped, as a decoration for chilled molds. If the stock is homemade, it should be clarified to be sure that it is translucent and bright (*see* Cooking Terms).

Avocado: This is really a fruit, but it is used chiefly as a vegetable. It originated in Mexico and Guatemala and was introduced to South America many years ago. Now many avocados are grown in the United States, for the most part in Florida and in Southern California. Our avocados vary greatly in size and, as we are inclined to do with all growing things, we have developed some huge varieties. Personally, I find the medium size most useful, as a half of one of the huge ones is more than most people could eat. An avocado is ripe when a gentle pressure of the fingers makes the flesh yield slightly. It is easy, however, to ripen them by leaving them out of the refrigerator in a fairly warm place. And if you can only buy ones that are not quite ripe, wrap each in several thicknesses of newspaper. They will usually ripen in a few hours, or a day at the most. If, for any reason, you want only to use half of an avocado, leave the pit in the unused half and put it in plastic wrap. It will keep in the refrigerator for a day or two without darkening much.

In general, it is best not to cut open an avocado or peel it until just before you are going to use it for whatever purpose, as they are inclined to darken rapidly when exposed to the air.

Avocados make delicious cream soup, especially when it's served cold in the summer. They also are fine for a first course, half an avocado for each person, with the hollows where the pit was filled with French dressing. Some people also serve them peeled, with the cavity filled with mayonnaise. Very rich and very good! Of course, everyone knows that this is a wonderful salad ingredient, just sliced on greens or mixed into a salad of greens, tomatoes, cucumber, and whatever else your fancy dictates.

Avocados stuffed with salmon, tuna, or shrimp salad make a perfect luncheon dish. Perhaps the best one of all in this category is avocados stuffed with mussels in curried mayonnaise.

Guacamole, the wonderful Mexican concoction, is made from mashed avocado with mayonnaise, salt, garlic powder, and chili powder to taste. It is especially good served as a dip with drinks, to be taken up with taco chips.

Too few people seem to realize that avocados are delicious cooked, as well as raw. An avocado stuffed with creamed salmon or tuna or any leftover white-fleshed fish, flaked, and topped with a sprinkling of grated Parmesan, then baked in a 400-degree oven until the top is nicely browned (about twenty minutes) is a rich and delicious entrée. Avocado slices, sprinkled with salt, pepper, and flour, then sautéed in butter and a little oil over fairly high heat for about eight minutes (turned once to achieve a golden color on both sides), are ambrosial eating and a perfect accompaniment to sautéed chicken livers.

B

Bacon: Bacon can be bought sliced, by the half pound or pound package, or in the slab, also by the pound. The only advantage of the latter is that it keeps better than the sliced variety. In either case, buy fat bacon. It is much tastier than bacon that is too lean.

There are, in my opinion, two satisfactory ways to cook bacon. The first is in a skillet, over very low heat, turning the bacon occasionally so that it browns on both sides. This method keeps it from shrinking and makes it beautifully crisp without ever browning it too much. It can take a half hour or more to be well cooked. Remove it from the pan and drain it on absorbent paper before serving. The second method is to bake it on a rack in a pan made for the purpose. This drains off all the fat into the pan as it cooks and is also a successful way to do it well, without much shrinkage. Keep the oven at low heat and check occasionally to see how the meat is coming along. It need not be turned while cooking. This is also a slow process and can take up to half an hour in a 250-degree oven.

Canadian Bacon is made by curing and smoking the lean muscle portion of boneless loins of pork. It doesn't really resemble sliced or slab bacon in any way. It can be bought in the roll in which you find it at the butcher's or you can buy slices if you're too lazy to do the job yourself. It can be cooked by frying the slices slowly in butter or by baking the roll and slicing it when hot. It is usually served for breakfast or brunch with eggs.

Sliced, slab, or Canadian bacon all can be frozen, but, as with all pork products, not for too long. If, for instance, you have opened a package of sliced bacon or a roll of Canadian bacon and you are going away for a few days, put them in the freezer by all means, but remember to use them up soon after you return.

Baking Powder: There are two types of baking powder, regular and double-acting. The latter reacts more slowly than the former, releasing part of its gas at room temperature when it is mixed with the other ingredients, and the rest upon being placed in the heat of an oven. The regular variety releases its gas at room temperature when mixed with the other ingredients.

The type of baking powder you buy will be clearly marked on the label, and it is wise to take the manufacturer's advice on the proportion to be used with a cup of flour.

Baking Soda (Sodium Bicarbonate): Baking soda, mixed with sour milk or molasses in making baked goods such as sour-milk pancakes —in the proportion of half a teaspoon of baking soda to one cup sour milk or molasses—gives off as much gas as two teaspoons of baking powder. The baking soda should be mixed and sifted with the flour required in the recipe. Baking soda is also most effective for absorbing odors, when the box is opened and placed in the refrigerator. A tiny pinch added to any green vegetable as it cooks makes it stay appetizingly and brightly green.

Bananas: If a banana has a few little dark specks on the skin, it is sweet and ripe and ready to eat. This is also true if the tip is green and just turning yellow. Bananas with large brown spots on them are probably on the verge of turning brown inside also. From experience, I tend to cling to the old adage that tells us never to store bananas in the refrigerator. The entire skin turns brown, if not black, and the fruit hasn't as much flavor when it's cold.

Bananas are very good when cooked. Banana tarts are a treat. Fried bananas (without sugar) are delicious with certain meats. Sautéed in butter, sprinkled with brown sugar and a bit of dark rum, they make a splendid dessert. And what is known in Hong Kong as "Spun Bananas"—two-inch pieces of whole bananas dipped in a light batter and deep-fat fried until golden brown, then dipped into a sugar syrup and served with a bowl of ice water into which the guests can dip their own with their chopsticks so that the outside becomes crisp and crackly and the inside is still hot—is one of the best desserts I know. Apple slices are cooked in the same way.

Bananas split, sprinkled with lemon or lime juice, then with brown sugar, nutmeg, and cinnamon, and finally with grated coconut are a fine invention.

Barbecue: The most usual modern definition of this is the grilling of meats, chicken, or other foods over an open fire, usually made with charcoal briquettes. Such food sometimes is marinated or basted, and always is served with a barbecue sauce. There are many versions of such a sauce, but it is usually based on tomatoes and contains any or all of the following: wine (usually dry red), onions, garlic, herbs, mustard, brown sugar, and other seasonings.

Bavarian Cream: This is a custard with gelatin, beaten egg whites, whipped cream, and flavoring incorporated into it. It may be flavored with fruit juices, chocolate, coffee, liqueurs, or wines. The same dessert is sometimes referred to as a "Cold Soufflé."

Beans (Green or Wax): If you really care a lot about eating fresh beans and have no vegetable garden, you will go to a market where they don't mind your picking over the beans available in order to have what you buy as near as possible the same size. This will make the cooking much simpler, as you will not have to overcook the small ones in order to have the larger ones done to your taste. In any case, do not overcook this delicious vegetable, or it will be a mush and not a bit tasty. A pound of these fresh beans serves four. Don't forget that the addition of slivered sautéed almonds, thinly sliced water chestnuts, sliced sautéed mushrooms, slivers of pimiento, or a sour cream sauce flavored with herbs can give a change of pace and new flavor to them.

Beans or Peas, Dried: This includes lentils, kidney beans, limas, white pea beans, pinto (pink) beans, navy beans, soy beans, flageolets, split peas, black eyed peas, chick peas (garbanzos), and more, all of which come under the heading of legumes, as the word is used in this country. They are high in protein value, among other assets, and can be substituted for meat frequently in your menus. A cupful of dried beans yields two to three cups, depending on their size.

The most familiar dried-bean dish in the United States is certainly Boston Baked Beans, which are usually made of white pea beans or navy beans. Lots of these dried beans and peas make wonderful soup, and they are soups of such hearty character that they easily make a meal-in-a-dish for most people. Lentil soup is an outstanding example, and it is particularly good with slices of frankfurter in it. The Dutch make the most wonderful split-pea soup in the world, known as *snert*. There's a restaurant in Amsterdam which gives students in the city a greatly reduced price for *snert* and black bread once a week. All legumes make a hearty side dish in place of potatoes or other starch. They must be soaked for several hours, then drained and cooked in water for several hours also. They should always be well seasoned with whatever your fancy or the recipe you are using dictates.

One delectable combination of fresh green beans and flageolets is baked in a casserole, well sauced, and nicely browned on top.

Beef: Beef is obtainable in USDA grades of Prime, Choice, Good, Standard, and Commercial. Prime very rarely appears in consumer stores, as it is bought up entirely by restaurants and clubs. Choice is very good beef and the best you are likely to find in the markets. Good is not as juicy or flavorful as the two higher grades, but is fairly tender and economical because it hasn't much fat. The two lower grades are seldom marked in any way, so you probably won't be able to identify them.

Rib roasts and most steaks are tender cuts. For that reason, it is possible to roast or broil them. It is not wise to cook less than a two-rib roast, and a three-rib one is still better. Steaks should be cut two to three inches thick to be broiled nice and brown on the outside and rare within. The exception to this thickness is steaks you prefer to sauté, as the French often do. These may be cut 1½ inches thick.

The kinds of steak available are porterhouse, rib, T-bone, filet mignon or tournedos (the same thing, though the latter are often cut a little thinner than the former), sirloin, pin-bone, and shell. There is something called a New York cut steak, a designation used only in the Middle West and West, which is a porterhouse without the fillet. In New York, this is called strip steak, *never* New York cut. A club, or Delmonico, steak is a boneless cut from the end of the loin. Or it can be cut from the rib, in which case the bone is left in.

Cuts like the round and chuck are less tender and should be pot-roasted or braised (*see* Glossary of Cooking Terms).

Rump, heel of the round, brisket, short ribs, flank steak, and plate are all good for braising.

The best cuts to buy for ground beef are round and chuck (a little more fatty than the former and thus, perhaps, more flavorful). "Hamburger meat," which you buy ready ground, is likely to have too much fat in it and thus be very wasteful in the cooking. So the best advice is to have it ground to your order.

Beef Dishes: This is a random list of interesting and fairly unusual beef dishes, many of which are of foreign origin, so that when you find you can afford to buy beef, you can vary the flavor and thus the interest. Check your favorite cookbook for recipes.

Beef Stroganoff: This dish should be made from fine fillet of beef, cut into thin strips and browned very quickly in butter, with a bit of sliced onion. To this is added consommé, sour cream, and a bit of to-mato puree, if you like, though purists think that a desecration.

Boiled Beef: This is a favorite dish in Austria and is served in every Vienna restaurant. It consists of beef chuck, with beef bones, sim-mered in water to cover with seasonings, parsley, carrots, celery, leeks, and onions for about three hours. The beef is served sliced with plain horseradish, apple-horseradish sauce, or chive sauce. It is delicious. The Austrians call it Tafelspitz.

Braised Short Ribs of Beef: Since these are very bony, you should allow a pound to a person. Season them, dust them with flour, and cook them in a 450-degree oven twenty-five minutes, or until well browned. Chopped onions, celery, mashed garlic, bay leaves, whole cloves, thyme, finely diced carrots, tomato sauce, Burgundy wine, and chicken broth are added, and the dish is then cooked in a 325-degree oven until the meat is tender (one and a half to two hours).

Carbonnade of Beef: This is a Belgian (Flemish) dish which consists of slices of beef rump, browned well, alternating with slightly browned onions, cooked long and slow in beer.

Cornish Pasty: This is an English dish consisting of chopped round of beef, chopped potatoes, and seasonings, baked in pastry. The pas-

ties, like little round pies, are eaten hot or cold, in which latter fashion they are wonderful for picnics.

Fondue Bourguignonne: The best fillet of beef is cut into inch-square cubes and cooked in a mixture of bubbling hot oil and butter by each guest according to his taste. Several sauces are also presented for dipping the cooked bits of steak before eating.

London Broil: A thin cut of flank steak, broiled rare (three to four minutes on each side) and sliced on a sharp diagonal. This cutting "against the grain" is very important and makes the beef much more tender.

Nargis Kofta is perhaps the best of the meat *koftas.* This version of it comes from Calcutta. Shell hard-cooked eggs and cut them in half. Mix ground chuck with ground cardamom seed, minced mint, salt, pepper, and ground coriander seeds. Cover each half egg fairly thickly with the mixture. Fry in butter to brown on all sides. Melt more butter in another pan and in it fry onion, ground red chilies, turmeric, mashed garlic, and shredded fresh ginger until the raw smell disappears (about five minutes). Add yogurt and chicken stock and heat through. Serve the *kofta* in the sauce. Delicious!

Pastitsio: The Greeks invented this dish, which consists of elbow macaroni, ground beef, eggs, milk, and seasonings—including a lot of garlic. Parmesan cheese is sprinkled over the top, which is browned in the baking.

Rump of Beef in Foil: A piece of whatever size beef rump you need for the occasion is placed on an ample sheet of aluminum foil. Sprinkle a package of dehydrated onion soup over the top. Bring up the edges of the foil all round the beef and pour in a half cup or so of dry red wine. Fold the edges of the foil firmly together so that the meat is totally enclosed. Bake in a roasting pan in a 350-degree oven one and a half hours.

Biscuits, Baking Powder: To make them flaky, be careful not to mix the flour and shortening too much. Roll the biscuits about a quarter-inch thick. If you prefer tall, puffy biscuits, roll the dough thicker.

Bouquet Garni: A combination of parsley, thyme, and bay leaf, used to flavor stews, soups, and sauces. If fresh, the herbs are tied together with string. If dried, they are put into a little cheesecloth bag and tied firmly. Sometimes other herbs, celery leaves, and the like are added, but in that case they are usually specifically required by the recipe. The bouquet is always removed and discarded when the cooking is finished.

Bourride: A dish of Provençal origin, this consists of small white-meat fish (one to a person), cleaned, but left whole, simmered in fish stock for about five minutes. Drain well, reserving stock for sauce—which is Aioli, made with garlic, egg yolks, olive oil, and fish stock. It is quite thin and served poured over the fish.

Bread, Baking: First, let it be said that all devoted cooks love to bake for a variety of reasons. The process of kneading, for instance, is a marvelous way to relieve frustrations. The smell of baking bread, cakes, cookies, and pies is delicious and heartwarming. And the pleasure which can be given to family and friends by the presentation of home-baked foods is exceedingly rewarding in this day of packaged products which bear little relation to the "real thing."

Sifting Flour: The small sifters are my favorites for home baking. Place a measuring cup on a piece of waxed paper, then sift the flour into the cup until it is heaping. Even the top off lightly with a flat knife.

Leavening: This word means "to lighten." In baking, it refers to one of three methods for making baked goods rise. First, leavening is air. This is added by beating egg whites or by sifting flour. Second, it is steam, which is the leavening for popovers and cream puffs. Third, it is carbon dioxide, which is derived from yeast, baking soda, and baking powder.

Yeast: There is fresh yeast (also known as "compressed") and there is dry yeast, which comes in little envelopes. Fresh yeast is sometimes hard to find, and the more familiar dry yeast, fortunately, gives good results. Two envelopes of dry yeast is the equivalent of one ounce of fresh.

Shortening: Butter, margarine, and vegetable shortening are all used in baking recipes. If the recipe calls for one cup of vegetable shortening and you want to substitute butter or margarine for added flavor, use one cup, plus two tablespoons of the butter or margarine. This is because butter and margarine contain only about 80 percent fat, but vegetable shortening is 100 percent fat.

Sour Milk: If a baking recipe calls for sour milk and soda and you wish to substitute fresh milk, use a cup of fresh milk for each cup of sour milk required and substitute one teaspoon of baking powder for each one-fourth teaspoon of baking soda.

Kneading Bread Dough: Place the dough on a lightly floured board. With lightly floured hands, fold the dough in half and press it with the heels of your hands about ten times. Now give the dough a quarter turn, fold, and repeat the process. Continue thus until the dough is firm and elastic. Add a very little more flour to the board if necessary. This takes five to seven minutes. If you have a bread hook for your mixer or an electric food processor, it will take no time at all. If you are arthritic or otherwise handicapped, it will be a blessing. But you will miss a lot of fun by not kneading it yourself!

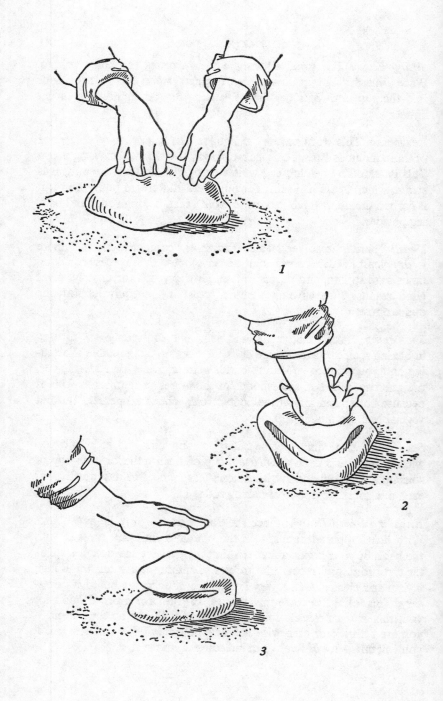

1

2

3

Temperature for Rising Dough: This is the most important factor in bread-making. It should be from 80 degrees to 90 degrees Fahrenheit, and the dough should be placed in a bowl, floured lightly, covered, and placed in a draft-free place. If all these conditions are met, the dough should double in bulk in forty minutes to an hour. If the temperature is too low, the rising period will be too long and your bread will be coarse. If the temperature is too high, the yeast may be killed; then the volume will be small and the bread not tender.

Punching Down Bread Dough: Usually, after the dough has doubled in bulk for the first time, recipes instruct you to "punch it down." This means exactly what it says and the punching, which flattens it a good deal, is another soul-satisfying way to get rid of frustrations. When it is well punched, form it into a ball again and let it rise for the second time under the same circumstances.

French Bread: Many people say that what we buy here as "French bread" isn't French at all. Unless it's imported, it certainly is nothing like the bread in France. Their flour is different from ours, for one thing. Another major reason for the difference is that they make their bread with water and we insist on using milk because the bread will keep longer. Proper French bread does not keep more than twenty-four hours, if that, but the flavor is great and much better than what our commercial bakers produce. If you want to eat French bread, better find a good recipe and make it yourself, unless you are prepared to buy it imported from France and pay a vast price.

Bread (Storing): Bread keeps much longer and better if stored in the refrigerator. It can also be frozen most successfully, but in thinking about this treatment, be sure you are not taking up space that might better be devoted to foods which *must* be kept frozen. If you have a large freezer, you can, of course, devote more space to bread if you so wish.

Brioche: This is a slightly sweetened yeast bread, baked in a shape which makes it look rather like a mushroom with a very thick stem. It is usually served as a coffee bread or cake for breakfast. There is also what is known as "common" brioche dough, which has very little sugar in it and is used in the making of hors d'oeuvres and for encasing small hot-entrée dishes. It is also used as the casing for the

Russian coulibiac, filled with salmon, baked, and served with a lovely rich sauce.

Brown Sugar: If your brown sugar has hardened to rock-like consistency, put it into the food processor, a modest amount at a time, and whirl it until it is soft and fine. Store in the refrigerator—and it will never harden again!

Bulgur: Also known as burghol, this is cracked wheat, an essential ingredient in many Middle Eastern countries. It is known in Russia as kasha. It is used in *tabouleh,* a typical Lebanese salad. After being soaked in cold water for an hour, it is squeezed out and mixed with finely minced parsley, tomatoes, mint leaves, onion, and scallions, then dressed with lemon juice, salt and pepper, and olive oil. It is also used in *kibbe,* mixed with ground lamb and seasonings and baked, or in raw *kubbe,* served as an hors d'oeuvre with a little olive oil added if desired. It can be substituted for rice in almost any menu.

C

Cakes:

Baking a Cake at High Altitude: Special recipes are required at high altitudes. Usually a decrease in the amount of leavening (baking powder or soda) or sugar, or both, and an increase in the amount of liquid, are needed. It is also sometimes necessary to reduce the shortening when making very rich cakes at high altitudes. Many cookbooks have a section on high altitude cooking. Check your local bookstore or library.

Dobos Torte is an Austrian cake of many thin layers (usually seven) sandwiched together with chocolate butter cream and topped by a hard layer of caramelized sugar.

Genoise is a sponge cake made with butter.

Lady Baltimore Cake is a white layer cake, filled and iced with a boiled frosting containing figs, raisins, and nuts.

Pound Cake received its name from the fact that it was made from a pound of flour, a pound of sugar, a pound of butter, and a pound of eggs, plus seasonings. Today's recipes do not require weighing all the ingredients.

Sacher Torte is a very, very rich Austrian chocolate cake, glazed with apricot jam and iced with chocolate. The Sacher Hotel in Vienna has never given the recipe to anyone, but there are many versions of it to be found in lots of cookbooks.

Upside-Down Cake: (*See* under "U".)

Canapés (also called Appetizers or Hors d'oeuvres): These are small bits of food served with drinks before a meal. They may be hot or cold, and it is most interesting and appealing to serve one hot and one cold one for a small group of diners, or two hot and several cold for more people. If the occasion is a cocktail party, not to be followed by food, you may offer a great variety of choices, limited only, perhaps, by the number of guests you are serving. There follow a few suggestions to put you in mind of the many possibilities available.

Cold Canapés—

Cheese Board: Serve two cheeses of contrasting flavor and texture to a few people, more to a crowd. In general, it is best to accompany them with crackers of very delicate flavor which does not interfere with the cheeses, but if you want to serve at least one cheese of strong flavor, you might offer with it wheat toast wafers or small pieces of pumpernickel or other dark bread, which can compete with the cheese.

Crudités: Raw vegetables, served well chilled, with a seasoned salt or a dip of some sort, are probably the most popular canapés in today's diet-conscious world. Cucumbers, carrots, celery, zucchini, green or red sweet peppers, and any other vegetables you find delicious to eat raw, cut into long, thin strips, are some of the possibilities.

Guacamole: Mashed ripe avocado, mixed with chili powder, garlic, onion to taste, and mayonnaise. Serve this with corn chips for dunking.

Mushrooms à la Grecque: A mixture of tomatoes, white wine, fresh mushrooms, and seasonings, cooked together, chilled, and served with crackers.

Pâté: You may make this yourself (many recipes are available) or perhaps do a little research to find a fine country pâté (the best are wonderful) which you can buy in a shop specializing in such goodies.

Potted Shrimp: For this English canapé (it is also served as a first course in Britain), melt butter and season it with mace, freshly grated nutmeg, and cayenne to taste, then add a can of tiny Alaskan or Gulf shrimp, drained well. Let stand for a few minutes to absorb the flavor, then put into little "pots" and chill in the refrigerator. *They also freeze very well.* Serve with fresh toast to spread it on—or with crackers, if you prefer.

Hot Canapés—

Bacon-Wrapped Crackers: Cut bacon slices in half crosswise. Wrap each piece of bacon around a club cracker. Place on a rack in a baking pan and bake one hour in a 250-degree oven, or until bacon is crisp and crackers are slightly brown.

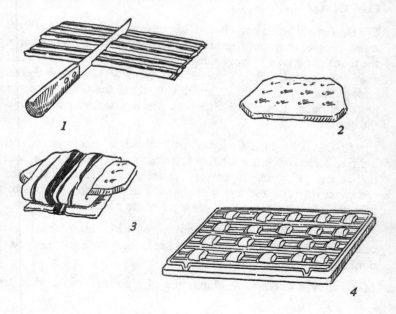

Fondue Bourguignonne: (See under "F".)

Meatballs in Sauce: In my opinion, the Scandinavians, particularly the Swedes, do best at these. So look up a good Swedish recipe and go from there. A chafing dish is the perfect object in which to serve them so that they stay hot. Toothpicks should be provided for picking them up to eat.

Onion Canapés: Make small rounds of white bread. On each, place a thin slice of onion of about the same size. Top with a generous dab of mayonnaise. Bake in 375-degree oven until golden brown (about ten minutes).

Rumaki: (See under "R".)

Caramelize: In the proportion of two parts sugar to one part water, melt sugar in a small skillet over low heat, stirring constantly with a wooden spoon until the sugar turns liquid and browns to the degree desired. Add water and mix well. Remove from heat and use in recipe as instructed.

Casserole Cookery: Cooking food in this way is particularly good for using leftovers. Mix together whatever foods you have in your refrigerator that you think will complement or contrast nicely with each other, add a good sauce, put all into a casserole, top with buttered crumbs or cheese dotted with butter, and bake. You can thus have a meal in a dish, easy to prepare and, usually, even easier to eat. You ought to have at least one casserole with a cover, as there may be times when you don't want to have a browned top—or when you'd rather cook on top of the range. And it's good to have casseroles of several sizes if you are, quite properly, addicted to this mode of cookery.

Celery Root (also known as celeriac): The French call it *celeri rave.* This is a special variant of celery which is cultivated for its large root, not for the stalks and foliage. It is a member of the carrot family. In Europe it is very popular, but here we know it all too little. It is perhaps best known for the dish Céleri Rémoulade, a first course made of blanched julienne of celery root and dressed with a mayonnaise-like dressing. Julia Child, in her first book, *Mastering the Art of French Cooking,* has a marvelous recipe for braising it. In fact, I like it better cooked than as salad.

Cheeses:

Natural Cheese is made by separating the milk solids from whole milk through curdling with rennet or bacterial culture or both. The curd is then separated from the whey by heating, stirring, and pressing. Occasionally, both milk and cream are used, as is skimmed milk.

Cheeses are then formed into characteristic shapes and given a coat of wax or other protective covering. Then they are allowed to ripen, under conditions of controlled temperature and moisture, until they are ready to eat. In this country, being always in a hurry, we are sometimes inclined not to ripen cheese long enough. Still, we make many excellent ones, like our own original cheddars, Liederkranz, and copies (in varying degrees of accuracy) of European cheeses.

Processed Cheese: This is a product made by mixing a variety of shredded natural cheese and pasteurizing (heating) it so that no further ripening occurs. Such cheese often contains pimientos, fruits, vegetables, or meats. Most true lovers of natural cheese regard the processed variety as a leathery abomination, the best part of whose flavor has been destroyed by the pasteurizing process. There are also pasteurized processed cheese food and pasteurized processed cheese spread, made in much the same manner as processed cheese, but usually in different forms and shapes.

Unripened Cheese: This is cheese that is consumed soon after it is made. These are relatively high in moisture and cannot be kept very long—like cottage cheese. Norwegian Gjetost, on the other hand, while it is an unripened cheese, has little moisture in it and may be kept for several weeks without damage to texture or flavor.

SEMISOFT, RIPENED NATURAL CHEESES

Bel Paese from Italy and the United States

Flavor — Domestic, very mild; imported (much better), fairly robust
Consistency — Medium firm, creamy
Color — Creamy yellow interior; slightly gray or brownish surface, sometimes coated with yellow wax
How Bought — Small wheel, foil-wrapped in a cardboard box
Uses — Appetizers; especially good with pears or other fruit for dessert

Brick from the United States

Flavor — Mild to strong
Consistency — Semisoft to medium firm
Color — Creamy yellow
How Bought — Brick-shaped loaf or cuts therefrom
Uses — Appetizers, sandwiches

Muenster from Germany

Flavor — Mild to strong, depending upon age and amount of caraway or anise, which is sometimes added
Consistency — Semisoft with many small holes
Color — Yellow interior; brick-red surface
How Bought — Circular cake or block
Uses — Appetizers, sandwiches, or in cooked dishes

Oka from Canada

Flavor – Aromatic; made by Trappist monks from secret method of the order which originated in France
Consistency – Medium soft
Color – Creamy yellow
How Bought – Round wheel
Uses – Appetizers, or for dessert with crackers or fruit

Pont l'Évêque from France

Flavor – Medium strong
Consistency – Semisoft
Color – Golden
How Bought – In box about 5 inches square
Uses – Definitely a dessert cheese

Port du Salut from France

Flavor – Superb mellow flavor; this is the original Trappist cheese
Consistency – Soft, creamy, buttery
Color – Creamy yellow
How Bought – Wheels and wedges
Uses – Appetizers, or for dessert with crackers or fruit

SOFT, RIPENED NATURAL CHEESES

Alouette from the United States—Our copy of Boursin and good (much cheaper, too)

Flavor – Delicate triple creme, flavored with herbs
Consistency – Soft
Color – White, with flecks of herbs
How Bought – Smallish round cake, wrapped in plastic
Uses – As canapé with crackers

Boursin (also Boursault) fines herbes from France—two companies with these names

Flavor – Faintly sourish, rich, triple cream, flavored with herbs
Consistency – Soft and delicate, somewhat crumbly
Color – White, with flecks of herbs
How Bought – Smallish round cake, wrapped in plastic
Uses – As canapé with crackers

Brie from France

Flavor – Mild, very delicate
Consistency – Soft, smooth, slightly runny when just ripe
Color – Creamy yellow, edible thin brown-and-white crust
How Bought – Whole, in a round wooden box, or cut in pie-shaped pieces, wrapped in plastic and sold according to weight
Uses – As canapé with crackers, or with fruit as dessert

Camembert from France

Flavor – Mild, distinctive flavor, quite different from Brie
Consistency – Smooth, soft, slightly runny when just ripe
Color – Creamy pale yellow interior; edible thin white or gray-white crust
How Bought – In foil-wrapped wedges in a box that is a half circle
Uses – As canapé with crackers, or with fruit for dessert; also makes a very rich soufflé

Explorateur from France

Flavor – Mild, beautiful, unique flavor
Consistency – Triple creme, very soft
Color – Creamy white interior, thin brown-and-white crust
How Bought – Comes in a five-inch round. Sold whole, by weight, or some shops will sell half a round
Uses – As canapé with crackers

Hablé Crème Chantilly from Sweden

Flavor – Delicate, fresh, rich
Consistency – Soft, butterlike
Color – White
How Bought – In wedge-shaped boxes of thin wood
Uses – With crackers, French bread, or toast for dessert

Liederkranz from the United States

Flavor – Strong flavor and fairly strong odor, but not unpleasant
Consistency – Soft, smooth
Color – Creamy yellow interior; pale orange edible crust
How Bought – Rectangular package
Uses – With crackers, French bread, or toast for dessert

Limburger from Belgium and the United States

Flavor – Very strong and pungent; strong, unpleasant (to many) odor
Consistency – Soft, smooth, with small, irregular openings
Color – Creamy white interior, reddish yellow surface
How Bought – Rectangular package
Uses – With crackers or dark bread; especially good with beer

SOFT AND FIRM UNRIPENED NATURAL CHEESES

Cottage, plain or creamed (also called pot or farmer cheese)

Flavor – Bland
Consistency – Soft; large or small curd
Color – White to creamy
How Bought – In round cardboard or plastic containers with lids
Uses – In salads, with fruits or vegetables, in sandwiches, dips, hot dishes with noodles, cheesecake, coeur à la crème, pastry

Cream from the United States

Flavor – Bland
Consistency – Soft and smooth
Color – White
How Bought – In 3- and 8-ounce packages, foil-wrapped (or sometimes in boxes)
Uses – In salads, sandwiches, dips, cheesecake; with crackers and guava jelly for dessert

Feta from Greece

Flavor – Slightly salty, a little sharp; made from sheep's milk
Consistency – Soft, curd like cottage cheese
Color – White
How Bought – By the pound, in cans, or in plastic packages
Uses – In appetizers, salads, omelets, cheese pie, and for fried cheese

Gjetöst from Norway

Flavor – Sweet, like caramel; made from goat's milk
Consistency – Firm, but not hard
Color – Brown
How Bought – In paper-wrapped rectangles
Uses – Best with dark bread; should be cut paper-thin

Mozzarella from Italy

Flavor – Mild
Consistency – Slightly firm, creamy white plastic
Color – Creamy white
How Bought – Small, round, wrapped in transparent paper or plastic, sealed with metal clip; also comes shredded
Uses – In hot sandwiches, pizzas, Italian pasta dishes, and casseroles

Neufchâtel from France

Flavor – Mild
Consistency – Soft, smooth; has less milk fat than cream cheese
Color – White
How Bought – In 4- and 8-ounce packages
Uses – In salads, sandwiches, dips, cheesecake

Ricotta from Italy

Flavor – Bland
Consistency – Soft, moist or dry curd, like cottage cheese
Color – White
How Bought – In pint and quart cardboard or plastic containers
Uses – In salads, appetizers, omelets, pasta dishes, desserts

VERY HARD RIPENED NATURAL CHEESES

Parmesan from Italy

Flavor – When young, slightly sweet; when hard, a bit sharper
Consistency – When young, soft enough to break
Color – Creamy white with black rind
How Bought – By the pound from a wheel
Uses – When young, with bread; when aged, grated and used in many hot dishes or sprinkled over soup and pasta

Romano from Italy

Flavor – Sharp and tangy
Consistency – When well aged, brittle
Color – Yellowish white with greenish-black rind
How Bought – By the pound from rounds flattened top and bottom
Uses – Grated, in cooked dishes and as topping for soups and pasta

Sapsago from Switzerland

Flavor – Sharp, pungent with distinct flavor of clover
Consistency – Hard
Color – Light green
How Bought – Small, truncated cone wrapped in paper
Uses – Grated: to be used with great discretion or it will overwhelm any cooked dish; often mixed with butter to make a spread

BLUE-VEIN-MOLD RIPENED NATURAL CHEESES

Blue or Bleu from France, Denmark

Flavor – Tangy, peppery
Consistency – Semisoft; sometimes crumbly
Color – White, marbled with veins of blue mold
How Bought – Large cylinders or cuts thereof; usually foil-wrapped
Uses – Appetizers, dips, salad dressings, sandwiches; for dessert with crackers

Gorgonzola from Italy

Flavor – Tangy, peppery
Consistency – Semisoft; sometimes crumbly; lower moisture than Blue or Bleu
Color – Creamy white, marbled with veins of blue-green mold
How Bought – Cylinders or cuts thereof
Uses – Appetizers, dips, salad dressings, sandwiches; for dessert with crackers

Roquefort from France (No copies; name may not be used for cheese made outside France)

Flavor – Tangy, with very slightly sweet undertone
Consistency – Semisoft; sometimes crumbly
Color – White or creamy white, marbled with veins of blue mold
How Bought – Large cylinders or cuts thereof, foil-wrapped
Uses – Appetizers, dips, salad dressings, spread on steaks; for dessert with crackers

Stilton from England

Flavor – Piquant; milder than Gorgonzola or Roquefort
Consistency – Semisoft, flaky; slightly more crumbly than Blue or Bleu
Color – Creamy white, marbled with veins of blue-green mold
How Bought – Cylinders or cuts thereof, foil-wrapped
Uses – Appetizers, with salads; for dessert with crackers

FIRM, RIPENED NATURAL CHEESES

Caciocavallo from Italy

Kaskaval from Rumania and Bulgaria

Cashkavallo from Syria

Flavor – Slightly salty with faintly nutty aftertaste
Consistency – Firm
Color – White
How Bought – By the pound, cut to order from a wheel
Uses – Appetizers, in cooking; for dessert with crackers

Cheddar from England and the United States

Flavor – Mild to very sharp
Consistency – Firm and smooth
Color – Pale yellow to bright orange
How Bought – Wheels and cuts therefrom by the pound
Uses – Appetizers, sandwiches, sauces, in hot dishes, for grating, with apple pie

Edam from the Netherlands

Flavor – Mellow, full flavor, very like Gouda
Consistency – Semisoft to firm; small holes; lower milk-fat content than Gouda
Color – Yellow to orange; red wax coating
How Bought – Cannonball shape. Sometimes in a crock with wine
Uses – For breakfast, as appetizer; for dessert with crackers

Gouda from the Netherlands

Flavor – Mellow, full flavor, very like Edam
Consistency – Semisoft to firm; small holes; higher milk-fat content than Edam
Color – Yellow to orange; red wax coating
How Bought – Round with flattened top and bottom
Uses – For breakfast, as appetizer; for dessert with crackers

Gruyère from French Switzerland

Flavor – Delicate, with a slight sweetness
Consistency – Semisoft with tiny holes
Color – White
How Bought – Wheels
Uses – Appetizers, sandwiches, in cooked dishes such as quiche Lorraine; for dessert with crackers

Jack or Monterey Jack from the United States

Flavor – Mild to sharp
Consistency – Firm and smooth
Color – Pale yellow
How Bought – By the pound from round loaves
Uses – Appetizers, cooking; for dessert with crackers

Noekkelöst from Norway

Flavor   – Mellow, full flavor with caraway seed
Consistency – Firm and smooth
Color   – Orange
How Bought – By the pound from rounds flattened top and
               bottom
Uses   – For breakfast, appetizers; for dessert with crackers

Provolone from Italy

Flavor   – Mellow to sharp, smoky, salty
Consistency – Firm and smooth
Color   – Creamy yellow interior, brown outside
How Bought – Pear-shaped, long like a sausage
Uses   – Appetizers, in cooking; for dessert with crackers

Swiss or Emmenthal from Switzerland

Flavor   – Sweet, delicate
Consistency – Firm, smooth with large round holes which should
               glisten if the cheese is properly ripe
Color   – Pale yellow
How Bought – By the pound from big wheels
Uses   – Sandwiches, in cooking (as for fondue), in sauces

Vermont Sage from the United States

Flavor   – Mellow with distinct sage flavor
Consistency – Firm and smooth
Color   – Pale yellow with flecks of green
How Bought – By the pound from round loaves
Uses   – Appetizers; for dessert with crackers

Chowder: Being of New England ancestry, I am one of those who say there is only one *real* kind of chowder—the New England variety. It is certainly the best. New England clam chowder, for instance, consists of chopped clams, potatoes, onion, flour, thyme, milk, cream, and clam juice. There is something known as Manhattan clam chowder which seems to me a vegetable soup (largely tomato) with a few clams run through it, though definitely not enough to compete with the other flavors present. There is also a Rhode Island clam chowder, which is a sort of mixture of the two previously mentioned. There are also fish chowders—the New England one being as white as its clam one, and as delicious. However, fish chowders in many guises, with many names and ingredients, are made in many countries of the world and are delicious, though totally different from the New England variety.

Coffee: If you really love coffee, you will grind what you need every time you make a potful. There are people who don't understand such matters, who think that this is a great waste of time and energy. It is not. It takes a few minutes—about one, in fact—to grind enough coffee for two for breakfast, especially if you have one of the very small, compact, and efficient electric grinders that are available.

If, however, you are not sufficiently fond of coffee or you are entirely used to the ready-ground variety, remember that you should keep it in a tightly covered can in the refrigerator. If you pour ground coffee into a canister, it is aerated and flavor escapes. When you buy ground coffee in a bag and the bag is not self-sealing, pour it into another container with a tight cap. Put the open end of the bag deep inside the container and pour as gently as possible. The less contact ground coffee has with air, the better. Ground coffee will stay comparatively fresh for a week in a tightly sealed container in a cool place. On the other hand, coffee in the bean keeps for a long time in a canister.

When buying ground coffee for a percolator, get the "regular" variety. If you use a drip pot, get the special "drip" grind. For a vacuum coffee maker, use the "fine" grind, which is even finer than the "drip."

Here's a guide to the amount of coffee and water you should use. Basically, it must be *plenty* of coffee.

Basic Coffee-to-Water Measure

Number of 5½-ounce Servings	Approved Coffee Measure	Tablespoon Measure (level)	Measuring Cups Water	Fluid Oz. Water
2	2	5	1½	12
4	4	8	3	24
6	6	12	4½	36
8	8	16	6	48
20	½ pound			1 gal.
40	1 pound			2 gal.

When you make coffee, the water should be cold before boiling. Let the water run for a minute to flush out stale water from the pipe before you put it into the coffee maker. Hot-water pipes are likely to have mineral deposits in them which alter the flavor of a beverage.

If you use a glass coffee maker with a filter paper, the water should be hot but not boiling. The grounds should be dampened with a little water first, then more water poured in.

If you use a percolator, bring the water to the boil before putting in the filled coffee basket. Thus you can time the perking action from the minute the basket goes in.

Never let coffee boil after it is made. It becomes bitter and oily, and the flavor is ruined.

Café au Lait: This is a combination of hot coffee and hot milk, usually half and half, served always for breakfast in France.

Café Diable and Café Brulot: These are essentially the same. They are a mixture of flamed cognac with sugar, spices, orange and lemon rinds, and strong black coffee.

Cappuccino: An Italian mix, half espresso coffee, half hot milk, with a piece of cinnamon stick put into the cup so that the liquid absorbs the cinnamon flavor as one drinks it.

Chicory: Whether or not you use chicory in coffee is entirely a matter of taste. Chicory is the roasted root of the chicory plant and has a quite decidedly bitter taste. In this country, it is used largely in the

New Orleans area. It appears to greater or lesser extent in most French coffee.

Demitasse: Small cup of coffee served after dinner.

Espresso: This coffee should be made double the strength of ordinary coffee. The espresso roast makes an excellent after-dinner brew. It is a dark roast—almost burned. When you have it in a coffee shop, it is made in a special machine, using steam pressure. There are also home "espresso" pots, some using steam, some not. You can make adequate espresso for demitasse with the right roast in any pot.

Iced Coffee: Use double strength coffee. Though most people put milk or cream into iced coffee, as an aficionado, I would like to recommend it without sugar or other embellishments. It seems to me that anyone who really likes iced coffee drinks it that way.

Irish Coffee: This is a combination of Irish whiskey and strong, hot coffee, slightly sweetened and served with whipped cream on top.

Turkish Coffee: A thick, sweet brew, made by mixing ground coffee and sugar, adding boiling water and letting it foam up and settle, which process is repeated three times. A dash of cold water is added as it is settling for the last time.

Viennese Coffee: A thick topping of sweetened whipped cream is used on strong black coffee.

Cole Slaw: There are many varieties of cole slaw and the one you choose to serve is entirely a matter of taste. The dish consists of either shredded or chopped red and/or white cabbage with one of many possible dressings and sometimes with the addition of other vegetables for color and flavor. The addition of celery salt or caraway seed to any cole slaw is a pleasant one.

Some people like a very vinegary French dressing for cole slaw. This is too tart for my taste. Mayonnaise or sour cream is more gentle, less competitive with the flavor of whatever you serve it with and, I think, more delicious.

Cole Slaw with Sour Cream: Shred or chop cabbage, then soak in cold water for an hour, drain between towels, and chill. Combine salt, sugar, pepper, lemon juice, and vinegar to taste and plenty of sour cream; mix these with the cabbage. Chill until ready to serve (not too long). Sprinkle with paprika.

Imperial Cole Slaw: In this version, the iced cabbage is mixed with seedless grapes and slivered toasted almonds in mayonnaise seasoned with mustard and onion juice.

Mexican Cole Slaw: Less complicated is this version which consists of shredded or chopped cabbage, green pepper, sweet red pepper, and mayonnaise with a dash of celery seed.

Pineapple Cole Slaw: This is a rather unusual and delicious salad, containing the usual cabbage, mixed with crushed pineapple and mayonnaise, seasoned with celery seed and freshly ground pepper.

Red-and-White Cole Slaw: Chopped red and white cabbage in the proportion of one part red to two parts white, mixed with mayonnaise and celery seed to taste.

Spanish Cole Slaw: This consists of the cabbage, shredded carrot, finely chopped sweet red pepper, diced celery, chopped scallion, and thinly sliced radishes. The dressing is mayonnaise, seasoned with prepared mustard, Tabasco, sugar, salt, and white pepper.

Cookies: Basically, there are two types of cookies: dropped cookies and rolled cookies. Dropped cookies are usually dropped from the tip of a teaspoon onto greased cookie sheets. There are seasoned cooks, however, who think that you get a far handsomer and more uniform result by putting the dough into a pastry bag and squeezing it through onto the sheets. If you've never used a pastry bag with a tube (for this particular purpose, Numbers 7 and 9 are just the right size), be assured that the pastry bag isn't at all difficult to use.

Rolled cookies should be made from dough that isn't too soft, but don't add too much flour to them or they will be nearly inedible. Chilling the dough first makes the rolling process proceed smoothly. Rolled cookies are usually cut into shapes with cookie cutters.

Having a full cookie jar of your own product is most satisfying. There's always a treat for children and a nice touch to add to desserts for everyone.

Corn, Fresh: If properly cooked, freshly picked corn is one of the great treats of summer. There are certain requirements for achieving the peak of sweet, delicate flavor. You must have either your own vegetable garden or access to a farm where you know the corn is picked fresh several times a day. *Never* remove the husks until the water in which the corn is to be cooked is boiling. Do not add salt to the water. Husk the corn and pop it into the boiling water. Watch it carefully and when it returns to the boil, cook the ears for exactly three minutes and drain at once. Serve on a platter, wrapped in a napkin which will keep it hot for a remarkably long time. Serve with butter, salt, and pepper, to be added by each lucky participant to his own taste. For my money, corn in this form makes a whole meal, with perhaps a simple lemon or raspberry ice as a topper-off.

Corned Beef: This is beef which has been preserved or pickled in a salt solution. It is a great favorite in New England, being the mainstay of a New England boiled dinner with the addition of cabbage, carrots, onions, turnips, and potatoes. It is one of the dullest dishes the United States has contributed to the cuisine of the world!

Red Flannel Hash, however, is a New England mixture of chopped corned beef, chopped cooked potatoes, chopped beets, and seasonings, browned in a skillet and served with a poached egg on each portion and is *very good* to eat.

Croissants: These are made from a yeast dough with butter rolled into it. After chilling, the dough is cut, then shaped into crescents and baked. The ones we buy in stores here are not usually as flaky and rich as the ones served in France for breakfast. But if you make them yourself, they are well worth the time, as they freeze perfectly, enabling you to make a big batch at one time and have plenty for future use.

Croquettes: Croquettes are made of ground meat, fish, or vegetables, mixed with a thick cream sauce, formed into cone shapes, dipped into a mixture of beaten egg and water, then coated with fine bread crumbs and fried in deep fat until golden brown. They are usually served with a sauce. There are also some sweet croquettes, usually made with fruit, served as desserts.

Croutons: Stale white bread is diced and sautéed in butter to a golden brown, or toasted, or simply dried in the oven to make croutons. These are scattered over hot soups or are used to decorate vegetable or meat dishes.

Cucumbers: Most people think of this lovely vegetable (it is really a fruit) as something to use in salads, to which it is a great addition. Cucumbers are also very good, cut into slim sticks, as one of the offerings in a plate of crudités, served with a seasoned salt or a "dunk" with drinks before a meal. There is a new kind of cucumber —very long and slim, and always encased in a plastic covering—which was originally seedless and very good, especially for people who must shun seeds of any kind. But now that variety *has* seeds in it and so is perhaps not worth the extra money that it costs in the markets.

Cooked cucumbers are something not well known in this country, though they have been favorites of epicures everywhere. One of the best ways to cook cucumbers is to cut them into long, thin strips and poach them in chicken broth until just tender, then remove them and keep them warm while you make a sort of cucumber Hollandaise, by adding to the broth butter, lemon juice, and egg yolk, then beating the mixture well with a wire whisk.

Cold Cucumber Soup: Peel the cucumbers. Slice them with a leek and sauté them in butter with a bay leaf. Cook the cucumbers slowly until tender, but not brown. Add flour and mix well. Then add a good quantity of chicken stock. Simmer this blend twenty to thirty minutes and whirl in the blender or food processor. Add another cucumber, grated (or whirled in the blender or food processor). Add cream, lemon juice, and chopped fresh dill. Serve with a dash of sour cream on top.

Stuffed Cucumbers: Cut the fruit in half lengthwise, remove the seeds, and hollow out some of the pulp. Whirl this pulp in the food processor, then combine it with coarsely chopped fish, shellfish, or cooked meat and seasonings to your taste and pile it back into the cucumber shells. Top with buttered crumbs and bake until crumbs are golden.

Of course, you do not peel the cucumbers to make the above dish, but for salads and some other uses, it is sometimes necessary to peel them because many of those obtainable in our markets have been waxed for preservation purposes.

Curries: There are many ways to make curried dishes. The simplest is to make a cream sauce and flavor it to taste with curry powder—a bit of grated fresh ginger root, some onion, and a bit of garlic. Then add whatever food you wish to curry: cooked meat or fish, vegetables, or hard-cooked eggs.

Some Indian, Thai, and Indonesian curries are much more complicated to make, but in this cook's opinion, well worth the time and trouble involved, as they are usually much more interesting and flavorful than the very basic, Americanized version suggested above.

Always buy the best curry powder you can find. Our own domestic varieties are a pretty sad attempt at copying the real thing. It also pays to buy the real Indian chutneys.

Custards: One major rule for successful custard-making is to use low to moderate heat; the other is not to cook too long. A reliable cookbook will give you specifics.

Baked Custard: Cook in a 325 to 350-degree oven. Test for doneness by inserting a flat, rounded knife in the center. If it comes out clean, the custard is done.

Boiled Custard: Eggs, slightly beaten, salt, and sugar have scalded milk stirred into them gradually. Then place the mixture over boiling water for five minutes, or until the mixture coats a metal spoon. Add vanilla and cool quickly. Use as a dessert or as a dessert sauce.

Floating Island: Use egg yolks instead of whole eggs, as in boiled custard. Chill the custard and float meringues of stiffly beaten egg whites, flavored with powdered sugar and vanilla, on top. The French call this Oeufs à la Neige and sometimes put raspberries or other fruits into the custard.

D

Desserts: Following is a list of desserts from a variety of countries. Some of them are famous, some not so well known, but all delicious and good additions to anyone's repertoire.

Ambrosia: A mixture of orange sections and banana slices, sugared lightly and chilled. Before serving, top with shredded coconut.

Apple Pan Dowdy: A Pennsylvania Dutch dessert of apples—peeled, cored, and sliced—mixed with spices, butter, sugar, and molasses, then covered with a biscuit crust and baked.

Baba au Rhum: This is a light yeast cake which is soaked in a syrup of sugar, water, and dark rum. It is sometimes served with whipped cream. It is usually made as individual, rather cone-shaped cakes, but can be made as one large cake, if preferred—sometimes in a ring pan. The center is then filled with whipped cream, fruit, or what you will. This form of baba is called a Savarin.

Baked Alaska: A mold or brick of very hard ice cream is placed on a piece of sponge cake which extends an inch wider than the ice cream all around. This is put on a board. The whole is covered with a thick meringue and baked in a 500-degree oven until the meringue browns delicately (this takes about five minutes). Serve at once, sliced. It is regarded as a great treat as a birthday dessert for school-age folk.

Beignets: These are fritters, frequently made of apples, strawberries, and other fruits and served for dessert with a custard type of sauce.

Biscuit Tortoni: This is an Italian dessert in which whipped cream is flavored sometimes with rum, sometimes with other flavorings, combined with macaroon crumbs, put into little paper cups, sprinkled with more macaroon crumbs or with ground almonds, and frozen.

Blancmange: A cornstarch pudding, often served with chocolate sauce, fruit sauce, or maple syrup. Rather dull, really.

Bombe begins with a mold of ice cream and/or sherbet, the outer lining being different from the inner filling. For instance, the outside might be orange sherbet, the inside vanilla or coffee ice cream. All sorts of combinations are possible, but when you plan one, be sure that the flavors are compatible. Use about half the capacity of the mold for the lining and half for the center filling. Put the mold into the freezer before you start to work. Then quickly line it with whatever you have chosen and return it to the freezer to make it very firm. Fill the center, cover the mold, and freeze the contents at least four hours—preferably overnight.

Bread Pudding: Soak half slices of bread (crust removed) in melted butter and sauté until golden brown. Pile the slices into a baking dish, then pour over them a mixture of milk, beaten egg, sugar, vanilla, and a dash of salt. Bake in a 350-degree oven until nicely browned on top (forty-five or fifty minutes). You may put raisins into this if you like. It is also exceedingly good (even elegant) flavored with melted chocolate.

Brown Betty: A hot pudding made of apples, soft bread crumbs, sugar, and spices. Served with hard sauce.

Buche de Noël: A rich French Christmas dessert of chocolate with a mocha filling, covered with a chocolate glaze and shavings, made in the form of a log.

Charlotte: The French version requires a mold to be lined with bread slices which have been soaked in melted butter, then filled with a fruit puree. These are baked, then turned out of the mold and served hot or cold with custard or whipped cream. In America, we line the mold with ladyfingers or macaroons. The center is filled with whipped cream, sometimes with nuts or fruit added. This Charlotte is frozen, unmolded, and served with whipped cream or fruit garnish.

Charlotte Russe: A combination of sweetened, flavored whipped cream and stiffly beaten egg whites, put into a bowl lined with ladyfingers and chilled thoroughly before serving.

Cherries Jubilee: Pitted black cherries in a hot sauce made from their juice are flambéed with cognac and then served over vanilla ice cream.

Cobbler: Fresh fruit, sugared, is put into a baking dish and covered with rich biscuit dough, then baked until the top is golden. A cobbler is served with whipped or plain cream.

Cold Soufflé: This title is often erroneously given to a Bavarian Cream. A real cold soufflé is baked like a hot one, then refrigerated, which causes it to sink and to shrink from the mold. It is then unmolded and served with a custard sauce.

Cottage Pudding: This is a yellow cake baked in a square pan, then cut into individual squares—or it may be baked in individual muffin tins. It is served hot, with chocolate, butterscotch, or fruit sauce.

Crème Brûlée: A very rich baked custard (all cream and egg yolks, no milk), thoroughly chilled, then covered with well-sieved light brown sugar and run under the broiler to caramelize the top. It must be watched every minute to see that it does not burn, then chilled again, so that upon being served, it cracks when cut into and is crisp. To my mind, this is one of the great desserts of history. Its origin is claimed by many places, including Cambridge University. The claim that it was invented in New Orleans seems more likely, as the French influence is strong and the dish is not good, plain English style!

Crème Pâtissière: A rich, soft vanilla custard, also used to fill cream puffs, Napoleons, and the like.

Crêpes: These are French pancakes made from a simple, very thin batter (about the consistency of light cream), using part water, part milk, eggs, and flour. Into a hot crêpe pan, in which a bit of butter has been melted, pour just enough batter to coat the bottom of the pan, tipping the pan to distribute the batter evenly. Cook the crêpe until very lightly browned. Turn it with your fingers (carefully!) and brown the second side.

Other uses for crêpes: These delicious thin pancakes can also be filled with jelly or jam, stewed fruits or fresh fruits. They may be flambéed with a liqueur or not, as you please. Crêpes are also filled with meat, poultry, seafood, and vegetable mixtures, rolled up, and usually browned under the broiler. They are sometimes covered with a sauce, sometimes not.

Crêpes normandes: French apple pancakes—made with the sliced or chopped apples incorporated into the batter. They are served with a sprinkling of powdered sugar and are absolutely delectable.

Crêpes Suzette: French crêpes are baked, folded in quarters, then placed in an orange-butter sauce in a chafing dish. Next, Grand Marnier and cognac are poured over the crêpes and ignited. As soon as the flames die down, the crêpes are served.

Floating Island: (*See* under Custards.)

Fruit Dumplings: European fruit dumplings are made of a simple dough wrapped around a piece of fruit or some jam and steamed or boiled. Fruit dumplings in this country are usually made with pastry wrapped around the fruit and baked in the oven. These are served with hard sauce.

Fruit with Cheese: This is one of the best possible desserts and has rapidly become popular in this country. Almost any fruit is good with cheese, but pears and apples are particularly delicious.

Gooseberry Fool: Gooseberries are cooked in sugar and water until soft, then pureed and cooled. They are then combined with whipped cream and chilled. "Fools" can also be made from other fruits.

Indian Pudding: A New England dessert made of corn meal, milk, molasses, brown sugar, and spices, baked long and slow. It is usually served hot with vanilla ice cream.

Jellyroll: It is helpful to have a jelly-roll pan to make this, because the size and shape make the whole process easier. Line the pan with buttered waxed paper. Put in the batter and bake it. During the baking time, put a sheet of aluminum foil or a clean tea towel on a cooling rack and sprinkle it with sugar. When the cake is done, invert it onto the foil or towel and peel off the waxed paper. Roll the cake up while it is warm. Cool. Unroll it and spread it with jelly or whipped cream or whatever you like. Roll the cake again and ice it or sprinkle it with sugar.

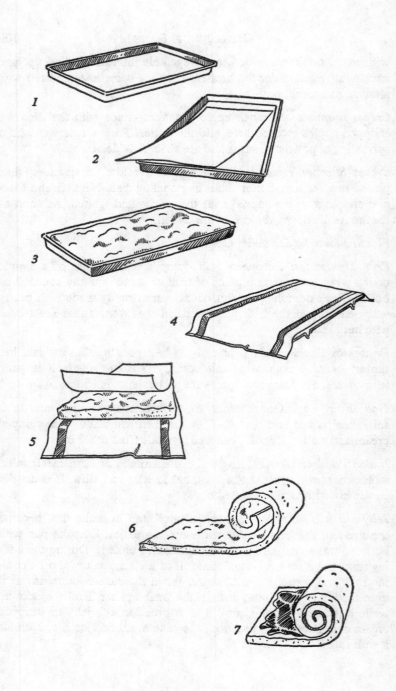

Lemon Snow: A gelatin dessert flavored with lemon rind and juice, with stiffly beaten egg whites folded in before chilling. It is usually served with a custard sauce.

Parfait: In this country, it is ice cream (sometimes more than one flavor) put into a tall, thin parfait glass with sauce poured so that it trickles down through the ice cream in an irregular pattern. The European version is made from scratch with heavy cream, whole eggs or egg yolks, and seasonings, then frozen in the parfait glasses. It is more creamy than ice cream.

Pot de Crème: This very rich chocolate pudding is made and served in little pots (custard cups). There is a variety of ways of making it, but the simplest and richest is to melt twelve squares of semi-sweet chocolate with two tablespoons of butter, then beat into it the yolks of seven eggs and finally fold into the mixture the stiffly beaten whites of seven eggs. Put into the pots and refrigerate at least two hours. A pot de crème can also be made with cream, sugar, eggs, and vanilla flavoring.

Profiteroles: Small cream puffs, made from Pâte à Chou, filled with ice cream and served covered with a sauce, usually chocolate.

Raspberry Whip: Half a pint of raspberries is combined with a cup of sugar and an egg white in a bowl and beaten with a rotary beater (this takes half an hour) or an electric mixer (fifteen minutes) until the mixture forms stiff peaks. Never try to do this in a blender or a food processor because they operate too fast and cannot do egg whites properly.

Rote Grütze: This is a German and Scandinavian dessert made from cooking raspberries and red currants together briefly in a little water, sieving them, then boiling them, stirring constantly, with sugar added. Gelatin is added and the whole is chilled and served with cream or milk (the Germans prefer milk).

Salzburger Nockerl: A beautifully light Austrian soufflé, made by baking a stiffly beaten egg-white mixture in a shallow layer of flavored milk.

Sherbet: This is an ice (usually fruit-flavored) made with milk.

Spanish Cream: A dessert made with gelatin, eggs, sugar, and vanilla. Not as rich as Bavarian cream, it is otherwise similar. It is usually served with whipped cream.

Strawberry Shortcake: The main point to remember is that the only proper cake for this is made from flaky biscuit dough, sweetened with sugar. This is baked, split, and buttered. Meanwhile, mash the strawberries coarsely and sugar them to taste. When you're ready to serve, pour the berries over the bottom half of the shortcake and cover them with the top half. Top the cake with whipped cream and decorate it with whole berries.

Stuffed Pineapple: Cut a ripe pineapple in half, right through the plume. Cut out the flesh, leaving a shell about an inch thick. Cube the flesh and combine it with other fruits which make a happy contrast of color, texture, and flavor. Pile the fruit back in the halves and flavor it with kirsch or other liqueur if you like. Chill well before serving. This is beautiful on a buffet table.

Syllabub: There is a variety of recipes for this English dessert, one of which starts out, "Take the mixture to the cow." However, it is easier to make it with sherry and bottled raspberry juice, seasoned with lemon peel, nutmeg, and rosemary, left to stand in a bowl with sugar overnight, then incorporated into whipped cream. There are some English recipes which make it with macaroons—a very different effect altogether!

Tipsy Pudding: This is our version of English Trifle, greatly simplified, as we simply soak the sponge cake with sherry and serve it with boiled custard poured over it.

Watermelon, filled with fruits: Hollow out a half watermelon and cut the fruit into chunks, then mix in other fruits, such as strawberries, cantaloupe and honeydew balls, blueberries, orange and grapefruit sections, sliced peaches, blue, red, and white grapes—anything you can find to vary the color, flavor, and texture. The fruits are heaped in the watermelon shell and may be flavored with wine or kirsch. They also may be flambéed with cognac. If they are ice cold when this is done, they will not be warmed too much, and the effect is spectacular.

Devonshire Cream: This is made by allowing unhomogenized milk to stand for six to twelve hours or until cream rises to the top. Next, the pan is set over very low heat until the milk is quite hot, though it must never be allowed to boil. The more slowly this process can be accomplished, the better will be the result. As soon as the milk is hot, it should be put in a cool place for twenty-four hours. The thick cream is skimmed off and stored in jars. It is usually served with fresh fruit.

Dressing (for poultry, etc.; sometimes called "stuffing"):

The simplest variety is made from dry and soft bread crumbs (in equal quantities), butter, boiling water, salt and pepper, and poultry seasoning. You can, of course, use in place of the poultry seasoning any combination of herbs you prefer. Very good stuffing has nuts (especially chestnuts) added to it occasionally. Many people put celery and onion, finely cut up, into stuffing, which adds a lot to the flavor of both the stuffing and the bird in which it is cooked. A particularly good stuffing for turkey has oysters added to it.

Some of the prepared poultry stuffings one buys in the grocery stores are excellent and a bag of this type is a good thing to have always on hand for a variety of uses—for instance, as a topping for casseroles instead of plain bread crumbs. Of course, this type of stuffing is much more expensive than that which you make yourself from scratch, but the prepared variety is indeed a great convenience.

Dressing (for salad):

French Dressing: A purist would say that this is a mixture of olive oil, vinegar, salt, and pepper—*period*. However, in this country we sometimes make additions of one or more of the following: mustard, garlic, paprika, curry powder, celery salt, grated onion, cheese, chives, chopped parsley, chopped shallots, sugar, and sometimes even catsup (of the last two I do not approve). Also, we substitute wine vinegar, herbed wine vinegar, or lemon juice for plain cider vinegar at times, as well as other oils for the olive oil.

Green Mayonnaise: Spinach leaves, watercress leaves, parsley, and any desired herbs are blanched briefly, dried, and either whirled in the blender or processor or pressed through a fine sieve, then stirred into mayonnaise, which they flavor and also color green. Especially handsome to serve with cold salmon or other fish.

Lorenzo Dressing: Chili sauce mixed with French dressing, in the proportion of one part to four, with chopped watercress added.

Mayonnaise: This is a rich, smooth cold sauce, which is essentially an emulsion of egg yolks and oil, usually olive. Important points in making a good mayonnaise are:

1. All ingredients should be at room temperature. (If the egg yolks are cold, warm the mixing bowl in hot water to take off the chill.)
2. Beat the yolks briefly before starting to add other ingredients.
3. The olive oil must be added *by the drop* until one fourth to one third of the oil has been absorbed, and the beating must be constant during the process of adding the oil. (This is most easily done with an electric beater at medium speed.) After that, the oil may be added by the tablespoonful.

The proper proportion of egg yolks to olive oil is as follows: Use half to three quarters of a cup of olive oil to one large egg yolk—*not more*. If this is exceeded, the mayonnaise will almost certainly curdle. The proper proportion of vinegar or lemon juice in good mayonnaise is two or three tablespoons to two egg yolks, depending largely upon taste. If the mayonnaise becomes too thick, thin it with vinegar or lemon juice, added by the drop.

It is possible to make good mayonnaise in a blender, but it is a fluffier, less rich-seeming dressing than that which you make by hand or with an electric mixer, particularly if you make it with whole eggs, which is possible with this method.

Mayonnaise should be stored tightly covered in the refrigerator if it is homemade. Commercially made mayonnaise may be stored on the shelf until it is opened. After that, it should be refrigerated.

Mayonnaise Chaud-Froid: Gelatin is added to mayonnaise. It is then mixed with chopped cooked vegetables or meat, or used to coat fish fillets and the like, then refrigerated until well chilled and jelled.

Roquefort Dressing: This is a French dressing with Roquefort cheese crumbled into it. A much less expensive, but similar, flavor is obtained by using Bleu (or Blue) cheese in place of Roquefort.

Russian Dressing: Mayonnaise with chili sauce, chopped pimiento, and minced chives added.

Thousand Island Dressing: Mayonnaise with chili sauce, Worcestershire sauce, chopped pimiento, chopped green pepper, and minced chives added.

Vinaigrette Dressing: This term is frequently used in France as interchangeable with our French dressing. It is also used here and in France for a dressing on cold cooked vegetables (especially artichokes and asparagus), cold meats, fish, or greens, and in this case consists of a plain French dressing with chopped capers, parsley, onion, hard-cooked egg, gherkins, and sometimes other herbs added.

Dips: See Dunks

Drippings: Fat and juices drawn from meat while cooking. Mostly used as the base for gravies.

Dumplings: There is a considerable variety of dumplings. The simplest one is made of flour, baking powder, salt, shortening, and milk. This is the type often served in stew and one thing that can certainly be said for it is that it contributes little to flavor, but is a good means of sopping up the gravy! The Czechs make what is my idea of the best dumplings in the world, known as Napkin Dumplings—or Třený Knedlík. They are composed of butter, eggs, salt, milk, flour, and small croutons made from stale white bread, sautéed until brown and then stirred into a dough made from the other ingredients. This is shaped into a long roll and slung in a napkin from a big wooden spoon or a rolling pin, set across the top of a large pot so that the dumpling in its napkin is submerged in water and cooked until done (thirty to forty minutes). It is sliced for serving and is particularly good when served with pork in a cream sauce, as it often is in Czechoslovakia.

Fruit Dumplings are a favorite dessert for many. Surely, the baked apple dumplings of our ancestors were a treat. For these, apples are

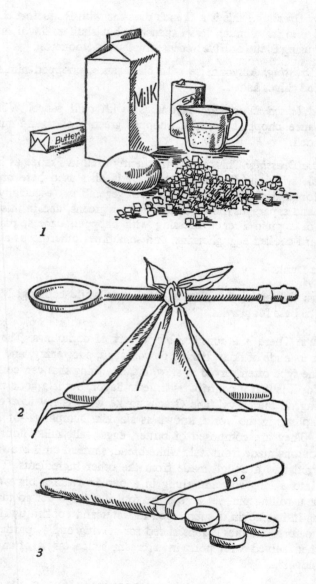

1

2

3

pared and cored, then each is placed on a square of biscuit dough, large enough to cover the apple when brought up to the top. Before the covering with dough is done, however, the cavities are filled with a mixture of brown sugar, seasonings, and raisins. After the dough has been brought up around the apples and pressed together at the top, it is brushed with slightly beaten egg white, sprinkled with sugar, and baked in a hot oven to brown them (about ten minutes), then at medium heat for twenty minutes longer. We always had these served with hard sauce. Cream would be nice, too.

You can make *fruit dumplings* by stirring seedless grapes or berries into a fairly stiff dumpling dough, then forming it into balls and cooking them in rapidly boiling water for about twelve minutes. Serve hot with any desired sauce.

"Dunks" (also known as "Dips"): A good "dunk" can improve the flavor of almost anything you dip into it. The possibilities are endless and take kindly to inventive experimentation. Here are a few examples, just to get you going on inventing your own.

Curried Cheese and Chutney: Cream cheese is mashed and diluted with enough milk or cream to soften it, then seasoned with curry powder, chopped onion, finely chopped Major Grey's chutney, and a dash of garlic powder.

Curry Sauce: Make a good rich curry sauce and serve it piping hot with ice-cold fingers of fresh fruit (pineapple, melon, apple, peach, papaya, or whatever else you like) to dunk into the hot sauce.

My Special Dunk: Mix mayonnaise, chili sauce, curry powder, chili powder, and garlic powder to your taste. It's really good with anything!

What to Dunk With: Potato chips, corn chips, frozen miniature fish cakes (hot), tiny meatballs (hot), little cocktail sausages (hot), raw vegetables, fried frozen shrimp, Italian breadsticks.

Duxelles are made by cooking very finely chopped mushrooms (stems and caps) in butter, over low heat, with finely chopped shallots and salt to taste, stirring occasionally, until all the liquid has evaporated and the mushrooms are quite black in color. Add more butter if necessary. Store in a covered jar in the refrigerator, where it will keep for a couple of weeks. It also freezes well. This makes a great addition to many sauces and to egg and vegetable dishes; it's a very handy thing to have around if you want to cook with flair.

E

Eggplant: Eggplant is probably most commonly fried, either in slices or sticks—the former usually sautéed in shallow butter or oil and the latter in deep fat. Eggplant, stuffed either with a combination of meat and vegetables or with vegetables alone, makes a delicious meal-in-a-dish. Simply cut the eggplants in half, lengthwise, take out all the seeds and some of the pulp. Grind the pulp and mix it with whatever filling you choose. Parboil the shells for about fifteen minutes. Drain well and fill, then top with crumbs or grated cheese and bake in a 350-degree oven for thirty minutes, or until the eggplant is tender and the topping is brown. Serve half a medium or small-size eggplant to a person, depending upon appetites.

Eggplant Caviar: A dish of Middle Eastern origin in which peeled and cooked eggplant is mixed with onion, garlic, tomatoes, seasonings, and sesame oil. Olive oil may be used if preferred. The mixture is chilled and served as a first course.

Eggs (general): Buy according to grade and size. Always look for the USDA Grade Shield which assures you that the eggs have been certified for quality under USDA supervision and that they were packed in a plant that meets the USDA's rigid sanitary requirements.

Adding Beaten Egg Yolks to a Hot Sauce: Add some of the sauce to the egg yolks, a spoonful at a time, beating constantly with a wire whisk. Return this mixture to the sauce and stir well to incorporate. *Never* let a sauce come to the boil after the egg yolks have been added.

Bits of Yolk in the Whites: Carefully remove these with a teaspoon or with the edge of an egg shell. Egg whites will not whip properly if there is any yolk in them.

Blood Spots: Ordinarily, the candling of eggs for quality eliminates those with blood spots, but if very small spots of this sort escape detection, they in no way affect the desirability of the egg for cooking.

Calories: A large egg has about eighty calories, sixty of which come from the yolk.

Color of Eggs: Some breeds of poultry produce eggs with brown shells; others with white. Nutritive value and cooking performance of white and brown eggs of the same grade are identical.

Cooking Temperatures: Always cook eggs with low to moderate heat. High temperatures and overcooking make them tough.

Cracked Eggs: Only fresh, clean, unbroken eggs should be used in making milkshakes and other uncooked or lightly cooked dishes. Eggs that are cracked should be thoroughly cooked.

Cup Measures of Whole Eggs, Egg Yolks, and Egg Whites:

	Extra large	Large	Medium	Small
Whole eggs	5	5	6	7
Egg yolks	12	12–14	14–16	15–19
Egg whites	6	7–8	8–9	9–10

Double Yolks: The only special thing about a double-yolked egg is that it is rather unusual. They come ordinarily from pullets coming into their laying period. If they cost more in your market than other eggs do, it is only because they are something of a curiosity.

Freezing Whites and Yolks: They both freeze beautifully. The yolks are most useful for making Hollandaise or other sauces and for enriching almost any sauce. The whites are just what you want for that extra one needed to make a soufflé soar high. Many cooks freeze egg whites in the little plastic containers intended for ice cubes.

When you have separated the eggs for a soufflé, you can throw in a frozen egg white, and as soon as it has defrosted, it whips perfectly with the other whites.

Grades: Grade AA, when broken, covers a small area. The yolk is firm and stands high. The thick white is large in quantity and stands high and firm around the yolk. There is a small amount of thin white. Use for cooking in the shell, poaching, frying, and scrambling.

Grade A, when broken, covers a moderate area. The yolk is round and stands high. The thick white is large in quantity and stands fairly well around the yolk. The thin white is small in amount. Especially desirable for cooking in the shell, poaching, frying, and scrambling.

Grade B eggs are seldom found in retail stores. The white of these eggs may be thinner and the yolks may be enlarged and flatter than eggs of the higher grades. They are satisfactory for general cooking and baking where appearance is not important.

The grade of eggs does not affect their nutritive value.

Nutrition: Eggs are a source of high-quality protein, iron, vitamin A, and vitamin B_2. They are one of the few foods that contain natural vitamin D.

Refrigeration: Eggs should be bought only from a refrigerated case and should be refrigerated promptly at home, large end up.

Room Temperature: Some recipes call for eggs at room temperature —for instance, omelets. They should be removed from the refrigerator about an hour before they are to be used, to achieve the desired temperature.

Separating Eggs: Have ready a bowl for the whites and one for the yolks. Break the egg open and rock the yolk into one half, allowing the white to pour into the larger bowl. Keep doing this, using the edge of whichever half is empty to help cut the white away from the shell in which the yolk is reposing, until all of the white is in the bowl. Drop the yolk into the second, smaller bowl.

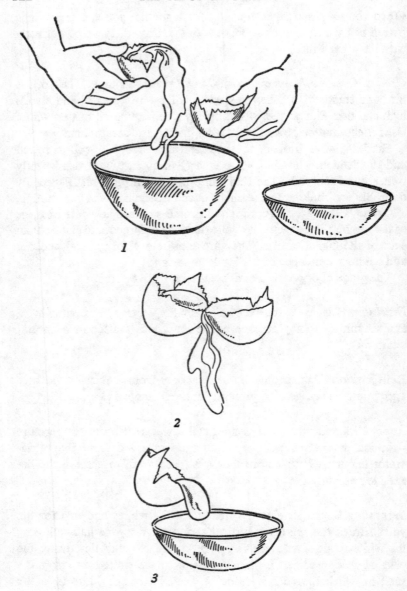

Sizes: Remember that size is not related to quality. Large eggs may be of high or low quality. High quality may be found in any size of egg.

The most commonly found sizes are	Minimum weight per dozen
Extra Large	27 oz.
Large	24 oz.
Medium	21 oz.
Sometimes available are:	
Jumbo	30 oz.
Small	18 oz.
Peewee	15 oz.

Eggs (suggestions):

Baked Eggs: Baked eggs are very much like shirred eggs, except that their entire cooking is done in the oven: in sauces, in hollowed-out tomato or sweet-pepper shells, in nests of vegetables or rice, either in individual ramekins or in a large, shallow baking dish. One must be careful not to overcook them, and remember that they go on cooking for a moment after they are removed from the oven.

Eggs Benedict: A toasted half of English muffin, covered with a thin slice of ham, topped with a poached egg, and covered with Hollandaise sauce. Sometimes a slice of black truffle is placed on top, but this is not essential and, in these days, so expensive as to be other-worldly for most people. It is said that this dish was invented by a Mr. Benedict who, upon awaking with an awful hangover, instructed the chef of the old Waldorf Hotel in New York to combine in some fashion the only foods which appealed to him at the moment. He had them, of course, for breakfast, but they are usually served at luncheon or supper.

Eggs Florentine: Raw eggs are set in a shallow dish on a bed of chopped cooked spinach, covered with a thin layer of Mornay sauce, and baked in a moderate oven for about ten minutes. They are then removed, sprinkled with grated cheese, and run under the broiler to brown. If you make this dish with Eggs Mollet (see below), simply eliminate the baking.

Eggs Mollet: Eggs are simmered in their shells in water just under the boiling point, for six minutes, quickly cooled in cold water, and shelled. The white is set and the yolk runny. Eggs Mollet are used in much the same way as poached eggs: in Eggs Florentine, covered with a sauce or an aspic, etc.

Fried Eggs: The eggs should be broken, one by one, into a cup and slid gently into a skillet containing about half a tablespoonful of fat (usually butter or bacon fat) per egg. They are then cooked over gentle heat—basted occasionally with the fat or not, as preferred—until they are done to taste. If served at this point, they are "sunny side up." If desired, the eggs may be turned over carefully and fried on the second side for whatever time suits your taste.

Poached Eggs: The eggs are cooked in simmering water until they achieve the degree of doneness you like. The best way to keep them symmetrical in the water is to place metal rings (sometimes known as "muffin rings") in a skillet with enough salted water to cover the whites of the eggs. Break fresh eggs, one by one, into a cup and slip each one into one of the rings. Be sure that the water is simmering gently—never boiling. If you cannot find muffin rings, take both top and bottom from deviled-ham cans and use the rings thus made.

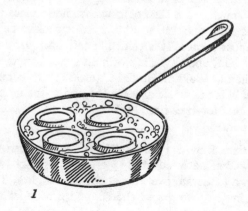

1

2

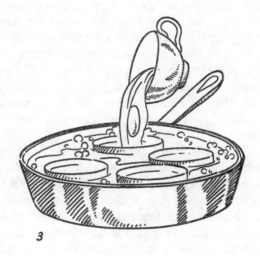

3

Eggs may also be cooked in a "poacher." This consists of a good-size pan with a rack into which several small round pans are fitted. Water is brought to the simmer in the larger pan. A bit of butter is melted in each little pan to prevent sticking, then an egg is slipped into each. The poacher is covered and the eggs cooked to the desired doneness. This method glazes the yolks over with steam, so that they are not as handsome as those poached directly in water.

Scotch Woodcock: Scrambled eggs, flavored with sherry, are served on toast spread with anchovy paste. A marvelous supper dish.

Scrambled Eggs: There are a variety of ways to scramble eggs. The one you choose will depend entirely upon your individual taste. 1. The simplest way to scramble eggs is to break them into a skillet in which there is about a teaspoonful of melted butter per egg. They are then stirred constantly with a fork over low heat until done to the consistency you like, which if you really care about eggs at all, will be soft and creamy. Season and serve at once. 2. Though many people regard it as a desecration and as the ruination of the eggs, sometimes they are broken into a bowl, beaten briefly, then mixed with about a teaspoonful of milk or cream per egg, seasoned, and scrambled in butter. I happen to like Method 1 better, but these are good, too. 3. Eggs can also be scrambled in a double boiler. This is perhaps of special interest to persons who cannot have butter. The eggs are beaten lightly and seasoned, then put into the top of a double boiler over gently bubbling water. They need only to be stirred occasionally until they reach the desired consistency. The addition of a bit of butter makes this dish taste even better, but is not necessary.

Shirred Eggs: An egg (or two) is broken into melted butter in an individual shallow baking dish (which the French call a *plat*), seasoned, and cooked for a minute over low heat on top of the range. A little melted butter is then poured over each egg and the cooking is finished in a moderate oven. Sometimes a couple of cooked sausages or chicken livers or some crisp bacon are added to the dish before it goes into the oven. Shirred eggs can also be started, as above, in a little butter, with a little cream or sauce then added before the dish is put into the oven to finish cooking.

Soft-Cooked Eggs: Place the eggs in water to cover them and bring the water to a boil. Remove the pot from the heat, cover it tightly, and allow the eggs to stay in the water for the time it takes to get them to the consistency you like. The consistency of the three-minute "soft-boiled egg" is achieved by letting the egg stay in the water for three and a half to four minutes after removing it from the heat.

Hard-Cooked Eggs: Done by the same method, these are left in the water for twenty minutes, then placed under running cold water to cool quickly. This way of cooking is also known as "coddling." It does not toughen the whites as boiling does.

Empanadas are little South American pies filled with chopped beef, highly seasoned and mixed with chopped black olives, chopped hard-

cooked egg, and white raisins. In miniature size, they make fine canapés.

Endive, Belgian: This is a delicious salad green, the leaves of which also make a marvelous addition to the crudité platter. Many people do not realize that endive is very good when cooked.

Endive, Braised: I do mine backward, according to the French and Belgians, but it comes out very well. First, in order that the leaves will not spread all over the pan, I tie each head with white string.

1

Then I brown them in butter to a nice golden color on all sides. Then I put in a bit of chicken broth (not too much—it is better to add more, if necessary, than to drown them), cover the pan, and cook them until they are tender—about fifteen to twenty minutes.

Entrée: In the U.S., this word is used to mean the main dish of a meal. In France, whence it came, it means literally "first," but in regard to a meal it stands for the third course, following the fish. In England, it denotes the course served before the roast. So, when you are at home, use it as the rest of the United States does, but when you're abroad, don't be surprised to find it used quite differently!

F

Fat: Some fat is necessary for good nutrition, but there is little question that most Americans eat altogether too much of it, by any standard. By and large, if we cut the amount of fat we use in cooking by half, our food would be interesting and good to eat—and better for us. Remember that fat is fat, and whether it be butter, margarine, vegetable oil or fat, olive oil, or any other, it contains the same number (9 to a gram) calories as all the others. On the whole, if you reduce your use of fats across the board, it doesn't matter which kind you choose—except for your own taste.

Filet, Fillet: Filet, coming from the French as it does and familiar to most in the name filet mignon, is pronounced "feelay." But fillet is pronounced "fillit," and is used, in the food world, to designate the meat of the fish, carefully cut from the bone and generally skinned as well, as, for instance, fillet of sole. Fillet is also a verb—one fillets a fish in the manner described above.

Fines Herbes: Properly, and according to Larousse Gastronomique, this term refers to a mixture of herbs such as parsley, chervil, tarragon, and chives, which in earlier times, had chopped mushrooms and even truffles added to them. However, nowadays, when one orders an omelet fines herbes here or in France, the fines herbes usually turn out to be chopped parsley, period—which, to me, for one, is a grave disappointment! It is possible to buy dried fines herbes in those lovely little crockery pots, imported from France, but it is even better to make one's own—definitely not including truffles, which, even if you like them, are outrageously overpriced these days. (*See also* Herbs and Spices.)

Fish and Shellfish

It is my opinion that the reason so many Americans say they "don't like fish" is that we have always been inclined to overcook it, which dries it out and detracts from the flavor. Fish is done when it flakes easily with a fork—an easy test to make.

Fresh fish should not have a strong, fishy odor. The eyes should be bright and bulging, the skin and scales shiny. The gills should be red and the flesh firm and springy to the touch. When buying whole fish, allow one pound per person. Of dressed fish (eviscerated, scaled, with head, tail and fins removed), steaks and fillets, buy one-third to half a pound per person.

If you have the privilege of dealing with fresh-caught fish, whether you caught them yourself or they are a gift, they must first be eviscerated. This means slitting them down the belly and removing the innards (any good fisherman would see to that before presenting them). They must be scaled and the head, tail, and fins removed.

A fishy smell on one's hands is most unpleasant. The best way to do away with it is to squeeze a little lemon juice on the fingers.

Ways to Cook Fish

Baking: Bluefish, mackerel, halibut steaks, pompano, salmon steaks, shad, pike, and whitefish are all good for baking. The traditional way to bake a fish is with the head left on. This adds a lot to the flavor. If this does not appeal to you, however (and I have known quite a few people who feel this way), have the head removed. Bluefish, mackerel, and shad are very good stuffed and baked, though they may be baked unstuffed if preferred.

Broiling: Bluefish, flounder, haddock (fillets or whole), halibut fillets or steaks, mackerel, porgies, salmon steaks, scrod, shad, striped bass, fresh-water bass, pike (whole steaks or fillets), whitefish (whole or fillets), perch fillets (ocean or yellow) are all good fish to broil. Any whole fish that is broiled is first split. It should be seasoned and liberally dotted with butter before it is placed under the broiler, and basted occasionally as it cooks to keep it moist and flavorful. Broil the fish in a greased pan, skin-side down, *without turning.*

Deep-Fat Frying: Butterfish, sea bass, halibut or haddock (cut into chunks), flounder fillets, catfish, perch fillets (ocean or yellow) are all good for deep-fat frying. Any fish that is deep-fat fried should be dipped in flour, beaten egg, then crumbs and fried in 375-degree fat until nicely browned—*not too long.*

Poaching: Usually large fish, such as salmon, cod, haddock, and halibut, are poached. However, carp, catfish, pike, trout, and whitefish can also be poached to good advantage. The fish are poached in a barely simmering court bouillon, which is a combination of water or wine with vegetables and seasonings. Sometimes fish heads and bones are added to the court bouillon, and the whole is cooked, then strained, before the fish is put in. If you find that you often wish to poach a big fish, it is a boon to own a fish poacher. This is a long, rather narrow pan with a lid, plus a rack by means of which you can lift the fish to a platter when it is done.

Sautéing: Trout, sole, flounder fillets, butterfish, porgies, smelts, catfish, whitefish, perch fillets (ocean or yellow) are all good when sautéed in butter or olive oil. They are usually served with a wedge of lemon to squeeze over them.

Clams: A good way to tell whether hard-shell clams are fresh is to find any shells that are open and tap them sharply. If the clam is fresh, it will close up tightly. Discard any that do not close.

Clams or Oysters Casino: Clams or oysters on the half shell, sprinkled with chopped green pepper, chopped onion or shallots, and topped with small pieces of "tried out" bacon are placed in tin plates half filled with rock salt, and run under the broiler until the bacon is crisp (three to five minutes). They can also be baked in a 450-degree oven, which will take about ten minutes.

Jambalaya: This is a New Orleans dish always involving rice and ham (jambon), usually with tomatoes and shrimp or other shellfish, together with seasonings, all cooked together in a fish stock until the liquid is absorbed.

Lobster: There are two types of lobster in the United States. First, there are lobsters with claws, which come from Maine and other parts of the New England coast, known in France as *homard.* Then there are the clawless lobsters, which the French call *langouste* and which come from California and Florida. The type with claws has always been preferred, though the meat of a langouste is delicious. South African rock lobster tails come from a member of the crayfish family, without claws, like the langouste type.

The green material inside the lobster is the liver, sometimes called the tomalley. It is delicious and should never be removed for serving. The pink you sometimes see in a lobster is roe and makes marvelous eating, so leave it in the shell for serving, too.

Boiled Lobster: Have water or fish stock (or better still, sea water) at a rolling boil in a big kettle. Plunge the live lobsters in, cover them, and cook them for the required time (four to five minutes to the pound). Remove the lobsters from the water. If the lobster is to be served hot, split it in half, starting at the head. Remove the stomach and the intestinal vein. Serve the lobster with melted butter. If it is to be served cold, first cool it, then chill it in the refrigerator. Split and clean it just before serving. Personally, I far prefer boiled lobster to the broiled variety, as broiling tends to dry the meat too much.

1

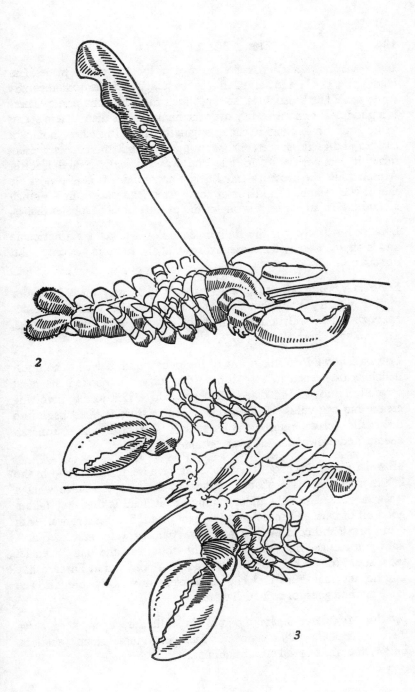

2

3

Lobster à l'Américaine: A French dish of lobster, cut in pieces (including the shell) and served in a sauce which includes tomatoes, dry white wine, and seasonings, among which there must be garlic. There is a good deal of controversy over the name of this dish. There seems to be little doubt that it came originally from Provence, home of tomato-and-garlic sauces, but some people think that in its present form, it came from Armorique and was originally called Lobster Armoricaine, the present name being a corruption. It is also possible that it was renamed in honor of some American patron in a French restaurant. In any case, it is one of the most famous of lobster dishes.

Lobster Fra Diavolo is the Italian version of Lobster à l'Américaine and is almost exactly the same, except that the lobsters are only split, not cut up.

Lobster Newburg: Sauté chunks of cooked lobster meat in butter until they turn pink (about three minutes). Flambé with warmed cognac, then mix with a sauce made of heavy cream and egg yolks, flavored with sherry.

Lobster Thermidor: This is one of the richest and, if well done, most delicious of French lobster dishes. The lobster is cooked, its meat carefully removed and diced, then put into a rich sauce, involving cream and egg yolks, well seasoned. The mixture is piled back into the shells (claws removed, of course), sprinkled with Parmesan cheese, and browned in the oven or under the broiler.

Mussels: Presently, about the least expensive item to be found in the fish market. This is probably because so few people realize what a treat they are. The only difficult thing about them is that they take a good bit of care and muscle to get them clean. Scrub them well with a stiff brush and cold water. Use several pans of water and keep at it until you can see no more sand in the bottom of the pan. Then let them stand for an hour or so, covered with cold water. Discard any that do not float. Now they should be clean and ready to cook. The same method goes for soft-shell clams.

Moules Marinière: Steam the mussels until they open, then serve them in the shells with a sauce of white wine, mussel liquor, shallots, butter, fine white bread crumbs, and parsley.

Mussels Ravigote: Steamed mussels, removed from their shells and chilled, then served in a Ravigote sauce (French dressing, mixed with herbs, capers, and onions).

Steamed Mussels or Soft-Shell Clams: Put them into a pot with about an inch of salted water in it. Cover the pot tightly and steam them until the shells open (about six minutes). Discard any that do not open. Serve with melted butter and cups of the broth.

Oysters: There are two forms in which you are most likely to purchase oysters—on the half shell, or shucked and put into a container with their juice. Although you may buy an oyster knife and learn how to open oysters at home, it is much easier and saves a lot of time to have your fish market open them for you if you're going to serve them on the half shell. You should keep them very cold and serve them on a goodly amount of crushed ice if you have them this way. Any good oysterman will tell you that they should be served only with a squirt of lemon juice and a bit of freshly ground pepper— never with that odd concoction commonly known as "cocktail sauce" which just masks their magnificent natural flavor and does nothing to enhance it.

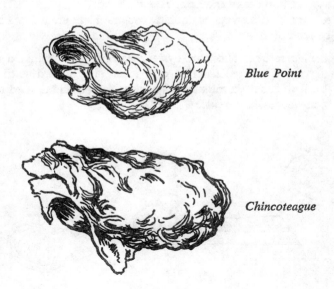

Blue Point

Chincoteague

When you are buying shucked oysters in their juice for a cooked-dish order, buy half a pint per person. Buy six oysters on the half shell per person, though there are people who would eat a lot more, given a chance. In fact, I have a friend in Mobile, Alabama, who often used to say to me before we were going to a rather grand luncheon party: "What do you say to a nice visit to the oyster bar before we go to lunch?" Since I love them, I would always accept with alacrity and eat my half dozen with great pleasure while he consumed *at least* two dozen.

There are many kinds of oysters available in various parts of the United States. Blue Points from Long Island Sound are excellent for cooking or eating on the half shell, being medium-sized and of very good flavor. The Chesapeake Bay produces many good varieties, most especially the great big Chincoteagues. Lynnhavens, also from Long Island, are excellent. For my taste, the tiny Olympia oysters of the Pacific coast are perhaps the most delicate and delicious we produce. The oysters that come from the Gulf of Mexico (those in Mobile, for instance) have relatively little flavor and a rather limp texture, probably because oysters in general seem to like cold water. That preference, by the way, is one very good reason for the "eat only in months with an 'r' in them." This is particularly true for such places as the Chesapeake and Long Island Sound.

There are countless ways of cooking oysters. Here are a few I happen to be fond of:

Angels on Horseback: These are oysters seasoned and sprinkled with chopped parsley, rolled in strips of bacon, and broiled until the bacon is crisp (about six minutes). They are served on buttered toast with lemon wedges on the side.

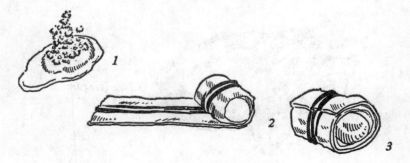

New Orleans Oyster Loaf: First, oysters are sautéed in butter, then stuffed into a hollowed-out loaf of French bread (which has been cut almost in half, but with a hinge left at the back). The loaf is closed and wrapped tightly in a piece of cheesecloth dipped in milk. The loaf is then baked for about a half hour in a 350-degree oven.

Oysters Rockefeller: Oysters on the half shell are placed on beds of rock salt in tin pie plates. They are then covered with a sauce composed of creamed butter, finely chopped cooked spinach, onion, parsley, and other herbs, plus anisette, if you can get it. If not, use a bit of anise seed. The pans are then placed in a 450-degree oven for five to eight minutes, until lightly browned on top, and the oysters are served at once in their tin plates.

Oyster Stew: Sauté oysters in butter with Worcestershire sauce and celery salt until their edges curl. Add milk, cream, and oyster liquor and bring just to the boiling point. Serve with generous pats of butter floating on top.

Scallops: We have two varieties—deep-sea and bay. The deep-sea scallops are quite large and far less delicate than the bays, but the latter are much scarcer and more expensive. In some restaurants, deep-sea scallops are cut into quarters and treated like bay scallops, but no true lover of the breed could be fooled by that maneuver. When buying scallops, get a quarter to a third of a pound per person, depending upon appetites.

The most delicious way to cook scallops is to sauté them in butter, with a dash of lemon juice and a sprinkling of parsley added before serving. They must first be washed and thoroughly dried with paper toweling (else they will not brown). They may also be breaded and deep-fat fried, or broiled on skewers with or without bacon. Scallops also take kindly to sauces, which should not be so strongly flavored as to top their own delicate flavor. They make a delicious stew.

Scallops may be eaten raw, with a squeeze of lemon over them, as an appetizer.

Coquilles St. Jacques is the French name for scallops—not, as many Americans think, for scallops in a rich sauce browned in the oven in scallop shells. They make a delicious first course and can be prepared with a variety of sauces, usually named in France for the restaurant in which they are served—for example: "Coquilles St. Jacques à la Façon du Restaurant Jacques-Coeur."

Seviche: This is a South American dish in which scallops are marinated in lime juice for at least eight hours in the refrigerator, then served with paper-thin slices of onion sprinkled over them, plus salt and pepper to taste. The marinating "cooks" the scallops. This treatment is also used on sole or any delicate white-meat fish. It makes a lovely first course.

Shrimp: In buying shrimp, remember that the bigger they are, the more expensive they are likely to be, which in no way indicates that they are of finer quality. When you get shrimp home, shell and devein them before cooking them. They will keep their shape better if you do this. Save the shells to make shrimp butter. Plunge the shrimp into rapidly boiling water and simmer them for three to five minutes. They should be drained immediately.

Butterfly Shrimp: This is a Chinese dish. First you shell the shrimp, leaving the tails on, and devein them. Then split them, but *not all the way through,* and flatten them. Dip them into a batter and fry them in deep fat. Sometimes a piece of bacon is pressed onto the shrimp before it is dipped into the batter. Sometimes the shrimp is simply coated with egg white to which a little cornstarch has been added, then fried. They look like butterflies when done.

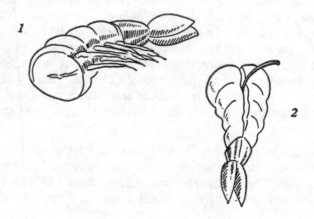

Shrimp Toast: This Chinese dish makes a fine appetizer for us. Raw shrimp is minced very fine and mixed with minute quantities of ginger, wine, other seasonings, and egg white, then spread on pieces of bread and deep-fat fried. Remarkably enough, the shrimp mixture clings, instead of falling off, as most cooks fear it will!

Tempura: A Japanese dish in which all sorts of fish and vegetables are dipped into a simple egg batter and deep-fat fried. We are inclined to think of tempura as shrimp alone done in this manner, but in truth, the variety is almost infinite. Various sauces are provided for dipping tempura—among them, soy sauce with slivered ginger.

Fish Roes: There are several fish roes that are great delicacies. At the top of the list, for me, is shad roe.

Cod Roe Caviar: This can be bought in a tube, imported from Norway. It can be squeezed from the tube like a ribbon and used to decorate canapés or whatever you will. It has a lovely flavor and color, and its use is limited only by your imagination—for instance, it is delectable in an omelet.

Herring Roe Cakes: This is a Southern dish, often served for breakfast. It can be bought in eight-ounce cans. You should drain the liquid from the roe, put it into a large bowl and mash it with a wooden spoon, then salt it lightly, add an egg, and beat until well mixed. Add enough cracker meal to absorb the liquid and enable you to form the mixture into patties two inches in circumference and three-quarters of an inch thick. Fry over moderate heat in bacon drippings until brown on one side, then turn and brown the other.

Salmon Roe: This is treated much like shad roe. It may be sautéed or poached.

Shad Roe: The best way to cook shad roe is to salt and pepper them, then put them into a pan with plenty of melted butter and cook, covered, at a fairly low heat until done (twelve to fifteen minutes). Be very careful not to ruin them by overcooking. Lots of people like to accompany them with crisp bacon. Shad roe, after being poached for about ten minutes, can be broken up and made into a delicious soufflé. Also, roe cooked in butter as described above, but only for ten minutes, may be placed in a flame-proof dish, covered with a béchamel sauce, and run under the broiler to brown lightly.

A Potpourri of Fish Dishes

Finnan Haddie: Smoked haddock, which comes whole or in fillets. It is best broiled or poached in milk.

Gravad Lax: This is Swedish salmon and got its name from the fact that it was buried in the ground for a time. Nowadays it is not necessary to do that to achieve success. The salmon is marinated in the refrigerator in salt, sugar, white pepper, and lots of dill, with a weight on top of it. It is turned a couple of times a day. It is sliced thin and sometimes served with a mustard sauce as a first course. At the Ställmastaregärden in Stockholm, it is cut thick and grilled so that it is browned on the outside and cold in the middle, topped with dill-flavored butter pats and served with a mustard sauce.

Quenelles: Ground fish, bread soaked in milk, eggs, and seasonings are shaped into small cylinders and poached. They are usually served with a Nantua sauce.

Salmon: Most of the salmon consumed in this country comes from the Columbia River, Puget Sound, Alaska, or Canada. It is a rich and delicious fish, the serving of which makes any meal elegant. If you are a fisherman or the friend of one, you really ought to own a fish poacher, as it offers the most convenient and excellent way of poaching fish of any kind and can take a pretty good-sized one with ease. Besides, salmon is perhaps at its best when poached.

Salmon can also be broiled (in the form of steaks) and can be sautéed as well. Salmon is such a rich and oily fish that it really needs no accompaniment except plenty of lemon to squeeze over it. On the other hand, if you go for rich sauces, either Hollandaise or Bearnaise sauce gilds the lily beautifully.

You may stuff a salmon and bake it. You may serve it with many kinds of sauces—like curry, for instance. Salmon takes beautifully to mushroom flavor and may be served with a mushroom sauce or with sautéed mushrooms as an accompaniment. In New England, along whose coastal rivers there used to be plenty of salmon until it was "fished out," which is sad, salmon was served boiled with an egg sauce. Having New England ancestry, I hope I may be permitted to say that they have some odd tastes up there!

Coulibiac of Salmon is a fascinating Russian dish and something you might like to try if you are bursting with energy and wish to make a real production—which it certainly is. I love it, but do not make it often. Salmon, cod or sole, shallots, mushrooms, kasha, many seasonings, and a lot of butter are involved in making the stuffing, which is eventually encased in brioche dough and baked, then served with Hollandaise sauce. If you want to make it, look it up in a Russian cookbook.

Gravad Lax: (*See* under Fish.) This is a remarkable way of treating salmon, originated in Sweden. Do try it!

Kedgeree: (*See* under "K".) This is particularly good if the fish used is salmon.

Smoked Salmon: Smoked salmon is sometimes used in cooked dishes —for instance, in place of other fish in a kedgeree. It is also browned with rice, put into pastry for a canapé, in fact used in any way your imagination dictates. However, in my opinion, smoked salmon is much better cold and not used in cooked dishes. On toast points with a lemon to squeeze over, it is a fine canapé. Served in thin slices and accompanied by a wedge of lemon and a pepper grinder, it makes a lovely first course at dinner. An especially delectable first course served at the Imperial Hotel in Copenhagen is cold white European asparagus with thinly sliced smoked salmon on top and a cold, creamy horseradish sauce to accompany it.

Trout: The best way to cook trout is outdoors—if you can! Dip the whole, cleaned trout, well seasoned, in cornmeal, then fry them quickly in bacon fat to a nice crisp brown. They are also lovely sautéed in butter with slivered almonds.

Trout au Bleu: The trout must be alive until almost the moment when it is cooked. It is given a blow on the head to kill it, quickly eviscerated, and plunged, whole, into a hot court bouillon, one fourth of which is vinegar, and cooked until just done (about five minutes). The vinegar causes the fish to turn a bright blue. These trout may be served hot with melted butter or cold with mayonnaise.

Trout Doria: Trout sautéed and served with oval-shaped pieces of cooked cucumber. Any fish dish served with cooked cucumber is called "Doria." Shad roe is sometimes prepared in this fashion. The combination is felicitous.

Flambé: Warmed liquor (usually cognac) is poured over food and set ablaze. Sometimes called here "blazing" or "flaming." The warming part is essential, otherwise it won't work.

Flour: There are many kinds of flours available these days, but the one most commonly available and still most used is enriched all-purpose flour, which does very well in all types of baking. Self-rising flours contain salt and baking powder, additions you can just as well make yourself (and spend less money). Cake flours are made from flour-starch blends in varying proportions. They are usually more expensive than all-purpose flours and produce lighter cakes in recipes using baking powder. However, with cakes leavened with beaten eggs, they really make no contribution at all. Bread flour, the kind used by bakeries, has a higher percentage of gluten than all-purpose flour, but is obtainable only from a bakery, which might be willing to sell it to you, or from a few health-food stores. Whole wheat flour, rye flour, cracked wheat flour, graham flour, bran flour, and the like are fairly widely available and add variety to your repertoire, plus a good deal of nutritive value. As a matter of interest, there is something known as "instantized" flour whose only attribute is, as far as I am concerned, that you cannot make lumpy cream sauce if you use it. However, most cooks are pretty good at making cream sauce and it is scarcely worth buying the smallest bag of this flour just for that purpose!

To measure sifted flour, sift it into a cup measure (there are small sifters which do this expeditiously) which stands on a piece of waxed paper. Hold the sifter up above the cup and fill it heaping full. Then even the top off lightly with a flat knife.

Fondue: First came cheese fondue, a Swiss dish, often called Fondue Neufchateloise. It is made of Swiss cheese (preferably imported) melted in dry white wine and flavored with kirsch. It is kept bubbling hot over an alcohol flame, and is eaten by dipping small cubes of French bread impaled upon forks into it.

There is also an American cheese fondue, which is a totally different dish. It is really a sort of cheese pudding, made with cubes of bread, grated cheddar cheese, eggs, and seasonings and baked in the oven.

Fondue Bourguignonne: The best fillet of beef is cut into inch-square cubes and cooked in a mixture of bubbling hot oil and butter by each guest to suit his own taste. Several sauces are also presented for dipping the cooked bits of steak. This is again a Swiss invention.

Frankfurters: This is a sausage made, usually, from a mixture of beef, pork, and dry milk solids, stuffed into a casing, smoked, and cooked. There are also all-beef frankfurters, sometimes flavored with garlic.

Boiled Frankfurters: Drop into boiling water for five to ten minutes.

Broiled Frankfurters: Split frankfurters and broil in moderately hot broiler eight to ten minutes.

Fried Frankfurters: Split frankfurters and fry in a small amount of butter or other fat until browned on both sides.

Stuffed Frankfurters: Split frankfurters about one inch from one end to one inch from the other end, and not all the way through. Into the slits, insert thin slices of cheddar cheese. Wrap each frankfurter around and around with a slice of bacon, securing it with toothpicks. Broil them under 350-degree heat, five inches from the broiler heat, for ten minutes or until the bacon is crisp, turning them frequently.

Serve any of the above frankfurters with mustard and/or catsup.

Fried Cheese: In Eastern Europe, slices of Swiss Emmenthaler cheese are cut about a quarter-inch thick, dipped into a batter of egg, milk, flour, and seasonings and fried in butter over brisk heat so that they will brown before the cheese melts. This is a wonderful luncheon dish, served with a simple green salad.

Fried Rice: This is a Chinese dish, originally found in Yang Chow, a province of China. Cold, cooked rice is fried briefly in oil (not to brown it) with meats, seafood, and seasonings, and all sorts of additions to suit the fancy of the cook or the area in which it is being served. Often vegetables, especially green ones, are added for color as well as flavor.

Fritters: A fritter is made from a batter containing either meat, fish, vegetables, or fruit (for dessert fritters), which is dropped into hot butter or other fat by the tablespoon. Here are a few examples:

Corn (or Other Vegetable) Fritters: Grate raw corn from the ears. Mix with egg yolks, milk, melted butter, and a very small amount of flour. Last, fold in beaten egg whites. This batter should be about the consistency of heavy cream, quite thin. Fry in butter or fat, by the tablespoon, until brown and crisp on both sides. These come out thin and lacy and absolutely delicious, bearing no relation to the puffed-up corn fritters containing baking powder (more fritter than corn) sometimes served. If corn kernels are forbidden in your diet and you have a food processor, grate the corn into it and give it a whirl. Your fritters will have all the lovely corn flavor and a completely smooth texture.

Fruit Fritters: The batter for these is like that for meat and fish fritters, with the addition of sugar to taste. Apples, strawberries, and any other fruit you care to try can be used in this way. They are served for dessert with a custard type of sauce.

Meat (or Fish) Fritters: The meat or fish is diced and mixed with a batter of flour, baking powder, egg, milk, and seasonings, then fried, by the tablespoonful, in either hot deep fat or in shallow fat in a skillet until a golden brown.

Frozen Foods

Defrosting: Although one is frequently told that various frozen foods will cook equally well in the frozen state as when they are defrosted before cooking, there are certain ones that cook much better if defrosted. In the case of meats that must be browned first, for instance, they will exude water to the extent that there is no possibility of their browning. This is disastrous, particularly in the case of stew meats, because the flavor is dependent on that achieved by browning before adding liquid. *Never* defrost fish by running cold water over it. It ruins the texture. Here are some of the foods which need to be defrosted first:

Defrosting times for frozen foods that should be defrosted before cooking:

	In Refrigerator	At Room Temperature
Meat	5 hours per pound	2–3 hours per pound
Shellfish	6–8 hours for 3 lbs.	1 hour per pound
Poultry	6–10 hours	3 hours
Fish	8 hours	4 hours

Defrosting Bread: Bread can be toasted from the frozen state (if it is sliced bread, that is!). It just takes a little longer than it would have if it had not been frozen. But for most other uses, it needs defrosting, which does not take long, especially if you separate the slices and lay them out on the counter.

Defrosting Prepared Dishes Before Reheating: Do not do this. They are best reheated without thawing, and take just a bit longer to cook than if you had just put them together without freezing them.

Filing Frozen Packages: Food cannot be frozen properly unless it is in direct contact with the freezer surface. After it is frozen, it can be stored in the door rack of your freezer or piled up to conserve space.

Foods That Do Not Freeze Well: There are few of these. Lettuce and other greens which are best eaten crisp do not freeze well. Neither do raw tomatoes, onion, celery, and green peppers. However, when these last are cooked or used as seasonings, they may be frozen without damage to texture or flavor. Cooked egg whites get tough when frozen, but can be grated and frozen successfully. Boiled potatoes get soggy when frozen. Custard and cream pies do not freeze well. Mayonnaise, as is, will separate when frozen, but can be frozen in combination with other foods. With these exceptions, the sky and your freezer's capacity is the limit.

Maximum Storage Periods for Frozen Foods at Zero Degrees:

	Storage Time (Months)		Storage Time (Months)
Butter	6–8	Crabmeat	2
Cheese	4–6	Shrimp	4
Eggs	6–10	Asparagus, beans, peas	8
Beef roasts and steaks	12	Cauliflower, corn,	
Lamb roasts	12	spinach	10
Veal roasts	8	Fruits	12
Veal cutlets and chops	6	Fruit juice concentrate	12
Fresh pork roasts	8	Bread and rolls	3
Cured pork	2	Cinnamon bread	
Bacon	2	and rolls	2
Sausage and		Doughnuts	3
ground meat	2–3	Angel or chiffon cake	2
Chicken, whole	12	Fruit cake	12
Chicken, cut up	6	Layer cake	4
Chicken livers	3	Pound or yellow cake	6
Duck, goose, and		Pastry shells	2
turkey, whole	6	Pies (unbaked)	8
Fish	2–3	Prepared main dishes	3–4
Cooked fish and		Sandwiches	½
shellfish	3	Soups	4

Baked Goods: These freeze well, but they are bulky and take a good deal of space, which is a consideration. Most of these foods freeze equally well, baked or unbaked. If you want to freeze a frosted cake, do so before wrapping it. Most cookies keep longer than other baked goods in the freezer—from six to twelve months. They should be cooled completely before freezing.

Bread: Bread freezes beautifully. Commercially made bread can be frozen in the covering in which it was purchased and kept for two weeks. Homemade bread and rolls and brown-and-serve bakery products can be kept, properly wrapped, for three months in the freezer.

Butter: It freezes well and can be frozen in the wrapping (or box) in which it comes from the market.

Cheese: It is possible to freeze cheese, with the possible exception of cream cheese, which does not yield a very acceptable product when frozen. However, cheese should be frozen in small pieces of a pound or less in weight and not over an inch thick. If properly covered and sealed, it may be held in the freezer for four to six months. The foil or other moisture-proof wrapping should be pressed tightly against surfaces to eliminate air and to preven evaporation; then the cheese should be frozen promptly. It will retain exactly the ripeness and flavor it had when you put it into the freezer.

Eggs: Eggs freeze very well, either whole or separated. Most people like to freeze either egg whites or yolks, each left from dishes requiring the other. (*See* Eggs.)

Fresh Fruits and Vegetables: This is an economical thing to do if you grow them yourself or if you buy local produce when it is most abundant. It is also economical if you take care to prepare and freeze them at once upon purchase. They must be packaged properly to avoid waste and spoilage. It is also economical if you keep your freezer well filled and rotate the products, using first the earliest ones frozen and filling in with other frozen foods so that space is not wasted.

Fried Foods: In general, these do not freeze well. French fried potatoes and fried onion rings are exceptions.

Game: Game freezes well and should be handled like other meat or poultry.

Herbs: They freeze very well, minced, and are a handy thing to have available at any moment. Freeze minced fresh herbs in season in small packages and enjoy them all year round.

Leftovers, Meats, and Other Foods in the Freezing Compartment of a Refrigerator: This is all right, but you must not be under any illusion that you have "frozen" these foods in the same way you would have if you had done the job in a freezer. The foods you buy in packages are *quick* frozen at temperatures of zero or less. The same result is impossible to achieve in a freezing compartment.

Leftover Turkey: As soon as possible after the turkey has been served, remove the meat from the carcass in large pieces. Wrap it in plastic film, heavy-duty aluminum foil, or other moisture-and-vapor-resistant packaging material. Freeze the meat at once. The turkey pieces will hold their quality a full month. Smaller pieces covered with gravy to keep out air should be frozen in rigid plastic, glass, or metal containers, tightly sealed, allowing a half-inch of space per pint at the top for expansion. Turkey thus frozen with gravy has a storage life of six months at zero degrees or lower.

Meat Pâtés: In my opinion, these do not freeze well, for though they may taste quite like the original mixture, they will have a *wet* quality which is far from attractive. But they will keep ten days in the refrigerator and in most households they will not last that long!

Meat Pies or Turnovers: It is best to freeze them unbaked, then bake them from the frozen state.

Milk Sauces: Sometimes sauces containing a relatively large amount of milk separate during freezing and thawing, but usually they can be stirred and beaten smooth again.

Nutmeats: They freeze very well and keep well also.

Pastry: Regular pie dough and puff pastry freeze very well.

Pork: Pork fat tends to get rancid much faster than other animal fats. So pork, unless it is very lean, should not be held long in the freezer.

Prepared Dishes: Here are some of the many that freeze well: meatloaves, pot roast, stews, hash, stuffed peppers, meatballs in sauce, meat birds, meat turnovers, creamed chicken or turkey, fish loaves or puddings, lobster or shrimp in sauce, chili con carne, Spanish rice, lasagna, macaroni and cheese (with or without ham).

Rice: "Converted" rice freezes better than the quick-cooking variety. It is a good binder for casseroles, too.

Sandwiches: Freezing sandwiches is a great time-saver and quality-keeper. Use day-old bread because it is easier to slice and spread (and sometimes is cheaper) and it is freshened by freezing. Make a lot of sandwiches at a time, using the "drugstore wrap" or plastic sandwich bags. Label them carefully, with the kind of bread, type of filling, and date frozen clearly marked. The variety of fillings is almost infinite and is limited, really, only by your imagination. It is better to use salad dressing, rather than mayonnaise, or else to send the mayonnaise along in a little separate container when the sandwiches go into their box. Since frozen sandwiches take two to four hours to thaw, they are perfect at lunch time if they are placed, frozen, in the lunch or picnic box in the morning—or if they are brought into the kitchen far enough ahead of mealtime.

Stews: Stews freeze well, but if the one you wish to freeze contains potatoes, put them in during the reheating, since whole potatoes, or quartered ones, do not freeze well.

Stuffed Poultry: This is a procedure of dubious safety. It is impossible to ensure, in the home, the rapid handling and freezing needed to produce a safe product. When poultry and stuffing are held at temperatures from 50 degrees to 120 degrees Fahrenheit, microorganisms associated with food poisoning may multiply and produce toxins. Even a bird taken directly from the refrigerator may reach room temperature while it is being prepared for freezing, and the stuffing is likely to be still warmer. At zero, the temperature of most home freezers, the freezing process is so slow that portions of the bird and the stuffing may remain in the danger zone too long, especially if the bird is a large one. It is better, therefore, to freeze poultry without stuffing, and stuff it just before cooking.

Unbaked Pie Shells: It is a very good idea to put an unbaked pie shell in the freezer before baking it. If you possibly can, you will get a better result if you put it into the freezer for at least an hour before baking. The pastry browns more evenly and lightly; if it is to be filled with liquid, it is less likely to get soggy.

Labeling Frozen Packages: Gummed labels, colored tape, special crayons, pens, and stamps are made for the purpose. Every label should carry the name of the food and the date on which it was packed and frozen.

Loss of Color and Flavor in Commercially Frozen Fruits and Vegetables: This is due to improper handling at any time after they are packaged. You should check at the market to make sure that the packages you buy are clean and firm—not torn, crushed, or juice-stained. If possible, also check the temperature of the food case. It should register zero or lower. It should be stacked with food no higher than the fill line. Buy frozen foods last when you market and ask to have them put in a double bag or an insulated one. Take them home at once and put them immediately into the freezer. Consult the storage time chart and see how soon you should use them up.

Packaging Materials for Frozen Foods: To retain the highest quality in frozen food, packaging materials should be moisture-and-vapor-proof to prevent evaporation, which dries out the food. Many of the materials obtainable for packaging frozen foods are moisture-and-vapor-*resistant* (not proof), and some of them can retain satisfactory quality in the food, but ordinary waxed paper, household aluminum foil, and cartons for cottage cheese and ice cream are not suitable. Rigid containers made of aluminum, glass, plastic, tin, or heavily waxed cardboard are suitable for all items and especially for liquid contents. Bags and sheets of moisture-and-vapor-resistant cellophane, heavy aluminum foil, pliofilm, or laminated papers and duplex bags consisting of various combinations of paper, metal foil, cellophane, and rubber latex are suitable for dry-packed fruits and vegetables. Bags are less convenient for liquid packs than are rigid containers. Remember that bags without a protective carton are difficult to stack. Rigid containers that are flat on top and bottom stack well in the freezer. Round containers waste space.

Partially Defrosted Meat: If frozen meat thaws slightly on the way home from the market, it can safely be refrozen if it has not thawed completely. However, the meat may be less tender and juicy when cooked.

Refreezing Totally Defrosted Foods: If foods have thawed slowly and gradually over a period of several days to a temperature of 40 degrees Fahrenheit, they are not likely to be fit for refreezing. This can happen when the current fails and the freezer is not operating. Under such conditions meats, poultry, most vegetables, and some prepared foods may become unsafe to eat. Fruits and fruit products develop a bad flavor and odor, at which point they really must be thrown away.

Rising Tops on Frozen Food Containers: Sometimes the tops on rigid frozen food containers rise up in the freezer. Almost invariably this is because enough head room was not allowed for the food to expand as it froze, as it always does.

The Safe Temperature at which frozen foods must be stored is zero degrees or lower. You can, of course, keep frozen foods for brief periods in the freezer compartment of a refrigerator, but the temperature there is never as low as zero.

Sealing Frozen Foods' Containers: Rigid containers are usually sealed by pressing or screwing on the lid. Some need to have freezer tape applied after sealing, to make them airtight. Glass jars must be sealed with a lid containing composition rubber or with a lid and a rubber ring. Many bags can be heat-sealed, or twisted at the top and secured with string, a good-quality rubber band, or another sealing device.

Seasoning Prepared Dishes Before Freezing: It is better to season such dishes lightly and add seasonings during the reheating. Pepper, cloves, and synthetic vanilla have a tendency to get strong and bitter. Curry sometimes acquires a musty flavor.

Soups That Freeze Well: Vegetable (without potatoes), split pea, pea, navy bean, chicken, onion, beef or chicken stock, and chowders all freeze well.

Topping a Dish Before Freezing: This is not a good idea. Crumb and cheese toppings are better added when the food is about to be reheated for serving.

Fruit, Dried: The most used and familiar dried fruits are prunes, apricots, dates, figs, and raisins. Any of these is good to eat from the hand "as is" and good for you, too. Prunes and apricots are usually cooked in water and sugar. Dates, figs, and raisins are often chopped and used in cookies and fruit cakes or fruit candies. They also may be chopped, mixed with chopped nuts, and rolled into little balls, making a delightful confection.

Dried fruits stored in tightly closed containers will keep well at room temperature for several months. When the weather is hot and/or humid, however, dried fruits should be refrigerated. Cooked dried fruits should be stored in covered containers in the refrigerator and used within a few days.

Fruit, Fresh: (*See also* specific fruit names.)

Figs: Ripe fresh figs are very perishable. Therefore, when you find them, plan to use them at once or they will be wasted. Never buy fresh figs with bruises on the skin, as they will probably have deteriorated already.

Fresh figs are delicious just "as is" to eat from the hand, or with cream if you like. They are absolutely wonderful when each is wrapped in a paper-thin slice of prosciutto ham.

Grapefruit: These are available all year, with most abundant supplies from January through May. Florida is the major source, but Texas, California, and Arizona also send us a good many. They are picked "tree ripe" and are ready to eat when you buy them. You should buy firm, well-shaped grapefruit, heavy for their size. Those with thin skin have more juice than coarse-skinned ones.

Grapes: If you're going to use grapes in a mixture of fresh fruits, and they are not the seedless variety, it is much nicer and pleasanter for the guests if you cut such grapes in half and remove the seeds before mixing them into the other fruits—very easy to do, too.

One of the best ways to serve little seedless grapes for dessert is to chill them, after washing them well, then serve them sprinkled with brown sugar and topped with sour cream.

Lemons: Most of our lemons come from California and Arizona and are available the year round. They should have a rich yellow color and smooth-textured skin with a slight gloss and should be firm and heavy. A pale or greenish yellow color means the lemon is very fresh and will have a slightly higher acidity. Coarse or rough skin is a sign of thick skin and not much flesh. Darker yellow or dull color and hardening and shriveling of the skin are signs of age. Soft spots, mold on the surface, and punctures of the skin are signs of decay.

Limes: Most green limes sold at retail (sometimes called Persian or Tahitian limes) are produced in Florida and are marketed when mature. Imported limes are mostly the smaller, yellowish (or Key) limes. Signs of age or decay are the same as for lemons.

Melons: Choosing a melon well is a difficult job. My advice is to search for a greengrocer who knows better than you do how to choose a good one and stick to that person whenever you buy the fruit.

CANTALOUPES—These are available from May through September and are produced mostly in California, Arizona, and Texas. When you buy, look for a skin with netting which is thick and coarse and stands out in bold relief over some part of the surface. Most ripe cantaloupes have a pleasant characteristic smell and yield slightly to light thumb pressure on the blossom end of the fruit. If you think a cantaloupe you have bought is not quite ripe, hold it at room temperature for two to four days, then refrigerate.

CASABA—This is pumpkin-shaped and slightly pointed at the stem end. It is not netted, but has shallow, irregular furrows running from the stem end toward the blossom end. The rind is hard, with a light green or yellow color. The stem does not separate from the melon and must be cut in the harvesting. The season is from July to November, and these melons are produced in California and Arizona.

CRENSHAW—One of the best. Large, rounded at both ends. The rind is smooth, with shallow lengthwise furrows. The flesh is pale orange, juicy, and delicious. Grown in California from July through October. Rind should be a deep golden yellow. The surface yields slightly to light pressure of the thumb. Crenshaws have a very pleasant aroma.

HONEYBALL—Similar to the honeydew, except that it is much smaller and very round. Slightly and irregularly netted over the surface. Choose with same criteria as for honeydew. (*See* below.)

HONEYDEW—Firm rind of creamy white to creamy yellow color, depending on ripeness. The flesh is pale greenish white and the flavor outstanding. The melons are large (four to eight pounds), oval, and very smooth, with only faint tracings of netting. Honeydews are available almost all year round, due to some imports during the winter and spring. Chief sources here are California, Arizona, and Texas, with the most abundant supplies available from July through October. Ripeness is most discernible by the detection of a slight softness at the blossom end.

PERSIAN—These resemble cantaloupes, but are more nearly round, have finer netting, and are about the same size as honeydews. The flesh is fine-textured and orange color. Grown primarily in California, they are available in fair supply in August and September.

WATERMELONS—These are available from early May through September, with peak supplies in June, July, and August. It is very hard to judge quality, unless the melon is cut in half or in quarters. They are extremely large, and a half watermelon goes a long way. The juicy red flesh is attractive in flavor and texture.

Nectarines: Available from June through September from California. Combine characteristics of the peach and the plum. Most varieties have an orange-yellow color between red areas. Bright-looking fruits that are firm to moderately hard will probably ripen normally within two or three days at room temperature.

Oranges: Oranges are grown in California, Florida, Texas, and Arizona. It is possible to buy one kind or another during the entire year, but for this customer juice oranges cease to exist when the Florida supply is out (usually in June), since I do not think that Valencias, which are available all summer, make good juice. Fortunately for the growers, there are plenty of people, I'm sure, who do not agree with me about this.

Navel oranges also come from California and Arizona. They are fine for skinning (easily) and eating out of hand, or for using in salads and mixed fruit dishes.

Oranges are required by strict state regulations to be well matured before being harvested and shipped out of the producing state. Thus skin color is not a reliable index of quality and a greenish cast or green spots do not mean that the orange is immature. Often fully matured oranges turn greenish (called "regreening") late in the marketing season. Some oranges are artificially colored to improve their appearance. This has no effect on eating quality and, personally, I prefer a less cosmetically dressed-up orange. I look for ones that obviously are not artificially colored.

Peaches: A great many varieties of peaches are grown, but only an expert can distinguish one from another. There are two general types: freestone (the flesh readily separates from the pit) and clingstone (the flesh clings tightly to the pit). Freestones are much better for eating fresh or for freezing. Clingstones are used primarily for canning. One does not find many of the latter in the markets.

You should buy peaches that are fairly firm or becoming a little soft. However, it is possible that unripe peaches may ripen quite satisfactorily at room temperature if they were not picked at an entirely immature stage. A creamy or yellowish ground color usually indicates that they are likely to ripen well.

There are white-fleshed and yellow-fleshed peaches. Which is better is purely a matter of personal taste. Either has wonderful flavor if it is ripe.

Pêches Cardinal: Peaches are poached, cooled, and chilled, then served with a puree of fresh raspberries poured over them.

Peach Melba: This is half a canned peach with a serving of vanilla ice cream in the center, covered with a raspberry sauce.

Peach Shortcake: This is made just like strawberry shortcake, except that you may either crush the peaches, as you do the strawberries, or just slice and sugar them.

Poached Peaches: You should have perfectly ripe peaches for this. Make a sugar-and-water syrup (half and half) and pour it, hot, over peeled halved or sliced peaches. Then chill them. This way they are not overcooked, and the fresh flavor is beautifully preserved.

Pears: Bartletts are the most popular. They are produced in California, Washington, and Oregon. They are used as fresh fruit and for canning and are available from early August through November.

Bosc, Comice, Anjou, and Winter Nellis come along later, are firmer, and keep better. These four are all good for poaching and other cooking uses. These are in season from November to May.

Colors:
Bartlett—pale yellow to rich yellow
Bosc—greenish yellow to brownish yellow
Comice and Anjou—light green to yellowish green
Winter Nellis—medium to light green

Pears that are hard when you find them in the market will probably ripen if kept at room temperature, but it is best to choose pears that are at least slightly soft, to be sure that they will ripen satisfactorily.

Pears Hélène: Poached pear halves, topped with vanilla ice cream and covered with chocolate sauce.

Poached Pears: Peel, core, and halve the pears and cook at a simmer in sugar syrup (half sugar, half water) until they are just tender but not mushy.

Pineapples: These are available the year round, and are at peak supply in April and May. They come to us chiefly from Puerto Rico, Hawaii, and Mexico. Because this fruit must be picked when still hard (but mature), they must be allowed to ripen before they can be eaten. They will normally ripen within a few days at room temperature, but many are already ripe when you find them in the market.

The fruit should be firm, bright, and clean—golden yellow, orange-yellow or reddish-brown in color. Usually the heavier the fruit is in relation to its size, the better its quality, provided it is mature. The mature fruit has a fragrant, highly characteristic odor, and a leaf pulled from the top comes out easily.

Plums: A number of varieties of plums are produced in California and are available from June to September. They differ widely in appearance and flavor, so if you are unacquainted with any of them, the USDA suggests that you buy one of each to try out and decide on your favorite. A plum of good quality is plump, clean, and fresh in appearance. It is fully colored for the variety it represents and soft enough to yield to slight pressure. The immature fruit does not ripen satisfactorily.

Tangerines: This is a delicious fruit to eat from the hand. The ease with which the peel can be removed is a great help. They should be deep yellow or orange in color and have a bright luster to give good flavor. Because of their loose skin, they frequently do not feel firm to the touch.

G

Game: Game is, in this writer's opinion, one of the greatest treats that can appear on any table. This is perhaps partly because it is rare enough in most places to be special. However, its tangy flavor and delicacy when well cooked give it high marks.

Dove: Known in the South as "birds," period, these tiny birds are delicious morsels. They can be roasted (very briefly and basted often with melted butter) or browned in fat and cooked in a casserole with wine, turtle soup, milk, or cream. In parts of the country where they are most plentiful, they are always served with hominy grits—frequently at Sunday breakfast parties. Depending on the size of the doves, from one to three are served to a person.

Duck, Wild: There are a great number of varieties of wild duck in this country, the commonest being Mallard, canvasback, and teal.

Probably the question most commonly asked by persons not accustomed to cooking these birds is whether they are hard to pluck. The answer is "Yes!" The only easy out is to take it to your butcher and pay him whatever he asks to pluck it! He will also draw it for you, though the hunter should eviscerate any bird or animal in the field, since this process not only prevents bacterial growth, but opens the body cavity to the air so the carcass can cool more rapidly. Plucking a wild duck is a fiendish job and should not be attempted except by an old hand at the task.

Wild duck should be hung at least a week at 40 degrees Fahrenheit. One way to reduce the gamy flavor of wild duck, which comes from the foods the bird has eaten, is to soak it in buttermilk for a couple of hours. A wild duck will usually serve two unless it is very small or the diners are very hungry.

Wild duck can be roasted, braised, or broiled with good results. It is a matter of taste to what degree of doneness you cook these birds, but, in case you're interested, I would like to tell you that my taste says they should be rare but not blue. The red juice should run freely and the meat should not be cooked thoroughly. This is achieved in a 500-degree oven, fifteen minutes to the pound, with frequent basting. However, if you like your wild duck well done and intend to roast it, you should stuff it. Rare wild duck is not stuffed, though you may put an onion, an apple, or some herbs into the cavity, if you like.

Small, young ducks are best for broiling. Split them, rub them well with butter, and broil them in a 350-degree broiler ten to twenty minutes, depending upon the degree of doneness desired, turning occasionally.

Wild duck is good served with wild rice or hominy grits, currant or grape jelly, and a green vegetable. A Burgundy wine goes beautifully with it, too.

Grouse: The most important American species is the Ruffed Grouse, which ranges from Minnesota through the New England states and from Pennsylvania to northern Georgia and Alabama. Other species are distributed widely throughout the country, except in the South and Southwest. The only one not favored is the Pinnated Grouse or "prairie chicken." For the other varieties, the rich, dark meat needs only brief cooking and is best when broiled or roasted. The birds are about the size of a small chicken, with the males weighing from one and a quarter to one and three-quarters pounds and the females six to eight ounces less. Depending upon size, each bird can serve one or two people.

Grouse, Scotch: This is a very different kind of bird, though it is about the same size. Perhaps because the Scots cook them so superbly, they seem to have a different flavor and texture. They used to be exported to us every fall, but were never cheap; now they are prohibitive in price. Even in Britain, they are too costly for most people, sad to say.

Partridge: The matter of which bird is properly named partridge in this country causes considerable confusion. In the South it is applied to several kinds of quail and in the North the Ruffed Grouse is sometimes called a partridge. True partridges are relative newcomers to the North American scene. Hungarian partridge came here from Eastern Europe about fifty years ago. They are plentiful in Wisconsin and sections of Oregon, Idaho, Montana, Illinois, Minnesota, the Dakotas, and, to a lesser degree, in some of the Eastern states. The Chukar partridge comes from the foothills of the Himalayas and after many unsuccessful attempts has caught on in California, Minnesota, Nevada, North Dakota, Washington, and Wyoming. The average partridge weighs twelve to thirteen ounces. Each serves one to two people. Roast or broil young ones (well larded—they are inclined to be dry). Braise or stew older birds. All partridge should be hung, or they will be pretty dull eating. Hang for at least forty-eight hours at 40 degrees Fahrenheit.

Pheasant: The first successful transplant of pheasant was made by the U.S. Consul-General in Shanghai in 1881, who shipped twenty-eight Chinese Ringnecks to the Willamette Valley in Oregon. Our pheasant today is a composite of species, including the English Ringneck and the Mongolian pheasant. The cock is a showy, arrogant bird weighing from two and three-quarters pounds to five pounds. The hen, which is chunky and colorless, ranges from two to three pounds. Both have white-meat breasts and wings and dark-meat legs. The young have short, round claws, the old have long, sharp ones. Cook according to age. Broil or bake young pheasants with a generous covering of bacon or salt pork and frequent basting. Fill roasted birds with a good stuffing and roast at 350 degrees for about an hour. Braise or stew older birds.

Pheasant should be hung for several days at 40 degrees Fahrenheit. One pheasant serves two to four, depending upon size.

Braised pheasant is very good, with sauerkraut or cabbage. The older birds are also delectable cut in serving pieces, sautéed, and cooked in a casserole with wine or fruit juice and with sour cream added just long enough before the end of cooking to warm through.

Currant jelly and bread sauce are almost musts with pheasant to some of us. Fried hominy is also excellent—or try German potato pancakes. Vegetables of the cabbage family—brussels sprouts, red cabbage, or cauliflower—have an affinity for pheasant, too.

Quail: The large quail family in the United States is represented by six distinct genera: the Crested, Eastern, Upland, Plumed, Spotted, and Western quail, each of which is divided into various subspecies. They are distributed widely throughout the country and are known by such popular names as Bobwhite, Desert, Massena, Scaled, Mountain, and Valley quail. The Bobwhite is most abundant and flourishes especially in the Southeast, where it is frequently called a partridge. Quail are small birds, weighing five and a half ounces to six ounces apiece. The delicately flavored white meat is prized highly and commands a premium price in restaurants.

Quail should not be hung more than a day or two. It should be eaten quite fresh. A quail serves one or more persons, depending upon appetites.

Quail can be roasted, sautéed, broiled, or braised. They are dry, like most game birds, and must therefore be well larded, or cooked in plenty of butter.

Rabbit: More wild rabbits are taken by hunters in this country every year than any other type of game, big or small. Yet rabbit is not a universally popular dish, however inexpensive. I think this is because people don't cook them properly, plus the fact that few know the difference between rabbit and hare, which is great. The Cottontail, Brush, Marsh, and Idaho Pygmy are true rabbits. The larger, infinitely stronger flavored (if the one you have has a very strong odor, marinate for several days), and tougher Jackrabbit, Snowshoe, and Idaho are hares. Young, tender rabbits have light meat and can be cooked like young, tender chicken. The larger, dark-meated hare should be marinated in wine or beer, then braised or stewed, just as older chicken is cooked. Rabbits weigh from two to three pounds and hares range from four to twelve pounds. The Cottontail is the most abundant rabbit of the United States and is found in every state from the Atlantic to the Pacific.

Civet de Lapin is a French rabbit stew in which the rabbit is marinated in red wine, spices, and vegetables overnight, then cooked and thickened at the end with the blood, which is exceedingly important in achieving the right flavor, which is delicious.

Hasenpfeffer: A German dish in which one hare or two small rabbits, cut up, are marinated for two or three days in vinegar, water, and spices, then patted dry, floured or crumbed, and fried to a nice brown. Some of the marinated liquid is added and the rabbit gently stewed until done. Sometimes beer is added to the marinade.

Jugged Hare is an English dish and, when well done, one of the best. The hare is cut into serving pieces and marinated in red wine and spices for several days, then stewed in the marinade with vegetables. A sauce is made from the stock, plus the liver, heart, and blood (now congealed) of the hare. The blood is essential in making this dish right, so if you have the butcher prepare your hare, make sure that he saves it for you. Garnish the cooked hare with crisp bacon, mushrooms, and croutons; serve currant jelly with it.

Squirrel: The Gray Squirrel is found over a wide range of this country. Others, in much less abundant supply, are: the California Gray Squirrel, the Tassel-Eared or Albert Pine Squirrel, and the larger Fox Squirrel. Gray Squirrels weigh about one pound and the Fox Squirrel averages two pounds. The white meat is tender and delicately flavored. Young squirrels can be broiled or fried. Only the oldest and toughest require stewing. An average gray squirrel serves one or two.

Brunswick Stew: This is the most popular squirrel dish in this country. It is a Southern concoction of squirrel, vegetables, and seasonings. Nowadays it is often made with chicken, but squirrel was the original base.

Venison: This meat must be properly hung. Fresh venison meat is not tasty and is inclined to be tough, no matter what the cut or the age of the animal. The meat should be hung for eight to ten days at 40 degrees Fahrenheit. If you have a full carcass, take it to your butcher for hanging.

Marinade for Venison: Some people marinate all venison and one might say it does no harm and often does considerable good. However, the tender cuts from a young animal—the tenderloin, saddle, and fillet—need no marinating and should be roasted or broiled rare. If the meat has been properly hung, they will be tender and delicious.

If you want to marinate your venison, here's how: Use red wine to cover, plus vinegar, salt, cloves, and a stick of cinnamon. From there, you are on your own. You may add garlic, onion, peppercorns, juniper berries, bay leaves, thyme, carrots, celery—any or all of these. The venison should remain in this marinade for at least two days. If you are then going on to make a stew or pot roast with it, use the strained marinade as part of the liquid for cooking. Venison may also be marinated in beer with seasonings.

Broiled Venison: Loin chops, fillet, and tenderloin, cut into mignons, are best for broiling.

Roast Venison: The tenderloin, saddle, or leg are roasted. The first two can be cooked without marinating, but should be well larded. The leg is best marinated before roasting.

Stewed Venison: Shoulder, shank, and breast, well marinated, are used for making venison stew.

To Serve with Broiled or Roast Venison: Pureed chestnuts and a tart jelly are indispensable to serve with such meat. In addition, noodles or potatoes in any form you like, plus a great vegetable, are good accompaniments.

Garlic: Garlic is a seasoning of the lily family, indigenous to Southern Europe. It is a bulb, known as a "head," made up of several parts or bulbils, known as "cloves." The skins of these cloves are white or dull purplish. While some people object to the odor and taste of garlic, no cook worth his salt would be without it in his kitchen.

Garlic Powder: This is just what it says it is and, while not as strong or as fresh-tasting as what you get from the fresh cloves, is a very useful cooking aid in an emergency.

Garlic Salt: To me, this is anathema. It has almost no taste and tends to make some dishes too salty. If you stock the powder, who needs the salt?

Garlic, Mexican: To be used as a canapé. Cloves of garlic are peeled and fried in olive oil, with constant turning, until well browned, then drained and sprinkled with coarse salt and served at once with beer or cocktails. The oil is saved also for future cooking.

Garnishing: Garnishing dishes of food with sprigs of parsley or other colorful and decorative bits is often a pleasant and appetizing thing to do, but if the food itself is arranged neatly and tastefully, it is really not necessary to gild the lily.

On the other hand, the matter of garnishing the platter upon which a roast is to be served is more serious. If you have the carver's best interests at heart, the platter should not be garnished at all. These extra bits of food simply get in the way when the bird is being carved. The platter should be ample in size and an extra warmed plate should be provided so that the carver can put the slices on it as he carves them, thus keeping the decks clear for further work.

Gazpacho: This is a cold Spanish soup made of tomatoes, well seasoned with garlic and vinegar. It is served with a lump of ice in the middle of each soup plate. Chopped green peppers, tomato, cucumber, and toasted croutons are provided for sprinkling over the top.

Gelatin: In making gelatin dishes, use one tablespoon granulated gelatin to two cups of the liquid in which you soften it. The greater the amount of acidity in the liquid (lemon juice, vinegar, or other fruit juice), the longer the time required for setting. Gelatin made with fresh pineapple will not set. When fruit or vegetables are arranged around the inside of the mold before the gelatin mixture is added, it is helpful to rub the mold lightly with oil before proceeding with the decorating or filling.

The most satisfactory way to unmold a gelatin dish is to set it, open side down, on the plate upon which it is to be served and then cover it with a dish towel, which has been soaked in hot water and thoroughly wrung out. If the dish is difficult to unmold, run a round-ended knife carefully around the top of the contents about an inch down. Turn the mold onto the plate again and cover it with the rewarmed towel.

Genoise: A sponge cake made with butter.

Ginger: *Fresh ginger root* is used in Chinese dishes, curries, and chutneys. The best way to keep it is to peel it and cut it into pieces, then put it in a freezing container and cover it with water or white wine and freeze it.

Candied ginger comes in either jars or tins and is particularly delicious to serve with after-dinner coffee.

Preserved Ginger is sold in jars and is ginger root preserved in a syrup. It is used in desserts and as a sauce.

Glace de Viande: This is a highly concentrated brown meat jelly, which is used in many sauces. Making it is something which no one but a skilled chef would, or should, undertake. It can be bought in jars and is usually called meat glaze or meat extract.

Gnocchi: This is a pasta that is made in two forms. The one made from potato is a sort of tiny pasta dumpling. The one made from semolina mush is quite different—usually cut into rounds, sprinkled with butter and grated Parmesan, and broiled, or served with a rich mushroom sauce. This variety is, to my mind, infinitely preferable to the potato one.

Gratin Dauphinoise: This dish consists of thinly sliced white potatoes mixed with scalded milk, beaten eggs, seasonings, and grated Gruyère cheese, then put into a shallow baking dish, sprinkled with more cheese, and baked fifty to sixty minutes in a 350-degree oven.

Gravy

Brown Gravy: Skim off excess fat from the fat and juice in the pan after roasting whatever meat or bird you may have cooked. For each cup of gravy, use two tablespoons of flour and two tablespoons of drippings, plus one cup of liquid (water, stock, or part milk). Stir the flour into the drippings and cook until lightly browned. Gradually stir in the liquid and cook the gravy until smooth and thickened. Season to taste with salt and freshly ground pepper.

Giblet Gravy: The giblets should be cooked as soon as the bird is brought home. Put gizzard, heart, and neck into a pan and cover them with water, adding salt and pepper and a little minced onion. Bring to the boil, then simmer about one hour. Add the liver and simmer twenty minutes longer. Discard the neck and chop the gizzard, heart, and liver. Return the giblets to the liquid if the gravy is not to be made at once; refrigerate, well covered. After the bird is cooked, remove it to a hot platter. Discard most of the fat in the roasting pan. Place the pan over low heat, add flour, and stir to blend well, scraping up all the good brown solids from the pan. Add giblets and broth, plus water, and stir until thickened.

Leftover gravy is very perishable and should be kept, covered, in the refrigerator for not more than one or two days. Or freeze it, again, for not too long a time—a week or so.

Greek Salad: This consists of lettuce, sliced cucumber, cubed tomatoes, Greek Feta cheese, pitted Greek black olives, sliced onion, cubed beets, chopped anchovy fillets, capers, and oregano. These are tossed gently with a French dressing, made with a dash of mustard.

Green Sauce: This is a sauce, known in its native Genoa, Italy, as *pesto*. It is made by mixing two cups of blanched basil leaves with a cup of grated Parmesan cheese, a mashed clove of garlic, and a quarter cup of pine nuts, then gradually adding olive oil, beating constantly with a fork, until the desired degree of thickness is reached. Then a dash of milk is added and the sauce is served over spaghetti or noodles.

Gumbo, Creole: A meal-in-a-dish soup that originated in New Orleans. It may be based on chicken or on seafood (usually crabs and shrimp) and it contains vegetables plus either okra or filé powder (sassafras). It is dark brown and rich and is served over hot rice.

H

Ham: The ham is cut from the upper part of the pig's hind leg.

You will have noticed that it is possible to buy a ham "fully cooked" and also "ready to eat." Fully cooked ham is just what it says it is and may be eaten "as is" or reheated, if preferred. Ready-to-eat ham is perhaps safe to eat as is, but it will be far more palatable if you treat it as you would an uncooked ham—that is, boil it, then bake it.

Boneless Smoked Shoulder Butt (sometimes called by the meat packer a "Porklette"): This can weigh from about one and three-quarters to three pounds. It is a most convenient cut for a single person or a small family. It should be boiled for about thirty minutes to the pound, cooled, and chilled. It also freezes very well and is handy to have available for things like eggs Benedict or ham omelets and the like.

Canned Hams are fully cooked, but they may be reheated or glazed if desired. Observe the label carefully to see whether your canned ham should be refrigerated.

Picnic Ham comes from the front leg, or shoulder, of the hog. It is cured and smoked (the picnic cut can also be obtained in fresh pork). These hams contain a higher percentage of bone, skin, and connective tissue than other ham and are less expensive.

Smithfield Ham is a long-cured ham of very characteristic (and excellent) flavor, which must be prepared in Smithfield, Virginia, to carry the name. These hams are dry-cured and aged for about eighteen months. Such long-cured hams can be kept for a considerable length of time without refrigeration.

Hamburger: Most Americans like hamburgers—indiscriminately—and a lot of other people like them if they're of good quality and properly cooked. The best cuts to buy for ground beef, of which a hamburger is made, are chuck or round. I prefer the chuck because it has more fat in it and therefore flavor is added to the finished product, though a good deal of the fat in the meat is lost in the cooking. In any case, do not buy it all ground and wrapped up in a package. Have it ground when you order it. Even supermarket meat departments will do this. By law, the proportion of fat to solid meat in ready-ground meat is 30 percent, but you can count upon it that there will be too much fat and thus a lot of waste when the fat cooks out and the hamburger shrinks greatly.

People who really care about how food tastes like their hamburgers rare. They are not in the majority, but there's always hope. The best way to broil a hamburger so that it is rare is to put it into the broiler fairly close to the heat and brown it quickly on both sides. Then pull it open a little with a fork and see whether it has reached the degree of doneness you like. If not, lower the heat so that the hamburger won't burn and continue cooking to the right degree.

Hard Sauce: Mix softened butter with granulated sugar, using the back of a spoon, until you achieve the consistency you like. Flavor with vanilla, rum, brandy, or other liqueurs if you like, and if whatever you use fits the dessert with which the sauce will be served. Hard sauce can also be made with brown sugar.

Harvard Beets: These are sliced cooked beets, glazed with a sauce of sugar, vinegar, and cornstarch, with butter added.

Hash: A hash is usually made of leftover scraps of meat, poultry, or fish. It is practically infinite in the possibilities of variations and seasonings. The scraps are usually finely diced, but sometimes are minced very fine. Here are a few examples:

Chicken Hash: My favorite way of making this is the way it was done in the old Ritz Hotel in New York. The chicken is ground fine and stirred into a rich cream sauce, put into individual shallow "plats," piped with a border of pureed peas, then run under the broiler to brown the top of the hash lightly. It is known as Chicken Hash St. Germain. Some people like chicken hash made of cubed chicken in a cream sauce and served poured over toast. It is good, but not superb like the St. Germain variety.

Fish or Shellfish Hash: The fish or shellfish is broken into fair-sized pieces and mixed with a béchamel sauce, then served in hot patty shells.

Roast Beef Hash: For this, the beef should be cubed fine, mixed with cooked cubed potatoes, seasoned, and browned well in a skillet.

Hearts: (*See* Variety Meats.)

Herbs and Spices: (*See also* Seeds.) When you buy these indispensable aids to good flavor in your cooking, always buy them in small quantities because they are inclined to lose flavor and potency with age. It is better to buy more frequently in small quantities. When you get them home, it is best to keep them in jars with tops that can be screwed on tightly. Exposure to air depletes aroma and flavor quickly.

People often ask whether fresh herbs are stronger than dried ones. Just the reverse! Dried herbs have stronger flavor and should be used in far less quantity than fresh ones. As with all herb cookery, you should taste as you add herbs, using great discretion at the start, and arriving at a seasoning that pleases you. Fresh herbs have, to be sure, better and more pleasing flavor than dried ones, and if you can grow them or find a shop in which to purchase them, you are in luck.

In learning how to use herbs in cooking, it is best to start by using far less than you can possibly believe to be right (a tiny pinch at the start), taste, then add until you achieve subtle flavoring. Herbs should never be used in such quantity that their flavor overwhelms others in the dish.

Fines Herbes are a mixture of fresh parsley, chives, chervil, tarragon, and sometimes rosemary. They are used, for instance, in an Omelet Fines Herbes.

To mince fresh herbs, use a French cook's knife. Grip the tip of the blade on top with the left hand, the handle with the right, and turn the knife about as you lift the handle end, coming down on the herbs to be minced from the pointed end, which is never lifted. Use the knife also to scrape the minced bits back into a pile. Once you master this technique, it is very speedy and thoroughly satisfactory, as it does not *mash* the herbs, merely gets them into as fine a mince as you desire.

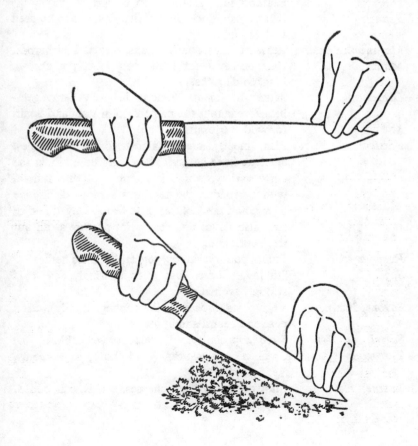

Herbs to Use with Specific Foods:

Basil, Sweet:	Tomatoes, soups, salads, and sauces.
Bay Leaf:	Meats, stews, and pot roasts. Strong. Use with discretion.
Chervil:	Eggs, salads, vegetables, soups, fines herbes. Delicate.
Chives:	Salads, omelets, potatoes, butter, fines herbes. A member of the onion family.
Dill:	Seafood, some salads, lamb, butter.
Fennel:	Salads, fish, duck. Its licorice flavor is to be used with thought.
Marjoram, Sweet:	Peas, stuffings, soups, salads, meats, fines herbes.
Mint:	Carrots, sauce for lamb, pea soup, pot cheese, long, cold drinks.
Oregano:	Sauces for meats, tomato dishes, other vegetables. Oregano is the name used in Italy and Spain for wild marjoram.
Parsley:	Fish, meat, sauces, salads, soups, vegetables, omelets, fines herbes. There are three kinds: the curly variety, which is commonest; the Italian, with a broader, flat leaf and a more distinctive flavor; and the Chinese, also broad-leaved and of strongish flavor and really not parsley at all but fresh coriander.
Rosemary:	Lamb, poultry, sauces, vegetables, fines herbes.
Sage:	Stuffing, sauces. Use very sparingly, as it is strongly aromatic.
Savory, Summer:	Vegetables (especially the cabbage family), dried peas and beans, and in soups.
Sorrel:	Soup (especially cold), salad, or vegetables.
Tarragon:	Chicken, fish, sauces (cold, hot), mushrooms, meats, fines herbes.
Thyme:	Chowders, tomatoes, cheeses, salads, fish, soups, other herbs.

Spices to Use with Specific Foods:

Allspice: Fruit pies, fruit salads, red cabbage, boiled fish, some meat dishes.

Cayenne: Cheese dishes, sauces, meat dishes. Very hot.

Chilies, Whole: Curry, Mexican dishes, meat dishes, sauces. Very hot.

Cinnamon: Applesauce, many desserts, especially rice pudding, toast, some meats, fruit pies, blended into chocolate ice cream, dessert sauces, hot beverages. Comes ground or whole.

Clove: Ham, tongue, desserts, pies, soups, hot or iced tea, mulled wine. Comes ground or whole.

Curry Powder: Curry powder is not a spice but a mixture of ground spices. It always contains turmeric and chili peppers. Other spices sometimes included are cumin, coriander, cardamom, mustard, cinnamon, allspice, black pepper, and minced fresh ginger. Every household in India (and every restaurant, too) has its own version of the curry powder to be used in every dish they make. They vary greatly in texture, flavor, and spiciness. The mixture, whatever it contains, is called the *masala*.

Ginger,
Fresh Root: Curry, Chinese dishes, chutneys.

Ginger, Ground: Baking, meats, poultry, puddings, sauces, vegetables, cooked fruits.

Ginger, Preserved: Dessert sauces, cakes, puddings.

Ginger, Candied: With after-dinner coffee.

Mace: Desserts, seafood stews, sweet spiced cakes and cookies. Mace is the outer shell of the nutmeg. To be used with discretion, as the flavor is most distinctive.

Mustard: Sauces, especially for fish, with meats, cheese dishes, deviled eggs, salad dressings. Comes dry or prepared in many variations.

Nutmeg:	Desserts, applesauce, beverages, cakes and cookies, cooked fruits, meat dishes, sauces, vegetables (especially spinach). Comes ground, but much more flavorful if bought whole and ground fresh at home.
Paprika:	Stews, sauces, chicken and veal dishes, eggs, fish, meats, salads, vegetables. Hungarian paprika, which is the best, comes sweet, medium, or hot.
Pepper, Black:	Good on or in any dish that is not sweet! Buy it whole and grind it fresh for greatest flavor.
Pepper, White:	White or light sauces. White pepper is sweeter and less pungent than black, though they can be used interchangeably. If you use white pepper, have a grinder devoted to it and grind it fresh—much tastier!
Saffron:	Rice, Spanish and Italian dishes, sauces, breads and cakes. Used more for color than flavor, for if you use too much, the dish will become bitter. Comes ground and in leaves (much cheaper, but never *really* cheap anymore) of which you make an essence for cooking.
Turmeric:	Curry, fish, rice, sauces, pickles, chutneys.

Hollandaise Sauce: This is made in the proportion of one egg yolk to one and a half teaspoons lemon juice and half a stick of butter (this may be doubled or tripled successfully). Melt the butter. Blend the egg yolk and lemon juice in the top of a double boiler, over hot, *not boiling,* water. Add butter gradually to the egg yolk, beating constantly with a wire whisk. Continue beating until sauce has reached the consistency you like. The more you beat, the thicker it will get. Remove from heat and let stand until ready to serve. It is not supposed to be served hot.

Hominy: This is hulled corn with the germ removed. A more familiar form, particularly in the South, is hominy grits, which is hominy in fine uniform particles. Hominy grits are never missing from a proper Southern breakfast, embellished usually with butter. Grits are also sometimes tossed with cheese just before serving so that the cheese melts and melds into the grits. It is also possible to make a casserole of cooked grits, mixed with butter, one or two well-beaten eggs, and a little milk, poured into a buttered baking dish and baked for fifteen to twenty minutes in a moderate oven until browned.

Hors d'Oeuvres: These foods are more frequently referred to in this country as Canapés (*see* Canapés) and are, by definition, something outside the meal. The French, at the time Larousse Gastronomique was written, served them at the table before the soup. The Russians, who call them *zakuski,* served them in an antechamber adjoining the dining room, accompanied by plenty of wine or liqueurs. As most people know, we serve them with drinks before a meal.

Hotchpotch: This is a dish of the Netherlands, to be found almost everywhere in that country, but particularly famous in Leyden, where it is always served to celebrate the lifting of the siege of Leyden, at which time it was given to the starving populace. Hotchpotch consists of flank steak, carrots, onions, and potatoes. At the end of the cooking, the vegetables are mashed and served on top of the meat with the cooking liquor as a sauce—not very exciting, but substantial.

Hungarian Goulash: This is a stew of many variations. Usually made of beef, it also sometimes contains pork. Often, but not always, it has sour cream added at the end of the cooking. Occasionally it contains sauerkraut or other vegetables.

I

Ice Cream: This is probably the most popular dessert in the United States and is certainly to be had in every gradation of quality, from rich and delectable to absolutely awful. If you make it at home, you are likely to reach a highly respectable degree of excellence for far less money than you would pay for equal quality store-bought.

The question of what is the best way to freeze ice cream at home is a matter of opinion. Those who are devoted to the old hand freezer will never admit that there is a better way than theirs. As a matter of fact, it does make wonderful ice cream if properly done. But many people cannot or will not take the time to turn the handle, so they freeze ice cream in the freezing compartments of their refrigerators and achieve good results. There are also quite expensive electric ice cream freezers, which are fine to have if you have a large, always-eating-ice-cream family!

To make ice cream with a hand freezer, fill the container three-quarters full and place the lid on securely. Pack the freezer with four to six parts chopped ice and one part rock salt. Turn the handle slowly and constantly until it becomes difficult to turn it. Take out the dasher and pack the ice cream down solidly in the container. Put the lid on securely and repack the freezer with ice and salt. Let stand for several hours so that the ice cream will mellow. And don't forget to let the best helper lick the dasher!

To make ice cream in the freezer compartment, you must be sure that your mixture is very rich and creamy. Make a custard of eggs and milk. The eggs act as a stabilizer, in addition to providing richness. Add whipped cream, which helps keep the ice crystals small. If desired, stir the ice cream up, or beat it with a rotary beater, when it has frozen enough so that there is a thick mush around the edge of the pan. Freeze at the coldest setting.

Ices: Usually fruit-flavored, ices are generally made with a base of sugar and water syrup, plus the juice and sometimes the crushed pulp of whatever fruit you choose. Sherbets are also fruit-flavored and sometimes have light cream or milk added. Ices and sherbets used to be served between the heavier courses of huge dinners in France, but even there the menus are far shorter now and the sherbet or ice is more likely to be served for dessert.

Instant Rice: In my opinion, the fact that instant rice can be made in a few minutes less than other rice is not enough advantage to make up for the lack of flavor and the less attractive texture.

Irish Stew is made with lamb and vegetables and could scarcely be duller, the meat being a dull gray color, as is the gravy, and the whole is frequently overcooked to the point that there is very little texture.

Italian Salad: This is a mixture of chilled cooked vegetables, diced and mixed with mayonnaise. They are then arranged in a dome shape and garnished with strips of anchovy, sliced Italian ham or salami, tomato wedges, olives, and capers—any or all, but the anchovy is never omitted.

J

Jams and Jellies: In the days when these delicious condiments were made by the old-fashioned, long-boiling method, the whole process was not only much more difficult, but also far more "iffy" than it is today. I know this well, because I got my start in those days. Now we add natural fruit pectin to the juice of ripe fruit and boil it only a short time and our success is as assured as it is when we carefully follow any recipe. For specific recipes, check your favorite *modern* cookbooks.

Jerusalem Artichoke: A tuber which grows underground and produces a type of plant related to the sunflower. It is usually boiled and served in place of potatoes. There has been an attempt to change the name to "Sun Choke," but it has not gained widespread use.

Julienne: This is a French word referring to any foodstuffs which are coarsely or finely shredded. For example, julienne of chicken, mushrooms, gherkins, and any vegetable you care to present in this manner.

Consommé Julienne: A clear soup made from consommé with the addition of a mixture of finely shredded vegetables which have been cooked slowly in butter until they are tender, but not mushy.

Juniper Berries: These come from an evergreen tree (the juniper). The berries are used to flavor certain foods (sauerkraut, game birds, etc.). They are also used in the distillation of gin.

K

Kedgeree: A mixture of flaked cooked fish, rice, chopped hard-cooked eggs, butter, and seasonings, heated together and usually served for breakfast or lunch.

Kidneys: (*See* Variety Meats.)

Kippers: These are smoked herring and constitute a well-known English breakfast dish. They may be heated in the oven with butter ("oven broiled") or served, broken up, in a cream sauce with hard-cooked eggs.

Kipper Pâté is one of the most delicious canapés you will find. Buy filleted kippers if you can. If not, you must skin and bone the kippers yourself, which is a tedious job, but worth it. Place the fillets, broken up, in the food processor, using the steel knife attachment; add a quarter pound of butter to the fillets of two kippers, lemon juice to taste, freshly ground pepper, and a dash of Tabasco. Process the mixture and add a little heavy cream if desired. This freezes beautifully and is very nice to have on hand for unexpected cocktail guests as well as for yourself.

Kirsch: (Kirschwasser) This is a brandy made from cherries. It is frequently used to flavor fresh fruits and adds delicious flavor.

Kugelhupf: This is a coffee cake made from yeast dough with raisins in it, in a fluted tube pan made especially for the purpose. It is generally credited to Alsace, but is certainly more commonly served in Austria, where I think it probably originated.

L

Lamb: The USDA grades for lamb are Prime, Choice, Good, Utility, and Cull. The higher grades are more tender and juicy and have a smaller percentage of bone than the lower grades.

Buy a third of a pound to half a pound of lamb per person with the bone in. A quarter to a third of a pound per person is required for boned lamb servings.

Until fairly recently, lamb was not a popular meat in this country, and it is my opinion that the very good reason was that most people overcooked it. The French roast or broil lamb only until it is pink on the inside. We have been inclined to cook it until it becomes gray and stringy and loses much of its basically delicate flavor. There seems to be less of a tendency to overcook lamb as badly as we once did, but it is still only a few who have learned that lesson. Of course, when you stew lamb, like all other meats, you use a relatively inexpensive cut and it must be cooked long and slow to be tender; thus, that sort of meat is well done.

It is best to broil lamb chops, whatever cut you choose, just long enough to make them brown on the outside and pink in the middle. It is also possible to pan-broil or pan-fry them if desired—and if you're only cooking one or two, pan-frying certainly saves energy costs.

The best cuts of lamb for roasting are the leg: loin (with bone, or boned and rolled); boneless sirloin, shoulder (with bone, or boned and rolled); crown; and rack (or rib roast), can also be broiled.

In this country, there is much talk about how meat shrinks if you sear a roast at the start of the roasting. For my part, I think that the very small amount of weight thus lost is more than compensated for by the much better flavor achieved. The French always do it that way. Despite advice to the contrary, all good cooks here sear meat before roasting it, in this way adding flavor and sealing in the juices.

The best cuts of lamb to use for stewing are breast, neck, or shoulder.

Lamb Patties: Buy ground lamb from the boned neck, breast, shanks, or flank. It is best prepared as patties to be broiled, pan-broiled, or pan-fried. Ground lamb can also be made into a well-seasoned meatloaf.

Shish Kebab: This dish comes from the Middle East. It consists of cubes of meat (usually lamb) arranged on a skewer, alternating with mushrooms, onion, pieces of tomato, and whatever else suits your fancy, then broiled. Often the meat is marinated in wine with seasonings before being placed on the skewers. Similar dishes are served all over the world; the Russian one, for instance, is called *shashlik*.

Yogurt Kebab: This is a Turkish dish. Lean lamb is cut into small, thin pieces, seasoned with salt and pepper, and broiled briefly to brown. Slices of whole wheat bread (*pide*) are cut into pieces about one inch square. These are put into a serving dish and melted butter is poured over them. Then yogurt is beaten with a wooden spoon over low heat until it is warm and is poured over the bread. The lamb is placed on top and sprinkled with minced parsley. Turkish yogurt (in fact, most Middle Eastern yogurt) is far richer than ours, but this is also a tasty dish made with what is available to us.

Lard: This is a soft, white, solid or semisolid fat, obtained from rendering the fatty tissue of a hog. It used to be used a lot, frequently in the making of pastry (sometimes half-and-half with butter), which made the pastry very short and delicate. However, lard is very little used nowadays, probably because it is highly saturated fat. The result is that, even if you'd like to try it, it is often hard to find. A pork store would be the most likely source.

Larding: The process of placing strips of any kind of fat on top of lean meat. This may also be accomplished by filling a larding needle with fat and thus inserting the fat into the meat. That process may also be accomplished by making incisions in the meat with a sharp knife, but the needle is easier.

Leavening Agents: Leavening means, literally, to lighten, and in baking refers to one of three methods for making baked goods rise—and *lighten.* First, leavening is air. It is achieved by beating egg whites or by sifting flour. Next, it is steam, which is the leavening for popovers and cream puffs. And third, it is carbon dioxide, which is derived from yeast, baking soda, or baking powder. (*See also* Bread, Baking.)

Leeks: They are a member of the lily family and have been cultivated in the Mediterranean and North African regions since prehistoric times. A leek looks somewhat like an overgrown scallion and has a more delicate and interesting flavor. The French use leeks in many ways, in salads and cooked dishes, all delicious.

One very important point to remember about leeks is that they are inclined to have a good deal of grit in them and must be thoroughly washed before they are used. Sometimes it is necessary to split the leek lengthwise, to make certain of removing all the grit.

Cock-a-Leekie Soup: This is a famous Scottish dish and rightly so. It is made by stewing a chicken long and slow until it falls off the bones, then throwing out the bones and cutting up the chicken meat, adding sliced leeks and seasonings and cooking further until the leeks are done. A stick-to-the-ribs meal-in-a-dish for cold days.

Leeks au Gratin: Braise the leeks in chicken stock, drain them, place them in a baking dish, and cover them with a cheese sauce. Run them under the broiler to brown.

Leeks Vinaigrette: Boil the leeks in chicken stock, drain, and chill. Serve as a first course with a vinaigrette sauce.

Vichyssoise: (*See* under "V".)

Leftovers: (*See* Chapter XI.)

Lentils: Since prehistoric times, these plants have been cultivated in the Mediterranean region and in India. Their seeds are used in a great variety of dishes. There are two distinct varieties. One (the common French kind) is brown, yellowish, or grayish. The other, Egyptian or Indian, is reddish or orange-red and includes the *dhal* (small lentils both red and green) of India.

Dhal: Red *dhal* is cooked long and slow in chicken stock with bay leaf, a bit of turmeric, and sliced fresh ginger. This takes about one and a half hours. When done, remove any pieces of ginger, drain, and give the mixture a whirl in the food processor. Stir in very thinly sliced onions fried in butter. Serve the *dhal* with curries.

Lentil Soup: It is under this guise that we here most commonly eat lentils. The soup is rich and thick and is usually served with slices of frankfurter floating on top. It probably comes from the German version, only the sausage they use is knockwurst and their soup contains potato, which we don't generally use. There is a Syrian lentil soup, which uses the red lentil and has a lot of vegetables in it, making a nice diversion from the standard recipe.

Moudardara: This is a lentil dish often served in Lebanon as part of the *mazza* (hors d'oeuvres). Cook lentils in boiling, salted water until almost soft. Add half a cup of rice and cook about fifteen minutes longer. Slice an onion very thin and fry it in olive oil until golden. Remove the slices from the oil with a skimmer and dry them on absorbent paper. Mix the oil into the drained rice and lentils. Cool and chill the mixture. When ready to serve it, sprinkle it on the onion slices.

Lettuce: In this country lettuce is largely used as a salad green. There is an infinite variety of types. The most commonly known is my least favorite—iceberg. I think it is dull. But I love Bibb, romaine, California red, escarole, chicory, and Boston. New variations crop up every year and are worth trying by devoted salad eaters.

Lettuce is good in cooking, as well as raw in salads. It can be braised, like endive. It makes a lovely soup, either cold or hot. The Greeks make a delicious fricassee of lamb and lettuce. It's a good vegetable to experiment with; you can become as inventive as you like in the process.

Liver: (*See* Variety Meats.)

M

Madeleines: Very rich, deceptively simple little cakes containing a great deal of butter. To be quite authentic, they should be baked in shell-shaped molds.

Madrilène: This is a clear chicken consommé with tomato pulp cooked in it, served icy cold and jellied.

Margarine: Some margarine is made from vegetable oils, with no animal fats. The variety known as oleomargarine is made from beef fat—neutral lard. Most people use margarine because they have been instructed not to use saturated fats. A few mistaken people use margarine because they think it is less high in calories than butter. This is not true; fat is fat and contains plenty of calories.

It is quite possible to substitute one cup of butter or margarine for one cup of vegetable shortening in a baking recipe—but add two tablespoons extra to the cup of butter or margarine. This is because butter and margarine contain only about 80 percent fat, while vegetable shortening is 100 percent fat.

Meat: (*See* Beef, Lamb, Pork, etc.)

Meatballs: There is a great variety of meatballs, which are served in numerous guises in countries all over the world. Some are made simply of chopped beef, well seasoned, almost always containing a little onion—the commonest variety in the United States. They are frequently served with a brown gravy, and usually as a main course dish with mashed potato, pasta, or rice, and a colorful vegetable.

Danish (Frikadeller): Made from beef, salt pork, and onion, ground together, then mixed with a hard-crust roll, soaked in milk, plus beaten eggs. This mixture is seasoned with salt and pepper and rolled in cracker crumbs, then mixed with a raw egg and rolled into small balls. They are then browned in butter.

Indian (Kofta): There are many *koftas* available in India, including vegetarian ones, which are delicious and rather unusual. Here is a description of one I got from a vegetarian restaurant in New Delhi. Grate together zucchini, carrot, and fresh green beans. A food processor is fine for this. When grated, squeeze the moisture from the mixture, leaving only enough to enable the ingredients to stick together. Form the blend into small balls about the size of walnuts. Handle these very carefully. Sauté the vegetable balls in butter, turning them with two spoons so as not to break them, and brown them on all sides. Cover the pan tightly and allow the *kofta* to steam gently in the butter for about ten minutes (which leaves the vegetables a little crisp) or until cooked to your taste.

Italian: These consist usually of chopped beef mixed with egg and bread well seasoned with grated cheese, parsley, basil, and a bit of chopped prosciutto added. The meat is shaped into balls 1″ in diameter and cooked in boiling beef broth. Meatballs are usually served with a tomato sauce. The beef can also be shaped into tiny balls, cooked and served in soup.

Norwegian (Kjottboller): These are made with ground sirloin, seasoned with salt, pepper, ground ginger, and enough beef stock to hold the mixture together. This is rolled into large balls and sprinkled with flour, then browned well on all sides in butter. Now stock is added, not quite enough to cover. Cover the pan and simmer fifteen minutes or more. Serve with the gravy.

Swedish (Köttbullar): These are made of a mixture of two-thirds beef and one-third pork, ground together very fine, then mixed with chopped onions, sautéed in butter until soft but not brown, plus bread crumbs, milk, egg yolks, salt and pepper, and one egg white. This mixture must be worked or beaten for at least fifteen minutes. It is then chilled in the refrigerator two to three hours. Shape the mixture into small balls and fry them in butter, browning them on all sides—or they may be fried in deep fat. Serve with or without brown gravy, as an entrée or on the smorgasbord.

Scotch Eggs: Perhaps these are the Scottish version of Nargis Kofta (*see* Beef dishes)—or perhaps the fact is the reverse. In any event, there is a definite relationship. Whole hard-cooked eggs are covered thickly with sausage meat, then coated with beaten egg and bread crumbs and fried in hot fat until nicely browned. Each is then cut in half and served, cut side up, on croutons of fried bread, sprinkled with chopped parsley.

Lion Head (Yangchow, China): This is an enormous meatball—about the size of a tennis ball—made from ground pork, minced vegetables, and seasonings, which give it richness, then steamed and served with a rich brown sauce. Ask for it in any good Chinese restaurant—you'll love it.

Meringues: These are little cakes made of beaten egg whites, sugar, and flavoring, put through a pastry tube onto a cookie sheet, which is

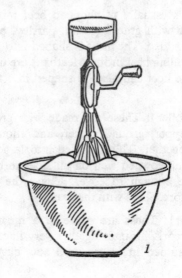

covered with ungreased paper. The meringues are baked in a very slow oven until they are very delicately browned, and dry on the surface. They can be made large or small. The very small ones are often known as "kisses." The same mixture (meringue) is used to top pies and cakes, as in lemon meringue pie.

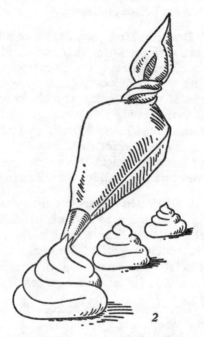

2

Milk (Instant, Non-fat Dry): This product is made by removing fat and water from pasteurized fluid milk. Most of the protein, minerals, and vitamins of the fluid milk are retained. Thus you have a product which is high in quality and wholesomeness and low in cost, with no fat content. It is good for cooking and for drinking. Manufacturers who decide to use the USDA grade shield go through a lot of checks in order to be approved for such use and are supervised from then on by the USDA. It makes sense to buy only USDA graded non-fat dry milk. When reconstituted, this milk should be kept in the refrigerator. However, the unopened package can be kept for several months on the shelf if temperatures do not exceed 90 degrees Fahrenheit.

Minestrone: This is a hearty Italian soup of good strong stock, vegetables, pasta, and sometimes meat, sometimes not. It can easily make a meal-in-a-dish.

Mole: This is a South American sauce of hot chili peppers and other seasonings, tomato, and chocolate. Strange as it sounds, it is very good. Used most often on chicken.

Mousse (Dessert): Most people think of a mousse as being a dessert —and it is a very good one. There are hundreds of recipes for chocolate mousse, for instance, and as many variations on the menus of restaurants, which obviously turn out to offer a mixed bag of quality and flavor. If you are going to make chocolate mousse at home, I urge you to try putting a little orange liqueur (like Grand Marnier) into the mixture. There's an affinity I'm sure you'll like. Orange mousse is another delicious cold dessert. So is coffee—and almost any fruit juice flavor you might care to try. Any mousse may be served in little pots, or unmolded if it is in a larger container like a mold.

Mousse (Cold Entrée): These are marvelous for summer meals and —some of them—for appetizers or first courses. They may be made out of chicken livers, any sort of poultry, ham, and many kinds of fish, salmon being a special favorite of mine. Most of them are made from jellied stocks, sometimes with whipped cream added. Wine is also a fine addition to many of these cold dishes.

Mousse (Hot Entrée): Ham makes a lovely hot mousse and is especially good when served with a mushroom sauce. Many kinds of fish can be used in making a hot mousse. These should be served with seafood sauce, Hollandaise, or Bearnaise.

MSG: Monosodium glutamate is used only to emphasize flavor already present in food. The amounts consumed are too small to make any worthwhile contribution to the diet, and many of us feel sure that the food we cook can stand on its own without needing a booster. Also, MSG is one of the more concentrated sources of sodium and should not be used by anyone on a low-salt or salt-free diet. It is used lavishly in some Chinese restaurants, but the really good ones never use it. In any case, if you ask not to have any used in what you have ordered, they will be glad, as a rule, to oblige.

Muffins: Here are a few tips about making muffins: Fill the pans about two-thirds full. Be sure the dough does not contain too much liquid and that it is not baked at too low heat.

When making fruit muffins, be sure to save enough flour from that required in the recipe to coat the fruit well before stirring it into the batter. This is done to hold the fruit suspended throughout the batter. Otherwise, it would be inclined to sink to the bottom of the muffin.

Be sure to remove muffins from the pan at once. They should not stand at all.

Muffins, English: Always tear English muffins apart with a fork. If you use a knife, it will squash the crumb of the muffin and make it far less interesting to eat. The best way to cook English muffins so that they do not brown in spots and not brown in others is to split them, butter them, and put them into a shallow pan, then place them in a 350-degree oven until they are browned to your taste. The browning is even and the butter melting into them gives them wonderful flavor.

Mulligatawny Soup: This is chicken consommé flavored to taste with curry and containing pieces of chicken. It is served over hot rice.

Mushrooms: There are, of course, thousands of kinds of mushrooms, grown all over the world. Many of these are poisonous and most authorities on the subject (they are few) advise strongly that amateurs stick to what they can buy—fresh, canned, or dried—in the shops.

As far as I am concerned, the addition of mushrooms to almost any dish helps that dish immeasurably. Raw mushrooms perk up salads and canapés and can make even a non-rabbit have a good time! Mushrooms have an affinity for other vegetables and, of course, for meat and fish as well.

When you buy mushrooms, choose only ones that are unblemished, and try to get them all the same size—about an inch and a half across is just right. Bigger ones are inclined to be leathery. Peel and stem them, then cook them whole or sliced or chopped, as your dish demands. *Always* save the skins and stems, however few. Simmer them in water for a good long time to extract every possible bit of flavor. The strained result is wonderful stock for sauces. If you want to make essence of mushroom soup (heavenly, hot or cold), add a couple of dried Italian or Oriental mushrooms—and the flavor will be much stronger and better.

In using dried mushrooms in any but the soup described above, first soak them well in warm water. Then drain them and proceed with the recipe.

Mutton: The British eat much more mutton than do we in this country. Here is at least one place where they are smarter than we are. We are inclined to think that mutton means old and tough lamb. Far from it. Mutton comes from either wethers (males castrated when young lambs) or ewes (females which have borne at least one lamb). The way these animals are fed and taken care of makes a world of difference. They should be brought up on grass or other sweet herbage and not allowed to exercise too much, which is conducive to making them tough.

A good mutton chop or roast is a real treat. The meat should be cooked like lamb—to be rare when done, but nicely browned on the outside. In texture, good mutton resembles venison, and it is an equally delicious thing to eat. Mutton is often served in England with a caper sauce, which has an affinity for the meat. Mutton is not always easily found in this country, but a very good butcher can get it for you if you ask politely!

N

Navarin Printanière: This is a French lamb stew for which the lamb is first browned before being stewed gently with spring vegetables. The browning makes it far more interesting than Irish stew.

New England Boiled Dinner: This consists of boiled corned beef with cabbage, carrots, onion, turnips, and potatoes added. It is one of the dullest of the few dishes that this country has contributed to the world!

New England Corn Pudding: If you want to be a purist about it, use kernels of corn scraped from the cob, eggs, milk and/or cream, and seasonings. If you want to add a little fun to it, put in some chopped green pepper, chopped pimiento, and minced onion, and use a little mustard in the seasoning. However you do it, the pudding is then baked in a 375-degree oven until brown and bubbling.

Norwegian Fish Pudding: Put carefully skinned and boned codfish and haddock through the meat grinder (or grind in the food processor) with egg white added, six times. Seasonings are added and the mixture is then beaten in an electric mixer for half an hour while milk and cream are gradually added. This is then baked in a loaf pan in a 350-degree oven for an hour, or until it is like a solid custard, dry enough to slice. It is served with a lobster or shrimp sauce and is marvelous.

Nuts

Blanching: Pour boiling water over shelled nutmeats and let them stand five minutes, or until the skins are wrinkled. Then drain and cool them. Rub the nuts with your fingers to remove skins. Dry thoroughly on absorbent paper or in an oven set for low heat. Do not blanch more than a quarter pound of nuts at one time, because they become soggy if they stay in water too long. Thin-skinned nuts (like walnuts and pecans) are used without blanching.

Calories: Nuts are fairly high in calories. You pay 50 calories for 6–8 almonds, 4–6 walnuts, 1 Brazil nut or 10–12 peanuts. One scant tablespoon of peanut butter costs 100 calories.

Fried Salted Nuts: Shelled nuts may also be fried in hot deep fat (360 degrees to 370 degrees) five to six minutes, using a frying basket. Drain them on absorbent paper and sprinkle them with salt.

Salting: Spread a thin layer of moist nutmeats in a shallow pan; sprinkle them evenly with salt. Heat them in a 350-degree oven about twenty minutes, stirring occasionally.

Sautéed Salted Nuts: Heat butter (half a cup to one cup of nuts) in a skillet. Add nuts to cover the bottom of the pan and cook them slowly, stirring constantly, until they are delicately browned. Remove the nuts with a skimmer, drain them on unglazed paper, and sprinkle them with salt.

Toasting: Place nuts in a thin layer in a shallow pan. Put into 350-degree oven fifteen to twenty minutes, stirring occasionally to toast evenly until golden brown.

O

Olive Oil: The best olive oil is usually imported into this country from Italy, Spain, or Portugal. It is the basis for a really good French dressing and is used a lot in Italian cooked dishes. To the best of my knowledge, no one has ever been able to copy the flavor of the real thing and it is essential for a proper French dressing. If you use it frequently and therefore use it up in a fairly short time, there is no reason why it must be refrigerated, though the advice is generally that you should do so. The oil may become cloudy and solidify in the refrigerator, but if left at room temperature for a sufficient time, it liquefies and becomes clear.

Olives: Most of us are familiar with green and black olives—with pits, pitted, or stuffed—and they are delicious. Few people seem to have discovered tree-ripened olives (says so on label), and I mention them here because, to my mind, they have the most delectable flavor of any olive I have had and should always be on hand for entertaining friends and family.

Omelets: The best omelets are the French ones, when made properly. Here is how it's done.

The eggs must be *fresh*. The eggs must be at room temperature. An omelet should be made with two or three eggs, never more. A three-egg omelet will serve one as an entrée or two as a first course. If you want to serve more people, simply make more omelets.

The eggs should be beaten with a fork, *lightly*.

To season, mix Tabasco (not pepper, it toughens the omelet), salt, and the required amount of water (one and a half teaspoons per egg) before adding these to the beaten eggs.

The pan should be heated over medium heat to the degree that a drop of water thrown on it bobs around and disappears fast. If the pan smokes, it is too hot. Cool it slightly by waving it in the air.

Put in one tablespoon of salted butter and spread it over the bottom and sides of the pan with the back of a fork, being careful not to scratch the pan. The heat should be kept at medium.

Instantly add your egg mixture and stir with fast circular motions, again with the *back* of a fork held in the right hand. Hold the handle

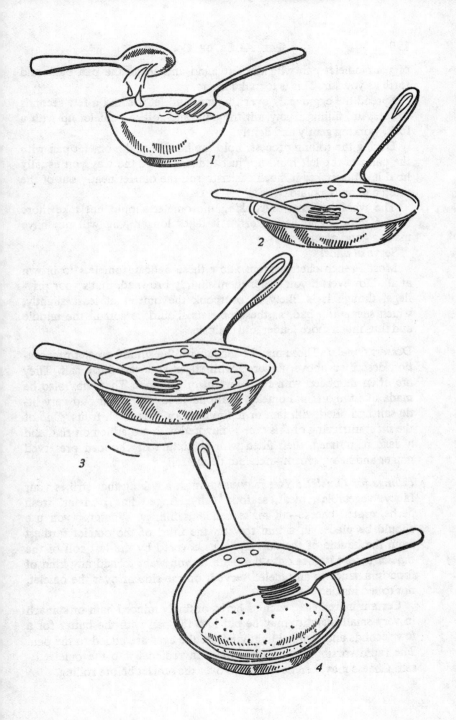

of your omelet pan with the left hand and shake the pan back and forth as you stir. This is to make layers.

Spread the egg evenly over the pan, and let it stand a few seconds to set. Add filling, if any, tilt the pan, and roll the omelet up with a fork, working gently and lightly.

During the rolling process, hold the handle of the omelet pan with the palm of the left hand *up,* just the reverse of the way you usually hold it. This makes it much easier to roll the omelet neatly out of the tilted pan onto a plate.

The whole process of cooking the omelet should not take more than a minute and a quarter. If it takes longer, you will not have made a good omelet.

Serve *at once!*

Most French chefs seldom allow these delicate omelets to brown at all. However, if you prefer them slightly browned, that's your privilege, though it is likely to overcook the omelet at least slightly, which seems too bad, as these omelets should be soft in the middle and thus much more tender and delicate.

Dessert Omelet: These may be made with the soufflé omelet preparation described above, flavored with sugar and very little salt. They are often flambéed with rum, kirsch, or kummel. They may also be made like the original omelet, again flavored with sugar and very little salt and filled with jam or marmalade or with fresh fruits. One of the most intriguing of this type is flavored with grated lemon rind and a dash of nutmeg, then filled with a mixture of chopped preserved ginger and heavy cream—rich, but delightful!

Fillings for Omelets: You may use almost anything that strikes your fancy: vegetables, meat, seafood (all chopped fine), caviar, fresh herbs, grated cheese—all make delicious fillings. Whatever you use should be placed in a thin row on the third of the omelet farthest from the handle of the pan and thus covered by the last roll of the omelet before it goes onto the plate. If you want to add any kind of food in a sauce to an omelet, serve it on the side or over the omelet, not rolled inside.

Certain ingredients, such as herbs or finely minced ham or spinach in very small quantity may be put into the pan with the butter for a few seconds and sautéed lightly before the eggs are added to the pan. The rapid stirring incorporates these ingredients into the omelet itself. Cheese may then be sprinkled over the omelet before rolling.

Soufflé Omelet: In the preparation of a soufflé omelet, the yolks and whites of the eggs are separated. The yolks are beaten with seasonings, then the stiffly beaten whites are folded in. The omelet is cooked slowly on top of the range until puffed and browned on the bottom. It is then finished in a 375-degree oven until dry to the touch. This type of omelet is often made in an "omelet pan," which folds in the middle. It is frequently called a puffy or a fluffy omelet.

Onions: These are probably the most indispensable vegetable in existence, from the cook's point of view. In fact, in any house that offers good food, onions are used every day, and often in several dishes. They are members of the lily family and come in a good many varieties—in this country, mainly the fairly strong yellow varieties. We also have available to us the sweet, red Italian onions and the big, delicate Bermudas, as well as tiny white onions, which are delicious and particularly suited to inclusion in beautiful sauces of great elegance.

Green Onions, Leeks, and Shallots: Green bunched onions are usually early white or bulbless varieties harvested in an immature condition when the desired size is reached. Leeks are considerably larger; they have broad, dark-green leaves and thick, white necks. They have a relatively mild flavor and are delicious cooked or raw. Shallots grow in clusters. They have almost straight stems with only slight bulb development and—like green onions—are harvested before they are mature.

All representatives of this bulbous family should be stored in a cool, dry, fairly dark place. The best is, of course, a root cellar—available to few of us. But even without that, onions will keep in a kitchen, in a vegetable "bin," for quite a long time. On the other hand, leeks and shallots keep best in the vegetable drawer of the refrigerator.

If peeling onions makes you cry, try doing it under running cold water—this helps a lot. A food processor is marvelous for chopping onions, but if you haven't one, get one of those glass jar types with a chopper and jar lid attached. They work very well.

Instant Onions: If you are a good cook and thus *must* have onions available, keep a jar of instant minced onions on the kitchen shelf for use in any cooking emergency. They aren't as good as fresh ones, but they are a lot better than no onions at all.

Oxtail: (*See* Variety Meats.)

Ozark Pudding: This delicious dish has been made most famous as "Mrs. Truman's Ozark Pudding," for which we all owe her a debt of thanks. Chopped apples and chopped pecans are mixed with beaten egg, sugar, and very little flour. The mixture (which may be flavored with rum) is turned into a shallow dish and baked. The pudding rises while baking, then falls (it is supposed to) and has a macaroon-like top. It is served hot or cold with whipped cream.

P

Paella: This is a Spanish dish containing saffron rice, browned pieces of chicken (with bone in), seafood (clams, mussels, shrimp, etc.) and sometimes bits of vegetable and pimiento, all cooked together in broth. In Spain paella is made in individual flat metal dishes with handles on the sides, with all the ingredients tastefully and neatly arrayed in an attractive pattern. The dish is quite dry by the time the cooking is finished.

Pancakes: Pancakes are certainly one of America's favorite breakfast dishes. The variety we like is fairly thick and we eat them generally with melted butter and maple syrup (for which there is no substitute) poured over them. My favorite recipe for this type of pancake is made with half a cup of white cornmeal substituted for half a cup of the flour usually required, the other ingredients being milk, baking powder, egg, salt, and vegetable shortening, which is cut into the dry ingredients, then mixed with the egg and milk to form the batter, which is cooked on a slightly greased griddle until golden brown and crisp on the edges.

Crêpes Suzette: (*See* under Desserts.)

French Pancakes are made with a very thin batter about the consistency of light cream, using part water, part milk, eggs, and flour. These are best cooked in a hot crêpe pan with a bit of butter melted in it. Pour in enough batter to coat the bottom of the pan, tipping the pan to distribute it evenly. Cook the batter until it is lightly browned.

Turn the pancake and cook the second side briefly, but do not expect it to brown. It is used as the inside of a stuffed, rolled crêpe, or the inside of the folded crêpe for Crêpes Suzette.

Potato Pancakes are best done in the German fashion. Raw potatoes are grated. All possible liquid is squeezed out of them. They are then mixed with eggs, seasonings, and a rather small amount of flour. They are fried to a good brown on both sides and turn out to be crisp and lacy.

Papadums: The most frequently served fried Indian bread, with the possible exception of Chapatis, which are cooked on a griddle. You can buy papadums in tins, ready for frying just before you serve them with a good curry. My favorite of all Indian breads is the Puri. These are rolled out very thin, then popped into deep fat, whereupon they turn into crisp, paper-thin balls which literally melt in the mouth.

Parsley: Most Americans are all too inclined to regard parsley as a decoration, period. It is known to many of my trade as "the photographer's delight," since a deft touch with parsley can cover almost any error in the outward appearance of a dish ready to be photographed. However, parsley is a great and necessary ingredient for many dishes and should be regarded with affection and respect. It is a member of the carrot family. There are a number of varieties of parsley obtainable in our markets. In addition to the delicate and fine leaves with which everyone is familiar, there is the stronger-flavored and broader-leafed Chinese parsley—and the Italian, also with a much broader leaf.

In Europe, more use is made of parsley in cooking than in the United States. For instance, there is no more delicious addition to fish dishes than fried parsley (leaves of parsley with a little stem attached for "handles," tossed into hot oil for barely a minute and drained on absorbent paper). Superb! And one of France's most famous summer treats is Jambon Persillé—made from ham cooked in white wine with a few vegetables. The ham is removed when done and sliced into a casserole. The stock is reduced, strained and mixed with gelatin, then cooled. A lot of chopped parsley is mixed with small amounts of garlic, heavy cream, and vinegar. This mixture is used to glaze the ham. This dish is usually served cold as a first course.

The minute you get parsley home from the market or the garden, wash it in cold water, shake out as much moisture as possible, and put it at once into a jar with a tight lid firmly affixed. Store it in the refrigerator; it will keep in this fashion for two weeks or more. Or chop the leaves of the parsley and freeze them at once. They will keep this way practically indefinitely.

Pasta: Pasta is a mixture of flour and water, sometimes with eggs added, which is made into many forms and shapes.
1. The string types: spaghetti; spaghettini; vermicelli
2. The tubular type with a hole through the middle: macaroni
3. The flat types: lasagna (broad); linguini; and fettucini (very narrow)
4. The filled types: ravioli, manicotti, cannelloni
5. The fancy shapes: stars, shells, wheels, etc., usually known as pastina

There are many, many more names and shapes and an infinite variety of sizes.

Homemade Pasta: The difference in taste and delicacy between homemade pasta and that which comes in a box is infinite. Making it takes time, but once you have done it, you will never be quite happy with the commercially made variety again. If you have a pasta-rolling and -cutting machine, the task is greatly eased. To dry the pasta, just spread it out on a flat surface for an hour or so. It then will be ready to cook, and the cooking time is far shorter than for the store-bought type. Do be sure to do some in the *pasta verdi* style, which means that it is colored and flavored with spinach juice.

It seems quite certain that Marco Polo brought pasta back to Italy from China (ravioli and won ton are very similar). The Russian piroshki is a good deal like fried won ton or ravioli. Middle European countries make many similar foods (such as spaetzle and tarhonya noodles).

When planning to serve pasta, remember that a quarter pound of fettucini, spaghetti, or similar pastas serves one Italian, but two or three Americans.

Pasta should be cooked briefly, compared to what most of us are accustomed to. One should be able to get the teeth into it (which is what *al dente* means) because it is not soft or mushy. Store-bought fettucini, for instance, is cooked eight to nine minutes. Homemade pasta takes far less time (fettucini about six minutes). Be sure when you cook pasta to put a little olive oil into the cooking water. This keeps it from sticking together.

Pasta is never served at the same meal with potatoes, but neither does it always accompany meat. One of the best first courses ever invented is either green noodles or fettucini tossed with butter and grated Parmesan cheese (and sometimes a bit of cream). After that, one serves meat and a vegetable or salad with no accompanying starchy food.

Pastry: Pastry can be blended with two knives or with a pastry blender. If you use the latter, get one made of stainless steel, rather than the wire type, which bends too much and gets out of shape. The ideal way to blend pastry in today's world is to use a food processor. It seems to me the most magical trick that great machine performs. Put in the ingredients, turn on the machine, and in less than three minutes there is a lovely big ball of perfect pastry before your eyes. You have only to chill it and roll it out and all is ready to cook!

You can use liquid oil in place of solid fat (preferably butter) in making pastry. For making a two-crust pie, shake together half a cup (minus one tablespoon) cooking oil and a quarter of a cup water, both at room temperature. Sprinkle this into the dry ingredients while blending with an electric mixer at lowest speed for three minutes, or stir it in with a fork. The dough appears dry, but can be molded easily by hand. Corn, cottonseed, soybean, and safflower oil work equally well, but none gives the flavor that butter does.

The best way to roll out pastry is to do the job on a board covered with a floured pastry cloth. A rolling pin with ball bearings makes rolling pastry simple. The rolling pin is the better for being covered with a cloth jacket. Cloths and rolling-pin covers can be purchased in housewares stores and departments.

Pastry dough, which is rich in fat, should be well chilled, but not so cold that it is hard to roll. On the other hand, if it is warm and sticky, the dough will be hard to handle and will probably require your adding more flour than you should in order to roll it out, thus changing its eventual texture. Remember that it is unwise to use hard pressure in rolling dough. This makes shaping difficult and also may make the dough thick in some spots and thin in others. The pressure should be even, but relatively gentle. When rolling, turn the dough on the board or cloth occasionally, so that you go at it from different angles to make it into the shape you want. If you are rolling on a well-floured cloth, the dough is unlikely to stick, but it may stick to a board. You should check occasionally by lifting the dough up on one hand. If it is sticking, add a light dusting of flour to the board before proceeding with the rolling.

Puff Pastry: This consists of many, many layers of flaky, delicate, paper-thin dough. Its making involves incorporating a large amount of butter into a flour-and-water mixture by means of repeated rolling and turning. It is used in many ways, one of the most familiar being to make patty shells. Once you have the hang of it, this is not hard to make, but it is exceedingly time-consuming. It is necessary to refrigerate the pastry dough after each "turn" (rolling out and refolding) for half an hour—and there must be at least five turns. Of course, you can do other things between times, but the whole preparation lashes you to the mast, to say the least!

Pâté: Larousse Gastronomique tells us that, properly, a pâté is a meat or fish preparation enclosed in *pastry*. It is admitted, however, that the term has come to be used for any preparation put into a dish lined with rashers of bacon and baked in the oven—though, Larousse points out, such a dish *should* be called a terrine. Well, few Americans have ever heard the term "terrine," but we are becoming more and more accustomed to the term pâté, used as Larousse thinks the unknowing use it. There are a great many types of pâtés available in fancy and unfancy food shops here—and a great many are made at home. You can undoubtedly find a lot of recipes that please you. Most of us could not make a pâté de foie gras, since we have no Strasbourg geese handy, but we can make a lot of very satisfactory pâtés from meat or fish or *game,* which is one of the supreme examples of what a good pâté should be. Country pâté (Pâté de Campagne) is great when it's well made and simple, too, as it should be. Pâté is served as a first course, with fresh toast, or as a canapé with drinks before dinner.

Pâte Brisé: This is a rich French tart pastry made with flour, butter, hard-cooked egg yolk, raw egg yolk, and flavorings. When baked, it has a cookie-like quality.

Pâte à Chou: This is the pastry used to make cream puffs and is made by turning the required amount of flour into a mixture of boiling water and melted butter and stirring vigorously until the mixture forms a ball, leaving the sides of the pan. Then eggs are added, one by one, off the heat. The mixture is shaped into the size you want and baked on a lightly greased sheet until puffed and delicately browned. When cool, the puffs are filled with Crème Pâtissière, whipped cream, or whatever else you like.

Polenta: This is a specialty of Northern Italy, consisting of cornmeal mush served with butter and cheese on it and as a side dish for meat, game, and various stews.

Popovers: This delicious bit of baked goods is a lot easier to make than many people suppose. A simple batter is made of flour, salt, beaten eggs, milk, and melted butter. It is beaten only until it is smooth. The big secret of making well-popped popovers is to do them in iron popover pans which have been made very hot in the oven before the batter goes in. It is the foolproof method of baking them. They can be baked in greased custard cups, but the result is never as spectacular. When you remove them from the oven, make slits in their sides to allow excess steam to escape and serve them at once with plenty of butter.

Pork: When buying pork, allow 3 to 4 ounces without bone, 6 to 8 ounces with bone. These amounts are average, though only you can know whether your family or guests will eat more or less. However, for roasts, do not buy less than three pounds, as less will not cook very well.

Pork should be stored in the refrigerator, loosely wrapped, for not more than a few days. Ground pork is perishable and should be eaten promptly, as should sausage. Uncooked cured pork may be stored longer than fresh pork, but the fat will become rancid if the meat is held too long. Cooked pork should be stored in the refrigerator and used promptly. Both cooked and uncooked pork can be frozen, but, again, should not be held in the freezer as long as other meats.

Pork must be cooked until well done because, in rare or underdone pork, there is danger of trichinosis, a very serious disease. Thorough cooking kills the parasites. On the other hand, it is possible to cook pork too long. It is done when all trace of pink color has disappeared. If cooked too long, pork will get dry and lose flavor.

Bacon: (See under "B".)

Cracklings: These are the little bits of crisp meat that are left from rendering to reduce the fat from salt pork.

Crown Roast: This is made from the rib section of the loin, cut so as to expose the ends of the rib bones, and shaped into a circle for

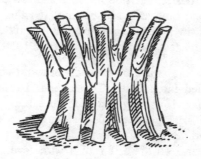

roasting. The center is not filled, as that of a crown roast of lamb, because this would considerably lengthen the cooking time.

Fatback: This is pure fat from the back of the pig. Most of it is rendered into lard, but some is cured and sold on the retail market. It is used in the South in cooking many vegetables, but elsewhere in the country is not liked in this manner. It appears also in canned pork and beans.

Frankfurters: (*See* under "F".)

Fresh Ham: This is the uncured leg of the pig. It will weigh from five pounds up. It is sold whole, by the half, or as steaks, butt end, and shank end.

Pigs' Knuckles: These are cut from the shoulder (front leg) of the hog. They are simmered long and slow in water, then sauerkraut or cabbage is usually added, cooked until just done, and served with the knuckles. Pigs' feet are cooked in the same way.

Pork Chops: They can be pan-fried, but in my opinion, they are best braised—that is, browned without additional fat, then covered with stock or water and cooked long and slow at a simmer. Gravy can be made from the liquid remaining in the pan.

Pork Spareribs: These can be roasted, using any basting material you like. They can also be braised, barbecued, or boiled. Sometimes spareribs are boiled for a time, drained, patted dry, then broiled or roasted.

Roasting Pork: The best cuts for roasting are the loin (center cut or blade); the sirloin roast; Boston butt; fresh ham; and crown roast. Pork should be roasted, fat side up, in a shallow pan on a rack, uncovered. Arranged thus, it is self-basting. It will be well done, with brown, crisp fat, in a 325-degree oven at twenty-five to thirty minutes to the pound. Meat thermometer will read 185 degrees.

Scrapple: This is a mixture of cooked pork and cornmeal, well seasoned and formed into a loaf. To serve, it is sliced off and fried brown and crisp. It is usually served for breakfast. It is properly referred to as "Philadelphia Scrapple," having originated in that city. I have never found very good scrapple in any other place, and consequently, whenever I go there, I return with several pounds of it. It freezes well, but, like most pork products, shouldn't be kept long in the freezer.

Potatoes: The white potato, sometimes known as Irish, is one of the most commonly eaten vegetables in the world. It is not a native of Ireland, but came originally from the high valleys of Peru, Bolivia, and Chile. The Spaniards, who discovered it in those regions, introduced the plant to Europe in the sixteenth century. At first, it was cultivated as a botanical curiosity. For years it was regarded as deadly poisonous. However, when it was introduced into England, it became popular with gourmets who could afford its very high cost. In 1663 the potato was introduced into Ireland in the hope of helping to prevent famines, which frequently struck that country. It became a staple of the diet—in fact, the only food crop. In 1864 there was a potato blight, which pointed up the fatality of developing a one-crop country. An estimated 600,000 persons died at that time.

Potato production in this country is now, of course, huge. Maine, Idaho, and California are the largest growers, but some varieties of the vegetable are grown in practically every state.

Potatoes should be cooked in their skins—boiled or baked. This saves a lot of nutriment for the consumer, as a lot of good nutrients are likely to be lost if the potatoes are peeled.

Baked Potatoes: Potatoes can be baked in about half the usual time by using metal rods sold for this purpose. The pointed ends of the rods are forced into the potatoes to conduct the oven heat straight into the center of the potatoes. In my opinion, this is preferable to the use of a microwave oven. It is a good idea to serve baked potatoes with the skins on. Once people get accustomed to eating them, they find that the skins have more flavor than the potato.

Duchesse Potatoes: Boiled potatoes are mashed and mixed with whole eggs and additional egg yolks and seasonings, then piped through a pastry tube to make the border of a dish, or piped onto a cookie sheet in any shape you like, and browned in the oven or under the broiler.

Gratin Dauphinoise: Thinly sliced white potatoes are mixed with scalded milk, beaten eggs, seasonings, and grated Gruyère cheese, then put into a shallow baking dish, sprinkled with more cheese and baked fifty to sixty minutes in a 350-degree oven.

Pan-Browned Potatoes: Traditionally, whole boiled potatoes are cooked in the roasting pan with the meat for as long as it takes to brown them. However, they are much better to look at and to eat if you brown them in butter in a skillet, turning them until all sides are golden and crisp.

Potatoes Anna: White potatoes are sliced into thin rounds, then put into a well-buttered baking dish in overlapping layers, each layer seasoned with salt and pepper and well dotted with butter. The dish is then baked in a 400-degree oven for forty minutes or until the potatoes are done and crisply brown on the bottom. They are inverted onto a hot plate or platter to serve. When the potatoes are layered with partially cooked carrots, this dish is known as Potatoes Crécy.

Röesti Potatoes: Although I hope I am not given to superlatives, this is, in my opinion, the best potato dish in the world. It is Swiss and appears everywhere in Switzerland. First, peel the potatoes and cut them into julienne strips. Next, melt butter in a heavy skillet over medium-high heat. When the butter is bubbly, add the potatoes. Season with salt and pepper. Cook the potatoes without stirring them, until they are beautifully brown on the bottom and tender on top. Invert onto a serving plate. In country restaurants, a great deal of butter or other fat is used, so the potatoes turn out quite greasy. Bits of ham or bacon, cut thin, sometimes are added. With a salad, this makes a very tasty luncheon dish.

Soufflé Potatoes: These are hard but not impossible to make—and absolutely delicious to eat. First, you must cut your potatoes in uniform pieces, about two inches long and one inch thick. Soak them at least half an hour in water. Pat them thoroughly dry. Then put them into 275-degree deep fat for four to five minutes. Drain them in a frying basket, then on absorbent paper, and refrigerate them until you are ready to finish them. At that point, put them, a few at a time, into 400-degree deep fat. When they are well puffed and brown (be careful not to burn them), drain them, sprinkle them with salt, and serve them.

Pot Roast: One great thing about pot roast is that it requires the less expensive cuts of beef. The long, slow cooking used for this dish breaks down the fibers in what is originally tough meat and makes it not only palatable, but delicious. Many pot roasts are first marinated in liquid (wine, stock, or whatever you like, with spices and herbs as you wish). When well soaked in the mixture, the meat is then removed and thoroughly browned in a Dutch oven type of pot. Then the liquid, sometimes with vegetables incorporated, is poured over the meat and the long, slow cooking begins. For this type of plain pot roast, the meat is removed when it is tender and the juices are strained, then thickened, if preferred, for use as gravy. Braised Beef à la Mode is the French name for a dish very similar to our pot roast.

Sauerbraten: This is a German pot roast of chuck, marinated for two or three days in vinegar, sugar, and spices, then cooked like any other pot roast, using the marinade as part of the liquid. It is usually served with those wonderful German potato pancakes.

Yankee Pot Roast: In the part of the United States where "Yankees" live, this is called Pot Roast with Vegetables. Carrots, potatoes, turnips, and onions are added toward the end of the cooking and are served surrounding the meat.

Poultry

POULTRY COOKING CHART

Poultry	Thermometer	Oven Temperature	Minutes per Lb.
Chicken	175–180	325	18–30
Turkey	185	325	20–25

Duck	175–180	325	20–25
Goose	175–180	325	20–25
Squab		325	45–60
Cornish Rock Hen		325	45–60

Note: If you prefer the searing method, to achieve especially crisp skin, start the bird in a 425-degree oven and cook it fifteen to twenty minutes, basting frequently, until it begins to brown nicely. Then reduce the oven heat to 325 degrees and proceed as above, counting the searing time in the total. The larger a bird is, the less time it takes, relatively, to roast.

Grading: The official grade shield on poultry certifies that it has been graded for quality by a technically trained government grader. The grading service is provided on a voluntary basis to poultry processors and others who request and pay a fee for it. Grade A birds are fully fleshed and meaty, well finished, and attractive in appearance. Poultry must be inspected for wholesomeness before it can be graded for quality. Often the inspection mark and the grade shield are displayed together. Grade B birds may be less attractive in finish and appearance and/or slightly lacking in meatiness.

You should select poultry by class as well as by grade. Class tells whether the bird is young or old. Young, tender-meated classes are most suitable for barbecuing, frying, broiling, or roasting.

Young chickens may be labeled as young chicken, Rock Cornish game hen, broiler, fryer, roaster, or capon.

Young turkeys may be labeled as young turkey, fryer-roaster, young hen, or young tom.

Young ducks may be labeled as duckling, young duckling, broiler, fryer duckling, or roaster duckling.

Mature, less tender-meated classes may be preferred for stewing, baking, soups, or salads.

Mature chickens may be labeled as mature chicken, old chicken, hen, stewing chicken, or fowl.

Mature turkeys may be labeled as mature turkey, yearling turkey, or old turkey.

Mature ducks, geese, and guineas may be labeled mature or old.

When buying chicken: Broilers: one-quarter to one-half a bird per person. Roasting chickens and fryers: two-thirds to three-quarters of a pound per person. Stewing chicken: one-half to two-thirds of a pound per person.

A *ready-to-cook chicken* is just what it purports to be. A *dressed chicken* has been plucked, but its head and feet are still on and the viscera are still in it. The butcher will "draw" it for you (remove viscera, head, and feet), but you usually still have to clean it up before you cook it. The ready-to-cook chicken is more expensive, but remember: You are paying for waste when you buy a dressed bird, so it may be a questionable bargain.

Washing Poultry: Many people wash poultry under cold running water before cooking it. I am inclined to go along with the French theory that this destroys flavor. Since our ready-to-cook poultry is usually beautifully clean, the washing process hardly seems necessary, but if you do it, be sure to pat the poultry thoroughly dry with paper toweling, or it will not brown well.

Singeing Poultry: Most poultry is so well cleaned that it rarely requires singeing. However, if you see signs of hairs or pin-feathers on a bird, hold it over an open gas flame and turn it about quickly to sear off any hairs or feathers—or use a match and quickly sweep it over the bird.

To Prepare Poultry for Roasting: Remove the giblets, which you will usually find in a bag inside the carcass. Remove all pin-feathers (an eyebrow tweezer is good for this chore). Singe off hairs. Feel inside along the ribs to remove bits of lung. Remove the oil sac above the tail. Wash the bird inside and out with cold running water, if necessary. Pat it dry with paper towels and place it in the refrigerator until you are ready to cook it.

When you are ready to cook the bird, season it lightly, inside and out, with salt and pepper. Just before roasting is the time to stuff poultry. It is not a good idea to stuff it and then store it in the refrigerator or freezer, because it takes so long for the heat to permeate the cold stuffing that the bird may be overcooked in the process.

Sew closed the cavity after the bird is stuffed, if you like, but the easiest way is to place several short skewers across the opening and then lace around them with heavy white string.

To Truss a Bird: Fold the wings back and press the tips against the back. Tie the ends of the legs together with white string and carry the string down around the tailpiece. Turn the bird over on its breast and bring each end of string forward over the front and tips of one of the wings and across the back to the other wing. Tie ends together in the middle of the back. Fold back loose neck skin and fasten it with poultry pins.

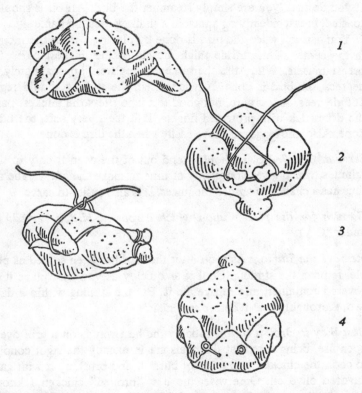

Roasting Poultry: The old-fashioned method is to sear the bird in a very hot oven twenty-five to thirty minutes, basting often, so that you get a crisp brown skin, then reduce the heat to 300–325 degrees and continue roasting until done, basting at least every twenty minutes. The second method is to roast the bird from the start in a 325-degree oven. There is not as much shrinkage in this method, but since the loss is relatively small anyhow, you may think it worthwhile in order to get a crisper skin'. Basting is of great importance in either method. If the breast or thighs of your bird become too brown before the whole bird is done, cover these spots with pieces of aluminum foil to protect them from further heat.

Covered Roaster: Birds should never be cooked in a covered roaster. If you do that, you are simply steaming the bird. All birds should be roasted, breast side up, on a rack in a shallow roasting pan.

You can tell when the bird is done by placing a meat thermometer in the center of the inside thigh muscle or the thickest part of the breast muscle. When the thermometer registers approximately 185 degrees, the bird is done. If it is stuffed, the stuffing should register 165 degrees. A less sure, but good test is to press the thickest part of the drumstick with protected fingers. If it feels very soft, the bird is done. Also, the leg joints move easily when the bird is done.

Serve at Once?: No! It should stand out of the oven twenty to thirty minutes, which gives you plenty of time to make the gravy. The meat thus has a chance to absorb the juices. It is also easier to carve.

Garnish for the platter upon which a roasted bird is served: (See under "G".)

Remove the Stuffing: As soon after the bird has been served as possible, remove the stuffing. Cool it as quickly as you can, place it in a covered container, and refrigerate it. Eat the stuffing within a day or two; thoroughly heat it before serving it.

Best Way to Broil a Bird: Probably the best way is on a grill over an open fire, being sure that the coals are in exactly the right condition to cook the chicken well and not burn it, and brushing it with garlic-flavored olive oil. Otherwise, the best "broiled" chicken I know is done in the oven! Season the broiler-fryer with salt and pepper, dredge it with flour and dot it liberally with butter. Place the chicken on a rack in a shallow roasting pan, and put a little water into the pan. Cook it forty-five to fifty-five minutes in a 400-degree oven, basting frequently.

Broilers and Fryers: It used to be that a broiler was a smaller, younger, and lighter bird, but nowadays there is no difference, though you may find chickens in the market marked either "broiler," "fryer," or "frying." All these can be either fried or broiled with equal success.

Capon: A capon is better for roasting than an ordinary chicken, because these birds are usually especially fattened and are especially tender. In fact, there is nothing better for making superb chicken salad and such dishes than a boiled capon. It is, of course, more expensive, but many consider it worth the price.

Chicken Breasts: The matter of ordering chicken breasts can be quite confusing. To some, a chicken breast means one side of the chicken's breast; to others, it means both sides. If the latter is what you want, be sure to specify a *full* chicken breast. If you order a *half* chicken breast, it should be clear to anyone that you do not want both sides. If you buy frozen chicken breasts, the package should specify how many "pieces" there are in it—and a "piece" in this instance means half of the full breast.

Chicken "Parts": Usually these "parts" are packaged as wings, drumsticks, thighs, and breasts. You buy whichever suits your pocketbook and your recipe. Chicken wings, legs, and thighs are relatively less expensive than whole broiler-fryers, so if you have recipes requiring any of these, it is definitely economical to buy them in pieces. If you want to make dishes out of chicken breasts only and do not wish to go to the bother of cutting off and freezing the remaining parts of the chicken, then buy the breasts, which will cost more, relatively speaking, than buying the whole birds.

The variety of chicken dishes for which recipes are available is perhaps the largest for any food. Here are a few examples I have collected around the world, just as examples of delectability:

Arroz con Pollo: The chicken is sectioned, sautéed, then cooked with rice, saffron, tomatoes, green peppers, and seasonings.

Chicken à la King: This is diced cooked chicken in a rich cream sauce, with diced mushrooms, green pepper, and pimiento added. It is usually served on toast or in patty shells.

Chicken Cacciatore: Sautéed chicken, after browning, is cooked with tomatoes, onion, green peppers, and sometimes other vegetables in small quantity, plus seasonings.

Chicken Chasseur: Sautéed chicken cooked in a tomato-and-mushroom sauce.

Chicken Fricassee: To most Americans, this is a stewing chicken cut into pieces and cooked long and slow in broth or water with seasonings. When it is done, the sauce is thickened. I have found that the dish is infinitely tastier, however, if the chicken pieces are first browned in butter or chicken fat, then stewed.

Chicken Jeannette is cold breast of chicken, covered with white chaud-froid sauce, set on a slice of pâté de foie gras, then covered with aspic and decorated with tarragon leaves and/or truffle.

Chicken Kiev: Boned breasts of chickens are rolled around very hard pieces of sweet butter in such a way that they completely enclose the butter. The rolled pieces are then dipped in egg and bread crumbs and fried in deep fat. Care should be taken in breaking into each piece, as the butter, which has melted inside, is likely to spurt out. Russian waiters are past masters, of course, at arranging not to have this happen.

Chicken Marengo: Chicken pieces are browned, then cooked in a casserole with wine, tomatoes, mushrooms, and seasonings.

Chicken Maryland: Chicken pieces, well breaded, are either fried or cooked in a casserole and basted with butter. This is served brown and crisp on the outside, moist and tender inside, with a cream gravy.

Chicken Mole: A South American dish of chicken in a sauce containing hot chili peppers and other seasonings, tomato, and chocolate. Strange as it sounds, it is very good.

Chicken Paprika: This is a Hungarian dish made in a variety of ways, but always with enough paprika to give the sauce a pink color and always with either sour or sweet cream involved in the sauce.

Chicken Pie: Cooked chicken (usually the stewing variety) is cut into good-size chunks; a rich sauce made from chicken stock and cream, carrots, tiny onions, peas, mushrooms—any or all of these—

and seasonings to taste, are put into a casserole, topped with biscuit dough or rich pastry, and baked until the crust is golden.

Chicken Salad: Cold, cooked chicken, cut in good-size chunks, should be mixed with homemade mayonnaise and served on crisp lettuce with a garnish of capers—or slivered almonds, if you prefer. The addition of lots of celery to a chicken salad makes it seem like just what it is—extended beyond the real and delectable point!

Chicken Sauté: Broiler-fryers, cut up, are browned in butter and oil, then cooked entirely at a simmer without the addition of any liquid. This chicken is served with a great variety of sauces, which are usually made in the pan after the cooked chicken has been removed to a hot platter.

Chicken Tetrazzini: Diced cooked chicken in a rich cream sauce with sherry in it, poured over cooked spaghetti in a casserole, covered with bread crumbs mixed with grated Parmesan cheese, and browned under the broiler.

Chicken with Forty Cloves of Garlic: This is a classic French dish of beautiful aroma (not a bit garlicky) and delicious flavor (you'd never know there was garlic in it, but for the name). Check your favorite cookbook.

Coq au Vin: This is chicken cooked in either white or red wine, but usually in France it is done in red, with mushrooms and onions. It is accompanied by parsleyed potatoes.

French Chicken Fricassee: The French use broiler-fryers for a fricassee. The chicken is cut into pieces, browned in butter, then simmered for half an hour in a relatively small amount of liquid. That liquid may be chicken stock, wine, clam juice, or tomato juice—what you will. Cream, with or without the addition of egg yolk, may be added at the end of the cooking. Mushrooms, onions, and other vegetables are sometimes added. In place of these, herbs are sometimes added, such as tarragon to make Chicken Tarragon.

Lemon Chicken: This is one of the most delicate, beautifully seasoned Chinese dishes. Boneless breasts of chicken are cut in half, then each half is split in two to make it thinner. Ginger, egg, flour, and salt (very small quantities) are beaten together and poured over the chicken breast and let stand a half hour. Then the chicken pieces are dipped into water chestnut powder and fried in shallow peanut oil until they are light brown and crispy. Slice them about half an inch wide and keep the pieces warm. Serve the chicken on a bed of finely shredded lettuce, with a sauce of lemon juice, sugar, soy sauce, and water, to which sometimes a little cornstarch is added, and also some slices of lemon which have been cooked in the sauce.

Suprême de Volaille: Skinned and boned breast of chicken. It may be cooked in many ways and takes kindly to an infinite number of sauces. A suprême takes only eight minutes to cook in butter. After this one removes the suprême and keeps it warm while proceeding with the sauce to go over it.

Cornish Rock Hen: This small domestic bird is a cross between two others; the man who achieved the cross will not tell which two. A little larger than a squab, this is a relatively uninteresting bird to eat.

Duck

Average Weight: Ducks weigh from about three to six pounds. The smallest are hard to find in many markets, but can be picked up in any Chinatown. However, larger ducks, while they contain more fat, also contain proportionately more meat, which is usually of the best quality.

Servings: A five- to six-pound duck serves not more than four, and it is often quite possible for three to consume such a bird. There is not a great deal of meat on a duck, but the crisp skin is so good and so rich that it helps to stretch the servings.

Boiled Duck: The Danes serve boiled duck, skinning it before carving it. They serve it with melted butter to pour over it and with frozen cream-horseradish sauce. Although one thus misses the lovely crisp skin of a roast duck, this is an utterly delectable dish.

Canard à la Presse: This is the great specialty of the famous Tour d'Argent Restaurant in Paris. It is duck roasted for a very short time, then carved. The bones are crushed in a duck press and the resultant blood is made into a sauce to go over the duck. It is known to many Americans as "bloody duck." It is not everyone's cup of tea, but the restaurant has many other very fine dishes.

Caneton à l'Orange: This is roast duck with an orange sauce, which is sometimes made separately and served with the duck, sometimes cooked with it. One of the best I know comes from South America and is cooked with orange marmalade spread over the duck and made into a sauce when the roasting is finished. This dish is known also as Caneton à la Bigarade.

Grilled Duck: Duck can be split and broiled on an outdoor grill or roasted whole on a spit. It takes a long time to cook—how long depends somewhat, of course, on the heat of your fire. A five- to six-pound duck will take about two hours to cook well.

Goose: For some reason, many people seem to think that a goose is hard to cook well. It is not difficult at all. A goose is a very fat bird. For that reason, the skin should be well pricked before the bird goes into the oven, to let the fat run out during the cooking. Otherwise, a goose is roasted like any other poultry, allowing twenty to twenty-five minutes a pound for the total roasting. Also, one should allow one and a quarter pounds per serving. A goose has relatively little meat on it, even compared to a duck, but it is a delicious thing to eat. Because it is so fat, a goose need not be basted.

Squab: A squab is a pigeon about five weeks old, usually weighing less than a pound. Stuff the bird or not, as you please. Tie its legs and place pieces of bacon or fat salt pork over the breast. Roast in a 325-degree oven forty-five to sixty minutes, or until well done, basting frequently. Remove the bacon or pork for the last fifteen minutes of cooking, so that the skin will brown. You can also braise the squab, either whole or cut up, and cook it in a casserole with a variety of sauces, including wine ones.

Turkey: When buying a turkey that weighs less than twelve pounds, allow three-quarters of a pound to one pound per person. If the turkey weighs twelve pounds or more, allow one-half to three-quarters of a pound per person.

It is more economical to buy a big turkey than a small one, especially since leftover turkey makes many fine dishes. At the same time, if you are a very small family, you may never be able to figure out how to use up a big turkey, in which case you will pay the penalty and spend more, relatively speaking, for a smaller bird. You might consider buying turkey in parts, too. It is sold in halves, quarters, or by the piece: legs, thighs, wings, and breasts, just like chicken.

Cooking Turkey in Aluminum Foil: This shortens the cooking time and prevents the oven from being splattered, which are advantages. However, a turkey cooked in foil does not turn out exactly like the one roasted in an open pan on a rack. Therefore, whether or not to cook in foil becomes a matter of taste. Some people feel that one never gets a properly crisp brown skin, even though the foil is folded back at the end of the cooking for browning purposes. Others, who prefer the foil method, think you cannot get a turkey as succulently moist by the ordinary method.

To Cook Half a Turkey: Season it with salt and pepper inside and out. Mound stuffing into the cut side of the half-turkey, cover the stuffing with aluminum foil, then tie strings around the meat and foil to hold in the stuffing—also to hold down the wing. Dredge the skin with flour and dot it with butter. Place the meat, foil side down, on a rack; roast it as you would a whole turkey.

Frozen Turkey: It takes about three days to thaw a twenty-pound bird in the refrigerator. The fastest way is to put it into a gas oven set at 150 degrees or into an electric oven at the "warm" designation. An eight-pound bird will thaw in three hours and a twenty-pound bird in five hours.

Smoked Turkey: Smoked turkey is, of course, already cooked. It is usually served cold, sliced, on a buffet table or as a canapé, in which case you can either cube it and impale it on toothpicks, or have crackers or hot buttered toast triangles handy to eat it on. Smoked turkey is a very rich meat, so a little goes a long way. It can be used in cooked dishes, but remember its richness in planning a sauce for it.

Turkey Roll: This is boneless turkey meat, made into a thick roll. It is cooked like roast turkey, but in a 350-degree oven until it registers 170 to 175 degrees on a meat thermometer.

Turkey Stuffing: Allow a scant cup of stuffing for each pound of turkey in birds under twenty pounds. The body cavity of very large birds does not vary much, so allow eighteen to twenty cups of stuffing for birds over twenty pounds. Place stuffing lightly into the neck and body of the bird. Stuffing expands in cooking, so be careful not to overpack.

The United States Department of Agriculture says that it is not a good idea to roast a large turkey partly one day and then finish cooking it the next. The roasting process should not be interrupted until a temperature of 195 degrees for an unstuffed or 165 degrees for a stuffed bird is reached, at which point it is done.

Turkey Divan: This was, of course, originally Chicken Divan, and is made in exactly the same way. Place hot cooked broccoli on a fireproof platter and pour a cup of béchamel flavored with sherry over it. Add a quarter of a cup of grated Parmesan to another cup of béchamel. Place enough thin slices of cooked turkey breast over the broccoli to cover it. Pour the sauce with the cheese over all and run the dish under the broiler to brown it delicately.

Using your imagination, you can invent dozens of delicious leftover-turkey dishes. Do use turkey all year round for all these good things.

Turkey Hash can be made just like chicken hash, with the meat either cubed or ground, according to your taste.

Turkey Pilau: Cubed cooked turkey is heated in a béchamel sauce. Meantime, currants and sugar are cooked in water to cover until the syrup becomes quite thick and the sauce is reduced. Pour the turkey over hot saffron rice, then pour the currant sauce over all and top with crisply fried, crumbled bacon.

Protein: It is a comfort, for those who are forced to plan meals in a time when most animal protein is too expensive for most people, to be told by nutritionists that most Americans eat too much animal protein. This is, of course, a matter of habit, and habits are not easy to change. However, dried beans, especially soybeans, peas, and lentils, are good sources of protein and can be served in many delicious ways. So plan to have several meatless or fishless dinners each week by substituting these dried legumes or adding more cheese, pasta, and other foods well supplied with protein. If you do, both your budget and your family will probably be in a far healthier condition.

Q

Quenelles: A quenelle is a sort of dumpling, made with very finely ground fish or meat (forcemeat) bound with eggs. They can be large or small. When they are used as a luncheon entrée, they are fairly large. When they are floated in a soup or used as a garnish for other dishes, they are small. After mixing them, one must be very sure to poach a test quenelle in simmering water to make sure that your mixture is of a consistency that will hold together during cooking. If the test quenelle falls apart, add an extra egg white or two (but never more than two, or the quenelles will be rubbery). A food processor saves a lot of work in making perfect quenelles, as it does for so many dishes. Quenelles de Brochet (pike) usually is served with a Nantua sauce.

Quenelles of chicken, which are delicate and delicious, generally are served with a mushroom sauce.

Quiche: This is an unsweetened cheese-custard pie, baked in a Pâte Brisé crust.

Quiche Lorraine: This variety contains bits of cooked ham or bacon in the cheese custard. Other possibilities for incorporation of flavor into the custard are: endive, mushroom, lobster, clam, crabmeat, spinach, leeks, onions, Niçoise (which is a tomato quiche with anchovies and olives, doubtless inspired by Pissaladière, the famous onion tart with anchovies and black olives, served in Nice).

R

Ragoût: This is the French word for stew. There are brown ragoûts, for which the meat is browned before the cooking (usually with other ingredients added) begins. Then there are ragouts à blanc, sometimes described in English as à l'Anglaise (in tribute, one would judge, to the typical lack of color in most British food). These belong in the category of poached food. They have no thickening, other than that provided by adding potatoes to the ingredients. A typical example is Irish stew. As you know, stews (or ragouts) are also made from chicken and fish.

Ragu Bolognese: A sauce from Bologna in Italy and is one of that city's magnificent contributions to North Italy's superb cuisine. It contains beef, veal, fat, salt pork (chopped), onion, carrot, celery, clove, and beef stock, cooked together for at least a half hour, after which tomato paste, salt and pepper, and water are added and the whole is cooked for another hour. The next addition is chopped mushrooms and chicken livers; then the mixture is cooked fifteen minutes longer. Just before serving, heavy cream is added and heated through. This is one of the best pasta sauces ever invented.

Raspberry Fluff: A half pint of fresh raspberries, one egg white, and one cup of powdered sugar are put into a large bowl and beaten until the mixture is stiff enough to hold its shape. By hand, with a rotary beater, this takes thirty minutes. With an electric beater, it takes fifteen to twenty minutes. Chill fluff until you are ready to serve.

Ratatouille is a Mediterranean vegetable stew, using eggplant, tomatoes, zucchini, onions, green peppers, and garlic—and additions of your own, if you like. Sometimes the sliced vegetables are layered in a casserole with olive oil in the bottom, seasoned as the layering goes on, then cooked either on top of the range or in the oven, covered until the last few minutes, when the cover is removed so that the sauce can thicken. Sometimes the vegetables are fried separately in olive oil, then mixed together. Ratatouille is good hot or cold.

Raw Vegetables: Raw vegetables, sometimes referred to as *Crudités* are a very popular (and sensible) offering with cocktails in this country, as this is written. They are generally served with a seasoned sauce to dip them into, and sometimes with a dip based on mayonnaise and well seasoned, which is delicious but takes away a lot of the sense in serving these low-calorie canapés, because the sauce is bound to be full of same. The vegetables can make a beautiful picture on the buffet or canapé table if you vary their colors well and arrange them attractively. Here are some of the ones you might choose: carrot sticks, radish roses, cucumber fingers, leaves of Belgian endive, green and red pepper sticks, celery curls, cauliflowerettes, scallions, mushrooms (sliced fairly thinly), and zucchini sticks. Some people like raw green beans, but the beans must be tiny ones, in my opinion.

Rice: The first mention of rice in recorded history was in 2800 B.C. in China. The cultivation of this grain has been traced to a plant, *newaree,* which was grown in India in an even earlier time, 3000 B.C.

Amount of Rice to Serve: It depends upon whether the rice dish is the main course of the meal or a side dish. It also depends upon whether one comes from a rice-eating country. For most Americans, a quarter of a cup of uncooked rice (which makes half a cup cooked), served as a side dish, is a great sufficiency. Italians, Far Eastern peoples, and Middle Easterners would serve at least twice that. If the dish contains meat and other ingredients that are filling, and thus becomes the main course, a third of a cup of uncooked rice would be plenty for Americans, but not for real rice-eaters.

Brown Rice: This is the whole grain of rice, with only the husk removed. It has more flavor and nutritional value than white rice.

Converted Rice: On the premise that most of the nutrients of rice are on the outside and are scraped away in the processing of white rice, converted rice has a special process which seals the said nutrients inside the grains. It is thus more nutritious than other rice and, since it is easy to cook, is well worth the effort in terms of flavor and family health. Follow the package directions for cooking converted rice.

Instant Rice: The fact that instant rice is ready to eat a couple of minutes sooner than long-grain rice, for instance, does not compensate for the fact that it has not as much flavor or character. However, lots of people eat it—probably because they think it's quick and maybe because their taste buds are at a low ebb.

Long-Grain Rice: The grains of this rice are four or five times longer than they are wide. When cooked and drained, the grains tend to separate and are light, dry, and fluffy. This rice should be boiled about fourteen minutes.

Short- and Medium-Grain Rice: These varieties of rice have short, plump grains which, when cooked, are tender and moist, with the grains tending to stick together.

Wash Rice?: The packaged rice you buy in this country is perfectly clean and not only does not need washing but loses food value if you wash it. However, if you buy rice by the pound in Chinese or other foreign food stores, you had best wash it before cooking it.

Wild Rice: This is just what the name implies. It grows wild in water in a few parts of this country and must be harvested by hand, which makes it exceedingly expensive. It has, however, great flavor and texture and is a delicious accompaniment to many dishes, if you can afford it. It must be cooked longer than other rice (thirty-five to forty minutes).

Rice Suggestions

Cold Curried Rice: Melt butter and in it stir raw rice until every grain is covered and a golden color. Add chicken broth and curry powder and boil fourteen minutes. Drain, cool, and chill. Mix with cooked, chilled peas and serve with bits of preserved ginger scattered on top. Lovely in summer with cold chicken, meat, or fish.

Fried Rice: This is a Chinese dish. Cold cooked rice is fried briefly in oil (not to brown it) with meats, seasonings, and all sorts of additions to suit the fancy of the cook or the area in which it is being served. It was invented in Yangchow, a province of China.

Green Rice: Cooked rice, grated Parmesan cheese, chopped parsley, minced spinach, eggs, milk, and seasonings are placed in a casserole and baked.

Nasi Goreng: This is an elaborate Indonesian fried rice dish, containing seafood, meat, many seasonings, finely chopped celery, and hot red peppers, and the necessary cold cooked rice. It is absolutely delicious.

Pilaf: This is the name usually given to rice dishes in the Middle East; they are made in many ways. They may contain meat, chicken livers, vegetables, raisins, and nuts. They are usually cooked in chicken broth, sometimes in the oven.

Pulao: An Indian dish of cooked rice, mixed with thinly sliced onion, raisins, nuts, spices, tomatoes, or other vegetables—any or all of these. Sometimes rice and spices are mixed with chicken or meat to make a main dish.

Rice Pudding: My cousin Clara had the best rice pudding I have ever tasted. It was very old-fashioned, but I assure you, truly wonderful! You put a cup of rice into a quart of milk, adding half a cup of sugar, half a teaspoon of vanilla, a quarter of a teaspoon of salt, and two cinnamon sticks, plus a teaspoon of butter—all this in a casserole or baking dish. Put into a slow oven (300 to 350 degrees) for two or three hours, stirring frequently, and being careful not to break the crust. Quite a job and well worth it.

Rijsttafel: This is the Dutch name for a fascinating Indonesian meal. Many servants, each carrying one dish, serve the guests. Everyone has rice and then whatever he wants from the other dishes—meats, vegetables, and eggs, some in hot sauces, some quite dry—all eaten with the rice and many sambals (Indonesian condiments, specially prepared for the occasion).

Risotto: An Italian rice dish, cooked in many ways in the various northern cities of Italy. Risotto Milanese (which I think is the best) is rice cooked in chicken broth with saffron and a little onion, tossed when done with butter and grated Parmesan cheese, and served with grated or sliced white truffle over it as a first course. In Venice, the risottos usually contain fish and/or shellfish, which makes them meals in a dish. In Florence they serve a Risotto alla Sherry, which is rice cooked in beef stock with onion and sweet red peppers. Before being served, it is tossed with grated Parmesan cheese and a little sherry wine.

Riz à l'Impératrice: This is a very elegant French dessert which might be described as Rice Cake with Candied Fruits. As a matter of fact, it is a gelatin dessert containing rice, milk, gelatin, rum, egg yolks, vanilla, sugar, and candied fruits. It is cooled and poured into a mold which has been lined with caramel and put into the refrigerator to set. When you unmold it, you may decorate it with more candied fruit, if desired.

Spanish Rice: Cooked rice is mixed with chopped green pepper, chopped tomato, chopped onions, and seasonings. It is sometimes served with grated Parmesan cheese.

Syrian Rice: Heat olive oil in a casserole, add raw rice, and stir the rice until every grain is coated, but do not brown it. Add beef bouillon and a clove of garlic and cook in a 375-degree oven until the rice has absorbed all the liquid and has a slight crust on top (about forty-five minutes). This can stand in an oven with the heat turned down almost indefinitely.

Rhubarb: This vegetable (though many regard it as a fruit) is said to have originated in Siberia, but is very easy to grow in temperate climates. It is, strange to say, a member of the buckwheat family. One of its most common uses is for pie and no respectable New Englander would think of calling it anything but "Pieplant." It is also exceedingly good stewed, especially with strawberries. Rhubarb makes a lovely spring dessert. It can be enjoyed at any time of year, if you use the frozen variety.

Stewed Rhubarb and Strawberries: Put one cup rhubarb, cut in one-inch lengths, into a saucepan with half a cup of sugar and two tablespoons water. Cover the pan and cook the rhubarb over low heat for fifteen minutes. Add strawberries and cook five minutes longer or until rhubarb is tender. Cool the mixture and chill it in the refrigerator.

Rumaki: This is a Polynesian invention which we use for a canapé. You slice chicken livers in half and divide any very large pieces in two. Sprinkle each with onion powder. Slice water chestnuts into three pieces each. Place a piece of water chestnut on each piece of liver. Pierce both with a toothpick, being careful to see that it goes through the middle of the chestnut slice, then through the other side of the liver. Divide bacon slices in half lengthwise, then crosswise. Wrap a piece of bacon around each chicken liver, securing it well on the toothpick. Place the rumaki in a marinade of soy sauce, curry powder, ginger, cinnamon, sherry, and garlic for two hours or more. When you are ready to cook them, remove the rumaki from the marinade and place them in a pan. Broil them about five inches from the broiler heat, turning them until they are browned on both sides (about ten minutes).

S

Salads

Cutting Up Greens for Salad: Never do it. Greens should be *torn* into whatever size pieces you prefer.

Greens Available: Chicory, dandelion, endive, Bibb, Boston, iceberg, romaine, sorrel, watercress. Of all these, I would hope that you omit iceberg lettuce, the dullest green offered and so commonly used that it gets very boring.

Vegetables Other Than Greens in Salad: Green or sweet red pepper, avocado, carrot, radish, tomato, onion, cucumber, celery, scallion, and fresh herbs—all raw, sliced or chopped—any or all are fine in a green salad. Another type of salad uses cooked vegetables.

Washing a Wooden Salad Bowl: Preferably, it should not be washed. Wipe such a bowl out well with paper towels when the salad is finished. Store the bowl covered with plastic wrap, which will cling and keep the bowl clean. If treated thus, the salad bowl will always be ready to receive the next salad. It will also be beautiful to look upon, as the rubbing with paper towels, when there is some oil left in the bowl, deepens the color of the wood and brings out the pattern of its grain.

Salad Suggestions

Beetroot Salad: Chilled cooked or canned beets are cut into julienne strips or thin slices, covered with very thin slices of onion, and marinated in a French dressing for a couple of hours before serving, decorated with minced parsley.

Caesar Salad: Greens are torn into a salad bowl, mixed with lemon juice, olive oil, seasonings, grated Parmesan, and crumbled blue cheese. A raw egg is broken into the salad and it is tossed thoroughly, so that the egg clings to every leaf and causes the cheese to stick to the leaves. At the end, garlic-flavored croutons are added and tossed lightly. It has sometimes seemed to me that every chef in California claims to have invented Caesar salad. In any event, it is Californian.

Celerie Remoulade: (*See* under "C".)

Chef's Salad: Julienne strips of chicken, tongue, ham, and Swiss cheese, in equal proportions, are mixed with watercress and other greens and served with French dressing.

Chiffonade Salad: This is a green salad with cold, cooked julienne slices of beets added just before tossing with the dressing.

Fruit Salad: Any fruits you wish to use are fine, well drained if they are juicy—and use fresh ones, please, if at all possible.

Guacamole: (*See* under "G".) This is sometimes served as a salad in Mexico and California.

Potato Salad: It is a good idea to marinate cooked potatoes first in French dressing with onion, green peppers, or any other additions you choose to make (perhaps none!) in the refrigerator for an hour or so at least. Then, at the last, mix with mayonnaise to taste.

Do not cook potatoes too long for salad. They should be just barely done—and will thus hold their shape much better.

Potatoes may be sliced or diced for salad, but remember that diced potatoes are not as likely to break up as sliced ones when mixed with dressing.

Russian Salad: Sometimes listed as Salade Russe, this is a mixture of cooked, chilled, and cubed vegetables, mixed with cubed ham or tongue, a few shreds of truffle, and mayonnaise.

Salade Maçédoine: A mixture of cooked vegetables, chilled and mixed with mayonnaise.

Salad Mimosa: This is a tossed green salad, flavored with garlic, if desired, with chopped hard-cooked egg sprinkled over it. The latter is what makes it "Mimosa."

Salade Niçoise: This is composed of one or more greens, quartered tomatoes, chopped green and/or sweet red pepper, thinly sliced onions and radishes, finely chopped white and red cabbage, white-meat tuna, anchovies, black olives, fresh basil, and sliced hard-cooked egg, tossed with a French dressing made with wine vinegar.

Salade Parisienne: A mixture of chilled, cooked vegetables, cut up small, with slivers of truffle, lobster, or crabmeat, plus mayonnaise, added. It is sometimes arranged in a mold lined with clear aspic and mixed with mayonnaise chaud-froid, then unmolded as a beautiful buffet dish.

Storage of Salad Greens: First, thoroughly wash and drain them. The French wire salad baskets offer the best method of draining greens well. When well drained, greens should be placed in plastic bags or wrapped in a tea towel and stored in the refrigerator's crisper.

Waldorf Salad: This is made of apples, walnuts, celery, and mayonnaise, served on a bed of lettuce.

Wilted Cucumbers: Cucumbers are pared and sliced paper-thin, then sprinkled with salt and mixed well, with the hands, in a bowl. Next, a plate is pressed down firmly on the cucumbers and they are left to stand for an hour, then drained, and dressed with vinegar, sugar, dill, and seasonings.

Wilted Green Salad: Lettuce or, preferably, dandelion greens are shredded. Diced bacon is fried until crisp, then sugar, seasonings, and vinegar are added. When the sugar is dissolved, this hot mixture is poured over the greens and they are tossed.

Salad Dressings: (*See* under "D".)

Sandwiches: It is practically impossible to be an American and never eat sandwiches. We have them on picnics, at school for lunch, at the office for lunch—and, for that matter, at home for lunch.

If you are in a situation where lunches are being taken to school and/or to work, the most expeditious way to prepare them is to make enough to fill all requirements for a week and freeze them. The one, or ones, you take out each morning will remain beautifully fresh and be just properly defrosted when you and/or your young ones are ready to eat lunch. Remember with sandwiches for freezing that there are foods that don't freeze well—cooked egg whites, tomatoes, cucumbers, lettuce, and mayonnaise are top examples. However, if you wish to include any of those ingredients in your luncheons, simply pack them in little separate containers and add them after the sandwiches are defrosted.

Wrapping sandwiches properly is very important, especially if they're to be frozen. They must be tightly sealed to preserve flavor and prevent "freezer burn." Sandwich bags are the easiest solution to this problem. Otherwise, use plastic, foil, or waxed paper, neatly and tightly folded.

No matter what kind of sandwich you take with you, try always to have some vegetable sticks ready in water in your refrigerator. They're also good for nutritious, nonfattening between-meals nibbling.

Be sure to vary the kinds of bread you use for sandwiches. It's a big help in preventing boredom. Grated carrot; corned beef, cream cheese, and spinach; baked bean (or brown bread); dried beef and cheddar cheese; date-nut-ginger (the preserved variety, chopped, with a little juice); sardine (take mayonnaise separately); liverwurst;

salami; sliced chicken and egg; ham and green bean sandwiches are just a few suggestions to put your own mind to work on what you and your family like. The variety can be endless and should be carefully planned.

Sauces

Béchamel Sauce: To some people, this is the same as a Cream Sauce. The French, who invented it, sometimes make it using chicken stock instead of milk, cooking it at a simmer for ten minutes with onion in it, then adding a few tablespoons of cream. Finally, they strain it before using. Other French recipes recommend making béchamel with veal stock and milk.

Bread Sauce: This is a sauce often served with game, particularly pheasant and grouse. It is made by cooking milk and fine, dry bread crumbs with an onion stuck with cloves, in the top of a double boiler. Coarse bread crumbs are fried in butter and stirred into the original mixture with seasonings to taste.

Brown Sauce: (*See* under Sauce Espagnole below.)

Cream Sauce: To make this, melt butter, stir in flour smoothly, add milk and/or cream, and stir until thickened, then season to taste. Proportions for cream sauce are as follows:

Thin	1 tablespoon butter	1 tablespoon flour	1 cup liquid
Medium	2 tablespoons butter	2 tablespoons flour	1 cup liquid
Thick	3 tablespoons butter	3 tablespoons flour	1 cup liquid

Hollandaise Sauce: (*See* under "H".)

Sauce Espagnole: This is a very important basic sauce which originated in France and is also sometimes called Brown Sauce. There are many recipes for making it, but it is basically a matter of browning chopped carrot and onion in fat (sometimes with bits of ham, which makes it very tasty), stirring in flour, then adding good strong beef stock and cooking the whole until it reduces and thickens. Tomato paste or fresh tomato is added at the end. It is cooked anywhere from three-quarters of an hour to one and a half hours. At the end, it is strained; it can be frozen or kept in the refrigerator. It is used as the base of many sauces and gives them wonderful, strong flavors.

Sauces That Go Well with Chicken

1. *Cream Sauce:* (*See* under Sauces.)

2. *Curry:* (*See* under Sauces That Go Well with Meat, in this section.)

3. *Ivoire:* Chicken is cooked in champagne, with rich chicken stock and sour cream added halfway through the cooking. When done, the chicken is removed and the sauce, with mushrooms added, is reduced until it bubbles fiercely and takes on an ivory hue. The chicken is then returned to the sauce and served at once.

4. *Mornay:* (*See* under Fish Sauces.)

5. *Paprika:* This can be a Suprême (*see* below) with good Hungarian paprika added. It can also be a cream sauce made with half sweet cream and half milk, or with sour cream. Chicken Paprika is a Hungarian dish.

6. *Périgourdine:* Reduce Espagnole until it is half the original quantity, then add Madeira wine and truffles. Very like Sauce Périgueux. (*See* under Meat Sauces.)

7. *Poulette:* (*See* under Fish Sauces.)

8. *Sauce Suprême:* Made like a cream sauce, but with chicken broth substituted for milk.

9. *Velouté:* (*See* under Vegetable Sauces.)

Sauces That Go Well with Duck

1. *Black Cherry:* The juice of black cherries is seasoned to taste, a little Sauce Espagnole is added, the whole is thickened with cornstarch, and the pitted cherries are heated in it.

2. *Olive:* Espagnole with white wine and whole pitted green olives in it.

3. *Orange:* Espagnole with wine, orange juice, seasonings, and slivered orange rind. When the duck has been roasted, add the pure juice from the pan, with the fat removed.

4. *Red Currant:* Stock thickened with a roux, with red currant jelly melted in it. May be flavored with dry sherry, if desired.

Sauces That Go Well with Eggs

1. *Aurore:* Tomato paste or tomato sauce is added to cream sauce or Mornay.

2. *Colbert:* (*See* under Sauces That Go Well with Fish, in this section.)

3. *Cream:* (*See* under Sauces, in this section.)

4. *Creole:* Based on tomatoes, with green pepper, onion, celery, garlic, and other seasonings. Also good for fish and seafood.

5. *Curry:* (*See* under Sauces That Go Well with Meat, in this section.)

6. *Hollandaise:* (*See* under "H".)

7. *Lamaze:* (*See* under Sauces That Go Well with Fish, in this section.) This is excellent on cold hard-cooked eggs.

8. *Mornay:* (*See* under Sauces That Go Well with Fish, in this section.)

9. *Mushroom:* (*See* under Sauces That Go Well with Vegetables, in this section.)

10. *Nantua:* (*See* under Sauces That Go Well with Fish, in this section.)

Sauces That Go Well with Fish

1. *Aioli:* (*See* under "A".)

2. *Béarnaise:* This is made just as Hollandaise is made, except that in place of lemon juice, vinegar and wine, boiled down with shallots and tarragon, is strained and beaten into the egg yolks before the butter. Minced fresh tarragon is then added.

3. *Colbert:* Bearnaise sauce (see above) with a little dissolved meat glaze stirred into it. Use for steak, chicken, and eggs, as well as for fish.

4. *Egg:* Cream sauce with chopped or sliced hard-cooked eggs added. A dash of Worcestershire is a good seasoning, also some minced parsley. This usually is served with poached or steamed fish.

5. *Horseradish Cream:* Cold, salted whipped cream, mixed with freshly grated horseradish to taste. Very good with cold salmon.

6. *Lamaze:* Mayonnaise mixed with an equal quantity of chili sauce and India Relish, plus mustard, Worcestershire, horseradish, chopped hard-cooked egg, chopped pimiento and chives, Tabasco, and other seasonings. Good with shellfish or cold fish of any kind— also on cold hard-cooked eggs.

7. *Matelote:* Red wine sauce in which fish has been poached is cooked down to thicken it a bit and reduce it, then finished off with seasonings and butter.

8. *Meunière:* Brown butter (not black) mixed with lemon juice and chopped parsley.

9. *Mornay:* White sauce with grated cheese (usually Gruyère

and/or Parmesan) blended well into it. It is usually poured over fish or eggs before the dish is run under the broiler to brown the top.

10. *Nantua:* Heavy cream, shrimp butter, and chopped shrimp are added to béchamel. Crayfish or lobster butter may be substituted for shrimp. This sauce is often served with Quenelles de Brochet.

11. *Newburg:* Make a thin roux of butter and flour, add cream and seasonings, including cayenne, and beat in egg yolks. Flavor with dry sherry. *Do not boil.*

12. *Poulette:* Minced shallots and mushrooms, sautéed in butter and added to a basic rich cream sauce with egg yolks beaten into it. Lemon juice and minced parsley are added at the end. This sauce is also used with poultry.

13. *Rémoulade:* Mayonnaise with anchovies, pickles, capers, herbs, and sometimes chopped hard-cooked egg added.

14. *Soubise:* To a cup of chopped onion, sautéed in butter until soft but not brown, add two cups basic cream sauce and cook gently for fifteen minutes. Puree in blender or processor, then add cream to taste. Add salt and pepper to taste. The basic cream sauce may be made from fish stock, if desired. This sauce is also used with lamb, veal, vegetables, and poultry.

15. *Tartare:* Mayonnaise made with hard-cooked, instead of raw, egg yolks and with minced pickles, capers, olives, and parsley added. It is generally served with fried fish and shellfish.

16. *White Wine:* White wine fish stock (court bouillon) is boiled down until it is a fumet (about three tablespoons left from a cup of stock). It is then substituted for the lemon juice in Hollandaise Sauce.

Sauces That Go Well with Meat

1. *Barbecue:* There are probably hundreds of versions of this sauce, but it is usually based on tomatoes and contains any or all of the following: wine (usually red), onions, garlic, herbs, mustard, brown sugar, and other seasonings. Used to marinate, baste, and serve with meats grilled outdoors or broiled indoors, mostly with beef.

2. *Béarnaise:* Particularly good with beefsteak.

3. *Bordelaise:* A red wine sauce with beef marrow in it.

4. *Caper:* Add capers to cream sauce and serve with boiled mutton.

5. *Chasseur:* Espagnole Sauce with tomatoes, garlic, and herbs. Very good with veal.

6. *Cumberland:* Port wine and melted currant jelly, with orange peel, shallots, orange juice, and other seasonings added. Served hot or cold, but usually cold with cold meat, especially game.

7. *Curry:* A proper Indian curry sauce is made by first grinding spices, either in the blender or with mortar and pestle, frying them for about five minutes, usually with onion and garlic, then adding flour or cornstarch, stirring until blended, and last stirring in stock and/or yogurt (in place of Indian "curd"). Spices used vary greatly, but always include hot (chili) peppers and turmeric (which makes the curry yellow). Other possibilities for the mixture are cumin, coriander, cardamom, mustard, cinnamon, allspice, black pepper, and minced fresh ginger.

8. *Horseradish:* Horseradish sauce can be made with sour cream, with whipped cream, or with applesauce, with grated fresh horseradish added. It is served usually with either hot boiled beef or cold beef of any description.

9. *Madeira:* Espagnole Sauce with Madeira wine. Very good with ham.

10. *Mint:* Made of vinegar, a little sugar, and chopped mint leaves. Served hot with lamb or mutton.

11. *Mustard:* The easiest way to make this is to add prepared mustard to cream sauce according to your taste. It is usually served with ham or tongue.

12. *Périgueux:* Espagnole Sauce with Madeira wine and truffles. With fillet of beef, ham, veal, and egg dishes.

13. *Raisin:* A thickened sauce made with stock, vinegar, brown sugar, and seasonings to taste, with raisins in it. Served hot with ham or tongue.

14. *Robert:* Espagnole Sauce with mustard in it.

15. *Smitane:* Sour cream sauce, seasoned with onion, a little white wine, and lemon juice, if desired. Very good on veal. Also used a good deal with poultry.

16. *Soubise:* (*See* under Sauces That Go Well with Fish.) Often used with veal, also lamb.

17. *Sweet and Sour:* A Chinese sauce which involves stock, vinegar, and sugar, and which is made in many ways, sometimes requiring pineapple, green pepper, carrot, ginger, and other seasonings. It

is thickened with cornstarch. We in the West think of it as being served with pork, but it is also used with fish and with other meats and sometimes with vegetables.

18. *Tomato:* Made at home with either fresh or canned tomatoes and good seasonings, this is a very different sauce from that you buy in a can. Try making it, and if you still like the canned variety or using canned soup as a sauce, go ahead! Especially good on hamburgers, but used with many meats, pastas, fish, and other dishes.

Sauces That Go Well with Pasta

1. *Bacon:* Diced bacon is cooked in lard until crisp, a good lot of freshly ground pepper is added, and the sauce is then poured over spaghetti.

2. *Bagna Cauda:* This means a "hot bath sauce." It is made of butter, olive oil, garlic, anchovy fillets, and truffles.

3. *Clam:* This can be red or white. For the red, heat olive oil with garlic, put in clams in their shells, tomatoes, and water. Cook until the clam shells open, then take the clams out and return them to the sauce, discarding the shells. Add parsley, salt, and pepper, then pour the sauce over the pasta. For the white, clams in their shells are steamed in a little white wine until they open. They are then removed from the shells and chopped. The broth is strained and boiled until it is reduced by half. Garlic and parsley are simmered in olive oil, then seasoned with salt and freshly ground pepper. The reduced broth and clams are added and heated through and the whole is mixed with spaghetti or noodles, as you prefer.

4. *Green Sauce:* Anchovy fillets, chopped parsley, watercress, capers, pickles, onion, and garlic, beaten with olive oil and either vinegar or lemon juice. The sauce should be creamy.

5. *Marinara:* A sauce of tomato, seasoned with onion, garlic, and oregano, and hot pepper, if you like.

6. *Meat:* A mixture of chopped beef, tomatoes, tomato paste, red wine, onion, garlic, and other seasonings, cooked down to a good thick consistency. Used mostly over spaghetti or noodles.

7. *Pesto:* This is a green sauce from Genoa, made by mixing two cups of blanched basil leaves with a cup of grated Parmesan cheese, a mashed clove of garlic, and a quarter of a cup of pine nuts, then gradually adding olive oil, beating constantly with a fork, until the desired degree of thickness is reached. A dash of milk is added and the sauce is served over spaghetti or noodles.

8. *Ragu Bolognese:* (*See* under "R".)

9. *Tomato:* (*See* under Sauces That Go Well with Meat, in this section.)

10. *Tomato and Mushroom:* Sliced or button mushrooms in a tomato sauce, flavored with garlic and onion.

Sauces That Go Well with Vegetables

1. *Aioli:* (*See* under "A".)

2. *Cream:* (*See* Cream Sauce under Sauces in this section.)

3. *Hollandaise:* (*See* under "H".)

4. *Lemon Butter:* Four tablespoons lemon juice are reduced by boiling them down to one, then beaten with a stick of butter, which melts in the process, over low heat until thick and creamy. Just before serving, add a couple of teaspoons of vegetable water. Also served with fish, in which case add fish stock.

5. *Mousseline:* Equal quantities of Hollandaise and whipped cream, heated but not boiled. Served also with fish.

6. *Mushroom Sauce:* Chop or slice mushrooms, sauté them in butter, then add flour and blend it in well. Next, add cream and/or milk and stir until thickened. Season to taste. Especially good with spinach or green beans.

7. *Ravigote:* French dressing mixed with herbs, capers, and onions. This is also served on cold fish.

8. *Velouté:* Made like cream sauce, but substituting chicken stock for milk and adding a little mushroom liquor and a little cream. Also used on fish.

Popular Dessert Sauces

1. *Butterscotch:* Brown sugar, mixed with a little flour, is cooked with boiling water and constantly stirred until thick. Then butter and cream are added. The sauce is usually served hot.

2. *Chocolate:* Probably the most popular dessert sauce of all. Best made by melting semisweet chocolate with a little unsweetened chocolate in a little coffee, then adding cream and stirring until smooth.

3. *Custard:* This is simply a boiled custard; it is poured over cakes, puddings, and the like.

4. *Foamy:* Butter, sugar, egg yolks, and flavoring (cognac or vanilla or wine) are beaten over hot water until heated through. Very good with plum pudding, flavored with cognac.

5. *Fruit:* Made either from pureed fresh fruit mixed with sugar

syrup, or from jams or jellies, melted in water. May be flavored with liqueurs.

6. *Hard:* Mix softened butter with granulated sugar, using the back of a spoon, until you achieve the consistency you like. Flavor with vanilla, rum, brandy, or other liqueurs and whatever else might fit the dessert with which the sauce will be served. (Can also be made with brown sugar.)

7. *Lemon Mousseline:* Sugar, water, and cornstarch are cooked together until thick, then grated lemon rind and lemon juice are added. Cool the mixture and fold in whipped cream.

8. *Zabaglione:* (*See* under "Z".)

Sauerkraut: Sauerkraut is shredded cabbage soaked in brine, made of its own juice with salt. I find the canned variety very good and the other a bother to make, but I am sure that a purist would frown on this attitude. All that's necessary is to heat it up with a bit of onion, butter, caraway seeds—whatever you like. Sauerkraut bought in the butcher store or a German market, of the homemade variety, should be cooked for thirty minutes. It is delicious cooked in champagne, but if that seems wild extravagance to you, use white wine. Sauerkraut is particularly good with game.

Sausage: Fairly highly seasoned minced meat (usually pork) is sold by the pound or stuffed into casings to make individual sausages. Sausage should always be well cooked because it is made of pork. Sausage meat may be frozen, but should not be kept long in the freezer, as it is among the most perishable of minced meats.

There are many other kinds of sausage, mostly of European origin, which can be bought here and are generally made here, such as: salami (Italian), Italian sweet and hot sausages, knockwurst (German), kielbasa (Polish), and many, many others, all worth trying.

Scrapple: (*See* under Pork.)

Seeds: Here is a brief list of the seeds most commonly used as flavorings in cooking.

Anise: Cookies, pastry, sauerkraut, cole slaw. Licorice flavor, so use with discretion.

Caraway: Sauerkraut, rye bread, cookies, soups, pork, and beef.

Cardamom: Scandinavian cakes and cookies, curries, pea soup. (Also comes ground.)

Celery: Pot roast, chowders, soups, stews, salads, sauces.

Coriander: Curry, cookies (especially ginger ones). (Also comes ground.)

Cumin: Curry, cheese, poultry, game, stews, chili dishes. (Also comes ground.)

Fennel: Bread (sprinkled on top), Bel Paese cheese, beef, pork, seafood (in the cooking water), sauerkraut.

Juniper Berries: Game, beef stew. Strong, so use with discretion.

Mustard: Curry, pickling, and preserving.

Poppy: Breads (sprinkle on top), cookies, canapés, cake fillings, sauces, noodles.

Sesame: Breads (sprinkle on top), casseroles (mixed with, or instead of, bread crumbs on top), topping for soups or vegetables.

Shepherd's Pie: This seems to be one of the British dishes we have turned into something even less exciting than it was in the land of its birth—and even that is not very interesting. We make it with mixed cooked vegetables, diced cooked meat, seasonings, and gravy. This is put into a casserole, covered with mashed potato, and baked in a hot

Shepherd's Pie

oven until the potato is brown. Properly British, it is made with ground beef, plenty of herbs and seasonings, and the mashed-potato top. It is a nourishing, if not outstanding, dinner in a dish.

Shortcake: (*See* under Desserts.)

Soufflés: There are two types of soufflés. First, there is the type that is made by folding beaten egg whites into a thick yolk mixture, to which may be added cheese, meat, vegetables, chocolate, liqueurs—

what you will. This takes thirty-five to forty minutes to bake in a 375-degree oven and is fairly solid all through. Second, there is the French dessert soufflé type, which is made by combining egg yolks with sugar and flavoring (usually a liqueur), then folding in the beaten egg whites and baking in a 500-degree oven twelve to fifteen minutes. This type is definitely wet in the center and feather light.

Ways To Be Sure That a Soufflé Will Rise Properly

1. Have the eggs at room temperature.
2. Add an extra egg white to all soufflés.
3. Beat egg whites until stiff but not dry.
4. Cool the yolk mixture at least slightly before folding in the whites.
5. Be sure to preheat the oven so that it has attained the right temperature before you are ready to put the soufflé in.
6. *Fold* the egg whites in gently. Never beat them into the yolk mixture. They should be pretty well incorporated, but it is not necessary, in fact not good, to mix them *thoroughly* with the yolk mixture.

Soufflé Collar: This is a strip of brown paper or waxed paper placed around the top of a soufflé dish, and rising about two inches above it. The paper is buttered. The soufflé mixture is then poured into the dish, coming just about to the top, and placed in the oven. Be sure the dish is small enough so the mixture will come to the top. When the soufflé rises, the collar keeps the top in shape. It is removed before serving the dish, and the results are spectacular. If you do not wish to bother about the collar, however, simply use a bigger dish, in which your mixture comes no higher than a quarter of an inch below the rim.

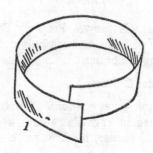

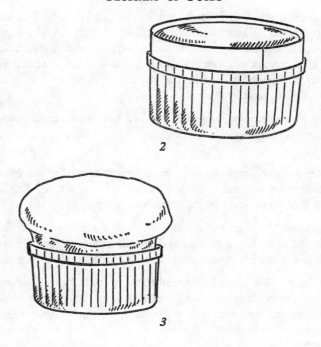

2

3

Opening the oven door when a soufflé is baking does *not* make the soufflé fall. That is an old superstition, and if you want to peek at a soufflé while it is cooking, go ahead. Do not leave the door open long and do not *slam* it shut.

Soups: First, let's discuss canned and dehydrated soups. Over 90 percent of the soup consumed in our homes is one or the other. My only caution would be to be sure to add seasonings, toppings, or whatever you feel would improve the taste. Remember that most foods prepared with the public taste in mind are under-seasoned rather than over-seasoned, except for the fact that most of them are too salty. Try combining two canned or dehydrated soups for new and interesting flavors. Dilute the cream soups with either milk or half-and-half, rather than water.

Billi Bi: A cream of mussel soup, which is served hot or cold, and despite its ridiculous name is delectable.

Bird's Nest Soup: This is really made from birds' nests. The nests are made by swifts on islands in the South Seas, and the edible part is a gelatinous substance which has to be very carefully cleaned, but is worth all the work and the cost, as it has a delicate, distinctive flavor which is like nothing else in the world. It is cooked in a chicken broth to make the soup.

Bisque: This term was originally applied only to seafood soups, such as lobster and crayfish. It is now given to any creamed soup, including tomato.

Borscht: A beet soup, Russian in origin, served hot or cold, with sour cream either beaten into it or placed on top. In Russia cold borscht is often served accompanied by a hot boiled potato.

Bouillabaisse: A Mediterranean fisherman's soup which contains at least six different kinds of fish, and usually some shellfish in the shell, though the latter is not essential. This is indeed a meal in a dish.

Boula Soup: This soup has nothing to do with Yale University, so far as we know. It is half cream-of-pea soup, half green-turtle consommé, mixed well, heated, put into individual flameproof casseroles, topped with salted whipped cream, and run under the broiler to brown.

Chowder: The old French word for caldron was *chaudière.* Vegetables or fish stewed in a caldron thus became known as chowders in English-speaking nations—a corruption of the name of the pot in which they were cooked.

Clam Chowder, Manhattan: A sort of vegetable soup, containing plenty of tomatoes (or sometimes just their juice) and a few clams.

Clam Chowder, New England: Made from clams, potatoes, onions, salt pork, and milk, it is the only proper clam chowder.

Cock-a-Leekie: (*See* under Leeks.)

Cold Cream Senegalese: A cold, curried cream-of-chicken soup with cooked white meat of chicken, finely chopped, in it.

Consommé Bellevue: Half hot chicken consommé and half hot clam broth, combined and served topped with salted whipped cream.

Consommé Double: A rich beef or chicken consommé which has been boiled down (reduced) to half its original quantity, thus doubling its strength.

Consommé Printanière: Consommé containing a mixture of cooked spring vegetables.

Consommé à la Reine: Chicken consommé thickened with tapioca or with egg yolks and heavy cream, sometimes with rice added, sometimes not.

Consommé Royale: Hot consommé served with diced or fancy-cut custard royale floating in it. Custard royale is a baked custard made with eggs and beef stock. Chilled, it is cut into fancy shapes or diced, and used as a garnish for consommé.

Fruit Soups: These are made from dried or fresh fruit and originated in the Scandinavian countries, where they are served either as the main course of a luncheon or supper, or for dessert with whipped cream. They have never been very popular in this country. I think this is perhaps because when we have tried serving them at all, we have offered them as a first course, as we would any soup.

Petite Marmite: Consommé containing meat and vegetables, and sometimes chicken. This is served in individual casseroles or "marmites" accompanied by toast or rusks, which are sometimes spread with beef marrow. It may also be served with a piece of toasted French bread, sprinkled with grated Parmesan cheese, and run under the broiler to brown.

Philadelphia Pepper Pot: A soup made from tripe and vegetables, highly seasoned with pepper (and sometimes a touch of Tabasco).

Potage St. Germain: Green pea soup. Whenever the title of a dish contains the designation St. Germain, you may be sure that it has peas involved in it somehow.

Pot au feu: A soup containing meat and vegetables, which is simmered long and slow. In French households there is always a pot of it on the back of the range. The soup and its contents are served separately, as two courses. The liquid is also used as stock for various sauces.

Poultry Soup from a Carcass: When you have had a roast bird, put the bones, with a little meat clinging to them, into a big pot, cover them with cold water, bring it to the boil, skim the fat, then simmer the liquid for an hour. Now add onion, celery, carrots, and seasonings and simmer for another hour or more. Strain. Before serving, remove the fat (it can be kept for cooking) from the top. This is good for a first course or for use in other soups and sauces.

Puree Crécy: A puree-of-carrot soup, sometimes with rice or tapioca added. Any dish with the name Crécy in it is either made of, or garnished with, carrots.

Scotch Broth: Made from lamb and vegetables.

Shark's Fin Soup: A clear chicken broth with soft, transparent shark's fin in it. This is one of the most delicious soups ever invented (it is Chinese). Shark's fins may be obtained in any Chinatown and are very expensive.

Snapper Soup: This is an invention from Philadelphia, where snapping turtles abound. It is made with the turtle, many vegetables, a veal knuckle, and fine seasonings, including sherry. In most parts of the United States, it is impossible to make this soup at home, lacking the snapping turtles, but it can be obtained in cans in specialty food shops and is very, very good.

Snert: The Dutch pea soup, which is the best in the world. It is made of split peas cooked for hours with pork knuckle, shin beef, and fresh bacon. Serve with slices of smoked sausage floating on top.

Won Ton Soup: Won ton is the Chinese original of ravioli—little dumplings stuffed with pork and/or shrimp and seasonings. In won ton soup, they are cooked in boiling water and served in hot chicken consommé, which also usually contains a bit of spinach and/or Chinese cabbage.

Soybeans: By this time, most people realize that soybeans are an excellent source of protein, but they instantly think of dried soybeans, since that is the form in which most of us have encountered them. Fresh green soybeans are less well known than they should be. They are an absolutely delicious vegetable, teeming with nutritive values. They are available in some areas in the late summer or fall and well worth buying for a treat in the long winter days ahead. If you have a garden, you will find they are easy to grow. They freeze beautifully. All you need to do is shell them, blanch them, and freeze them as you would any green vegetable. One interesting way to use these is to defrost them and let them come to room temperature, then serve them as a canapé with drinks—delicious! They are also good cooked as you would any green vegetable. They may take ten to twenty minutes to cook at a simmer. Serve with butter and a little salt.

Soybean sprouts can be grown at home from dry soybeans. They are an integral part of a lot of Chinese dishes, but you may use them as an addition—by making them part of a salad, for instance.

Spoon Bread: This is really not bread at all. It is a Southern dish in which cornmeal, eggs, milk, and baking powder are mixed and baked in a casserole. The resulting product is served with a spoon from the dish, usually as a side dish for meat.

Stifado: A Greek stew of beef round, cut into chunks, cooked with onions, garlic, tomatoes, and white wine.

Stocks: When a recipe calls for chicken stock, or fish stock, or beef stock, what do you do? I had thought to give you some hints at the methods of making these highly necessary cooking ingredients, but upon really going over what I once used to do without question, though it took hours, I have decided to give you this recommendation: If you insist upon having the real thing, look up a recipe in a cookbook of the 1930s or thereabouts and you will be able to do it. If, however, you are a working person or a very busy mother or for any reason your time is filled to bursting, use powdered chicken stock base or beef stock base, rather than bouillon cubes, which haven't half as much flavor. Lots of times, one is instructed to cook something in one of these stocks—vegetables, for instance—and they taste a lot better for this treatment, so you will want such dishes to be as good as they can without your slaving over a hot stock pot. The powdered way is the one to go!

Sweetbreads: (*See* Variety Meats.)

Tacos: These are small (four-inch) Mexican tortillas which are stuffed with whatever suits your fancy, rolled, and fastened with toothpicks. They are sometimes fried and served with various sauces, or left unfried so that people can partly unroll them and add extras to suit their taste. In the United States tacos are not rolled, but folded in half.

Tarhonya Noodles: These are a Hungarian pasta, usually translated as "egg barley." They are made of flour, salt, and eggs rolled out and cut into narrow strips, which are then chopped into small pieces "as fine as barley grains." Tarhonya are used in soups, and also dried out in a slightly warm oven, stored in jars, and later cooked in water, drained, then fried in butter to use as an accompaniment to meats. They are delicious.

Tea: There are many brands and types of tea available in our markets, both domestic and imported. The choice of what tea you drink is a wholly personal matter. Tasting is the only way to learn what suits you. For instance, nowadays there are innumerable herb (and other) flavored teas which some people love and others loathe. So be a taster first.

Making Tea: Tea should be made in a china or an earthenware pot. Silver or other metal spoils the flavor. The pot should be heated by putting scalding hot water into it. Bring cold water to the boil. Pour out the hot water in the tea pot and into it pour a teaspoon of tea for every cup you want to make, plus "one for the pot." Pour in a little boiling water, cover the pot, and allow the tea to steep for a minute. Then pour in the number of cups of hot water you need to make the desired quantity of tea. Steep until it has the desired strength.

No purist would use tea bags. However, it is obviously a losing battle to advise against their use, because not enough people care that much. In my opinion, the chief advantage of tea bags is that they can be lifted from cup or pot, whereas getting steeped tea leaves out is often quite a chore.

Iced Tea: Tea which is to be iced should be strong, to allow for the dilution by melting ice. Use 50 percent more tea than you do to make hot tea. It should then be kept at room temperature until used. Refrigerating it will make it turn cloudy. The cloudiness can be corrected by adding a little boiling water to it.

One of the best recipes for iced tea I know is to put seven teabags into four cups of boiling hot water (heat turned off) for about six minutes, making a very strong base. Add to it one can of frozen lemon juice, plus the amount of water required on the label. I then put this into a covered container in my refrigerator. All guests seem to like it as much as I do.

Tea in Punch: Tea gives interest and good flavor to punches, both alcoholic and non-alcoholic. It should be made double strength, as for iced tea.

Tempura: (*See* under Fish and Shellfish.)

Timbale: A timbal is a drum. A timbale is a creamy mixture of meat, fish, or vegetable, cooked in a drum-shaped mold (a custard cup will do). A timbale is also a small pastry shell of delicate texture, filled with a cooked timbale mixture. These are used for canapés or for decorating very fancy platters of meat or game.

Tomalley: This is a term often used to designate the liver of a lobster, which is the green substance found inside the shellfish. It is delicious and should never be removed before serving. The pink substance also sometimes found there is roe, known as the coral. Like the liver, it makes marvelous eating.

Tomatoes: Tomatoes were cultivated by the Peruvian Indians before Columbus reached this hemisphere. They were transported from Peru to Italy in the fifteenth century, and were then known as "love apples" and regarded as poisonous. Gradually, however, they were found to be entirely edible and their popularity was to spread afar. Thomas Jefferson grew some of the first tomatoes to be found in this country. Today, of course, there are tomatoes everywhere, and in a great variety of shapes and sizes. There are red, yellow, and green tomatoes. There are some red ones that grow to be four to five inches in diameter. There are also, sad to say, some that should be that way, but instead are hard and pale-colored—what many of my friends call "plastic tomatoes." That is the only kind most city folk can buy in the winter—and for that same city population, those available in the summer are not much more attractive or tasty. The only really good red tomatoes are grown on farms handy enough for some lucky people to reach them with ease and get the real thing. There are also cherry tomatoes and plum tomatoes—the latter being often the size and shape of the yellow variety.

Green Tomatoes: These are the big red variety before they begin to ripen. Most people—even some who grow them—hasten to take them indoors to ripen before the frost comes, and they miss the best tomato dish of all: fried green tomatoes. I always try to beg some green tomatoes from friends with vegetable gardens, just before frost time. If I succeed, here is how I cook them: Mix salt, brown sugar, pepper, and bread crumbs together well. Slice green tomatoes a half inch thick. Sprinkle slices on both sides with the bread-crumb mixture. Melt butter in a heavy skillet, put in the tomato slices, and brown them over low heat on both sides. The tomatoes must be well cooked as well as browned. They are delicious with meat when cooked in this manner.

The little cherry and plum tomatoes are at their best, in my opinion, served as canapés, with seasoned salt to dip them into. They can be hollowed out and stuffed in various ways, but this seems to me a rather fussy and time-consuming way to gild the lily.

There are, of course, hundreds of ways to cook tomatoes. I have only one real plea to make and that is that you bake fresh tomatoes, rather than broil them. The latter is too easy a way to burn them without getting them sufficiently cooked. If you cut them in half, sprinkle them with basil, seasoned salt, sugar, and chopped onion, then cover them with prepared poultry seasoning, dot them with butter, and bake them in a 375-degree oven for about half an hour, you will have something special to eat.

Peeling Tomatoes: If you have a gas range, impale a tomato firmly on a long-handled fork, then hold it over the flame, turning it constantly until the skin pops open in at least one place. Remove the tomato from the heat and, with a paring knife, slide the skin off with ease. If your range is electric, pop tomatoes, one at a time, into boiling water (heat turned off) and leave them there until the point of your knife tells you that the skin will come off easily.

Tongue: (*See* Variety Meats.)

Tortillas: These were the bread of ancient Mexico before the Spanish brought in wheat. All that's needed to make them is *masa harina*—the corn flour which is to be found in Mexican and Puerto Rican stores—salt, and water. A great time-saver is to have a tortilla press; otherwise you must pat a ball of the dough in your hands until you have formed a thin, round cake.

Tournedos: (*See* under Beef Cuts.) The tenderest beef of all, which should be served rare and beautifully browned, and is enhanced, often, by a Bearnaise sauce.

Trifle, English: I used to think, like most Americans, that English trifle consisted of sponge cake well soaked with sherry, served with boiled custard poured over it. Americans call the same thing Tipsy Pudding. However, one lives and learns, and finally an English friend gave me her recipe for trifle, made as follows: Stale sponge cake, sliced thin, is cut into two-inch squares. Every two squares are put together with raspberry jam, then cut across into triangles. These are piled into a glass bowl, filling it half full. Add enough sherry to soak the sponge cake (but not drown it). The whole is covered with a good, rich custard and placed in the refrigerator to set (about two hours). Before it is served, it is covered with whipped cream and decorated with slivered toasted almonds and silver sprinkles. *Quite* different—what?

Tripe: (*See* Variety Meats.)

U

Udung Sambal: This is a prawn curry, as served in Singapore. It contains shrimp, chili peppers, garlic, onion, dried shrimp, peanut oil, and tamarind water. It is hotly spiced and for this reason, I presume, is called a sambal—a word, familiar in Indonesian cookery, which means hot relishes. Sambals consist of ground hot red peppers, mixed with different spices, fish, shrimp, or nuts. I don't think there is ever a meal in Indonesia which hasn't at least one sambal included in it.

Upside-Down Cake: The most usual upside-down cake is made with fruit—fresh or canned. First, in a heavy skillet, you melt butter and add brown sugar, stirring until the sugar melts. Then put in the fruit, arranging it carefully, since in the end this will be the top of the cake. Now add the cake batter and put the skillet into a 350-degree oven for about fifty minutes. If you want to have a richer cake, double the amount of sugar called for in the first part of the recipe and when you turn out the cake, let the pan rest over it for about one minute so that all the caramel syrup will run onto the cake. May be served with whipped cream, if desired.

V

Variety Meats: The variety meats are brains, heart, kidneys, liver, oxtail, tongue, tripe, and sweetbreads—in other words, "innards." They are known in Britain by the (to us) unappetizing title of offal.

Brains: Those most commonly served are calf brains. They are very delicate and delicious. They are soaked and sometimes blanched before cooking. Then they may be sautéed, broiled, braised, or cooked in a liquid and served in a sauce. The most usual, and delicious, way to cook them is to sauté them to a delicate brown, then dress them with a sauce of butter which has been cooked to a darkish brown (Brains au Beurre Noire); lemon juice and capers are added before the sauce is poured over the brains.

Heart: Hearts, whether beef, veal, pork, or lamb, are best cooked by braising or simmering long and slow in liquid. They are also very good stuffed, baked long and slow in the oven.

Kidneys: One veal kidney, but two or three lamb kidneys, depending upon size, will serve one person well. One beef kidney will make sufficient stew for four.

Kidneys, Beef: Beef kidney is inclined to be tough; it should be cooked long and slow in salted water to cover, then cut up to make a stew or a beef-and-kidney pie.

Kidneys, Lamb: Are cooked just as you do veal kidneys (see below).

Kidneys, Pork: If you can get them almost immediately after the pig is slaughtered, they are delicious, but after only a day or two their flavor becomes too strong for most tastes.

Kidneys, Veal: They are best split (not all the way through), broiled, and served with either a butter or a deviled sauce (plenty of mustard). They can also be sliced and sautéed, then served in a brown sauce or a wine sauce.

Splitting a Veal Kidney

Liver: The people who can't bear to eat "innards" miss a lot, and there are quite a lot of them. At least we don't emulate the British in calling them "offal," which should take away anyone's appetite, but the fact that we choose the rather finicky term "variety meats" for them is a little too bad, in my opinion.

In any event, the various livers available to us are so good to eat and good for us that we're lucky to have them. They also adapt themselves to many treatments and recipes, thus offering good variety as well as delectable tastes.

Preparation for Sautéing or Broiling Liver: If your butcher has not removed the filament from the liver, peel it off, or the meat will curl up as it cooks. Otherwise, just add salt and pepper to it and dredge it lightly with flour. Sauté thinly sliced liver quickly in butter that is hot but not burning. For broiling, have the liver cut thick—about one and a half inches. Broil it four to five inches from heat. Cooked either way, the juices should run pale pink when the liver is pricked with a fork.

Cooking Liver: Calf liver is the most expensive and delicate of all livers and is best sautéed with great care not to overcook it. It should be pink inside when served. If it is overcooked, it will be tough. Steer liver can be treated in exactly the same way and produces an excellent dish.

Liver, Calves': If your butcher has not removed the filament from the liver, peel it off, or the meat will curl up as it cooks. Be very careful not to overcook liver. Just salt and pepper it and sprinkle it lightly with flour. Then sauté thinly sliced liver quickly in butter that is hot, but not burning. (Adding a little vegetable oil will aid the process.)

Liver, Chicken: Chicken livers are delicious sautéed in butter until just done, then sauced with wine and/or cream. They are also very good broiled on skewers, either alternating with mushrooms and other vegetables or not. Whatever way you cook these delicate livers, be careful not to overcook them, which dries them out. Chicken livers also make delectable pâtés, and there are many good recipes available, especially in French cookbooks. One more marvelous dish is sautéed chicken livers with avocado slices (salt, pepper, and flour the avocado slices and cook them right along with the chicken livers, if you have a big skillet).

Liver, Pork: This is delicious if you get it almost immediately after the pig is slaughtered, as is the case with pork kidneys.

Liver, Steer: Can be treated in exactly the same way as calves' liver (above). It produces an excellent dish if not overcooked, which will make it tough. It can also be boiled, ground, and put into a cream sauce flavored with sherry. Serve on toast—delicious! It is far less expensive than calves' liver.

Oxtail: This is best braised with herbs and other seasonings, vegetables, and sometimes wine to make a stew. With more liquid, it makes a fine soup.

Sweetbreads and Brains: They are very much alike, but brains are more delicate. They are handled in much the same way. They are soaked and sometimes blanched before cooking. Both brains or sweetbreads can be sautéed, broiled, braised, or cooked in liquid and served with a sauce.

Tongue: You might say a civil one is best, but for the purposes of this book, let us say that either beef, veal, lamb, or pork tongue makes good eating. However, beef is the most commonly used. It may be smoked or fresh, though the latter is harder to find in most markets. Cook tongue in water to cover, with an onion stuck with cloves and any other seasoning that suits your fancy, long and slow in a covered pot. When it is done, let it cool in the liquid in which it was cooked. There are many delectable sauces with which tongue can be served. It is excellent hot or cold. Slivers of tongue add greatly to a chef's salad.

Tripe: Part of the stomach of an ox. Plain tripe is taken from the walls of the rumen, or first stomach, and honeycomb tripe is taken from the second stomach, the walls of which have a net-like lining.

There are many wonderful tripe dishes, their delectability depending largely upon the sauce in which they are served. Tripe must be cooked long and slow in liquid, usually three to four hours. Sometimes it is cooked in the sauce in which it will be served; sometimes the sauce is added after the tripe is done. Tripe à la Mode de Caen is one of the most famous French dishes. In it, the tripe is served in a sauce containing vegetables, wine, and sometimes brandy, varying with the chef who concocts it. One of the best tripe dishes I ever ate was in Buenos Aires. It was cooked in champagne, with cognac added, and was superb. The Irish like tripe in cream sauce. In truth, it takes kindly to almost any sauce at all.

Veal: USDA grades for veal are Prime, Choice, Good, Standard, Utility, and Cull. The nearer the color of the meat is to white, the better it will be. The redder it is, the less fine and the tougher it will be. In buying veal, one should allow one-third to one-half a pound of boneless veal per person, and three-quarters of a pound of veal with bone in per person.

The veal one can buy in Europe is superior to ours. It is more delicate and whiter in color because it is milk-fed; milk-fed veal is very hard to come by here. Also, Europeans slaughter their calves at a younger age than we do, which means our veal has less flavor and is less tender than theirs.

Veal should be cooked long and slow, as in braising or stewing, because it lacks fat and has a good deal of connective tissue. It is especially good with fine sauces to enhance flavor. The only exception is in the case of veal scallops, which are so thin that they can take rapid cooking over high heat.

Cuts of veal that can be roasted are the rib, leg (shank half), loin, sirloin, shoulder, rump (standing or boneless), and breast. The rib is always roasted, but the other cuts are equally good, and in some instances better, if they are braised.

Blanquette de Veau: This is a marvelous French veal stew, fit to serve to the grandest company. It is best made with breast of veal, in which case you should allow a pound per person, as it is very bony. If you prefer to use boneless veal, allow one-third to one-half a pound per person. In this case, add a veal bone to the stew while it is cooking. The veal is cooked long and slow in a good white stock of chicken broth and is served with tiny onions and mushrooms in a sauce made from the liquid in which the veal was cooked, with plenty of lemon juice added, and thickened with egg yolks and heavy cream.

Veal Chops: Veal chops can be broiled or pan-fried, but they are best braised. This keeps them moist and provides them with a sauce or gravy, to which veal takes so kindly.

"City Chicken": This consists of cubes of boneless veal on a skewer. They are braised or pan-fried.

Mock Chicken Legs: Ground veal is molded into the shape of chicken legs, around a wooden skewer, which sticks out at the end to represent a leg bone. They are braised or pan-fried.

Osso Buco: A hearty Italian dish made from veal shanks with plenty of meat on them, braised, and cooked in wine with seasonings, which always include lemon rind.

Veal Scallops: These are very thin slices of cutlet, without bone, which are pounded almost paper-thin. They can then be cut into pieces of any size desired for the dish you want to make. Although they are sometimes referred to as scallops, most of our butchers understand what you want better if you ask for "veal cut for scallopine." In France, veal cut this way is referred to as "escalopes." A good butcher shop gives you veal scallops separated each from the other by sheets of thin paper.

Veal scallops will not brown well unless they are thoroughly dried with absorbent paper. Also, any transparent filaments, skin, or fat, must be removed, or the meat will curl and thus not brown evenly. Sometimes you can get a better brown on veal scallops if you flour them lightly before browning. They should be browned in butter (and/or olive oil) over moderately high heat for four to five minutes on each side. They are now not only browned but cooked, but may be reheated at a simmer in sauce, if they are to be served in one. However, they are excellent served at once, decorated with parsley and perhaps a few capers and with a lemon wedge to squeeze over them.

Schnitzel à la Holstein: A sautéed veal cutlet (not breaded) with a fried egg on top.

Vitello Tonnato: A famous cold Italian dish of veal with a sauce of tuna, seasoned with anchovies.

Wiener Schnitzel: Veal cutlet, breaded, and sautéed in butter.

Vegetables

	Servings per Pound		Servings per Pound
Beans, green or wax	4	Peas	2 or 3
Broccoli	3	Squash, winter	2 or 3
Carrots	3 or 4	Tomatoes	3 or 4
Greens, cooked	2 or 3	Other vegetables	3 or 4
Greens, salad, raw	8		

Cooking Vegetables in Stock: Most vegetables that are not going to be peeled later are improved by being cooked in chicken stock, because they take on delicate flavor from it. Sometimes sturdily flavored vegetables (like carrots) are cooked in beef stock.

Brussels Sprouts: These can be served with melted butter, but a lot of contrast and character is added by serving them mixed either with cooked chestnuts, broken up, or with warmed seedless white grapes.

Canned Mushrooms: If cost is the main thought, remember that if the price of a four-ounce can is one-third that of a pound of fresh mushrooms, they are equally good buys, based on the premise that a pound of fresh mushrooms gives six servings and a four-ounce can gives two servings. If flavor is more important than price, there is never a choice, as canning completely takes away the fresh mushroom taste.

French-Style Peas: These are peas braised with lettuce, onion, butter, and seasonings.

Jerusalem Artichoke: This is a tuber that grows underground and produces a type of plant related to the sunflower. It is usually boiled and served in place of potatoes.

Puree of Peas: The easiest way to make this is to do it in the food processor or the blender, using as much of the water in which the peas were cooked as you need to get the consistency you like. Using a food mill is harder, but is also a good way to make a puree. This not only goes for peas, but for any cooked vegetable.

Salsify: It is the root of a member of the chicory family and is also known as oyster plant, because some people think it has something of the flavor of oysters. Boil and mash it and mix it with egg and a little flour, salt, and melted butter to make a thick batter which can be formed into patties. Roll these in bread crumbs and fry them in butter until golden brown, or boil them and serve them with melted butter and seasonings, or a well-flavored cream sauce. Another way to use salsify is to boil it whole, cut it into halves lengthwise, dredge it with flour, and fry it in butter or bacon fat until it is golden brown.

Shallots: Small members of the onion family with reddish-brown skins, which have a sharper flavor than scallions, with a faint garlic flavor, in some people's opinion.

Snow Peas: Small pods in which the peas do not mature. They are primarily a Chinese vegetable, but are raised all over the world. They are cooked very briefly in hot oil (about one minute with constant stirring) and are crisp, sweet, and delicious to eat. They may now be purchased frozen, but these are not nearly as good as the fresh ones.

Spinach: When cooking spinach, do not add water. Simply use the water that clings to the leaves after washing. There is a lot of water in spinach, which will be drawn out in the cooking, so no more is needed.

To Vary the Flavor of Spinach: Finely chopped spinach is excellent in a cream sauce, seasoned with freshly ground nutmeg. Mushrooms are very good with spinach, either in a cream sauce in the center of a spinach ring or sautéed and mixed with the spinach. Also, spinach is very good finely minced, with a bit of onion, garlic, seasonings, and chopped clams with their liquor stirred in!

Plenty of vegetables, raw and cooked, are essential to a good diet. There are many ways of cooking them. They can be boiled, steamed, braised, sautéed, and stir-fried, to name a few of the possibilities. Vary your ways of serving them to keep your family interested in eating them.

Whether you serve vegetables straight from the garden, or preserved by you in the proper season, or in commercial cans or frozen packages is for you to decide. For instance, I happen to like fresh peas, frozen peas, and tiny canned peas, and to my mind they are three quite different vegetables. On the whole, though, I prefer fresh or frozen vegetables to canned ones.

Vichyssoise: A cold leek-and-potato soup, cooked with chicken stock, pureed, then blended with cream and served chilled, topped with minced chives. This soup was invented by Louis Diat of the Ritz Carlton Hotel in New York.

Vinegars: The vinegar to which most of us are accustomed is cider vinegar, pale gold in color and fairly sharp in flavor. It is used in salad dressings, and in some cooking. White or distilled vinegar is used mostly for pickling. There are also red and white wine vinegars that are used for salad dressings. Wine vinegars are often flavored with tarragon, garlic, basil, and other herbs. You can also make raspberry vinegar at home—something our ancestors found delicious to drink on a hot summer's day.

W

Waffles: You will, of course, need a waffle iron to serve these delicious breakfast treats. One thing to remember about that utensil is that you should grease it only the first time you use it. Brush it well with unsalted fat, then bake one waffle until it is good and brown. Throw that waffle out. From then on, wipe the waffle iron out after use. Never wash it.

Amount of Batter To Be Used: The compartments should not be full or the batter will overflow. Put about a tablespoonful of batter in the center of each compartment (depending upon the size of your waffle iron). The batter will then flow out to cover the entire compartment.

When the Waffle Is Done: Unless you have an electric iron, which signals when the waffle is done, the best test is to watch for the moment when steam stops escaping.

Waldorf Salad: (*See* under Salads.)

Water Chestnuts: The fresh ones, which can sometimes be bought in Chinatown, are far the best in flavor and texture, but the canned, which are widely distributed, make a satisfactory substitute.

Welsh Rarebit: Often called a "rabbit," probably because of frequent mispronunciation, a Welsh rarebit is a mixture of melted cheddar cheese, stale ale or beer, egg, and seasonings, stirred until smooth over hot, not boiling, water and served over buttered toast.

Wheat Germ: This is a part of the wheat kernel called the embryo, from which the new plant starts its growth. It is a concentrated source of protein, iron, vitamin E, and the B vitamins. Its nutritional significance in the ordinary diet is limited because such small amounts are eaten, alone or combined with other foods.

Wine in Cooking: The following list is a good basic one for the wines

you will want on your shelf for cooking purposes. They are used with
the suggested *types* of food.

Dry white:	Fish and chicken
Dry red:	Meats and chicken
Dry white vermouth:	Fish, chicken, veal, and soups
Sherry, dry:	Fish, chicken, soups (added at the end of cooking)
Sherry, sweet:	Desserts
Madeira:	Chicken livers, brown sauces, ham
Port:	Meats, duck, chicken
Marsala:	Veal, desserts

Alcohol in Wine-Flavored Dishes: Many people want to know
whether they are adding a lot of alcohol to dishes by using wine or liqueurs in them. They are adding practically none, as the process of
cooking or flambéing evaporates the alcohol, leaving only the flavor.
This would not be true in the case where you simply pour a liqueur
over dessert, but you do not use enough to make it very alcoholic!

Cheap Wines in Cooking: If by "cheap wines" one means wines of
inferior quality, they should certainly not be used in cooking. On the
other hand, there are lots of relatively inexpensive wines that are delightful to drink and thus fine for cooking. The premise, in general, is
that you do not use wines in cooking that you would not care to
drink. It is better not to use wine in your dishes at all than to ruin
their flavor with inferior wine.

Rules for Cooking with Wine: There aren't any. There are suggestions to help guide you in regard to which wines are best with which
foods, but as in all flavoring situations, you must experiment and
taste to discover what suits you best. You may be quite unorthodox
in your choices and still feel pleased with the results. Just remember,
as you start to use wines in your cooking, that the guidelines have
been developed over a long time by people who know how to cook
with wine, and they are worth following, at least at the start.

Same Wine for Cooking and Drinking: This is a pretty good rule to follow. If you do so, there will be no conflict of taste between the wine you serve and that used in the sauce. For instance, it would be a mistake to cook a chicken in white wine and then serve a red to drink at the meal. The red would overwhelm the white in the sauce. On the other hand, if you have cooked the chicken in red wine, you will do well to serve the same red to drink with the meal.

Sauterne in Cooking: There is a great American illusion to the effect that sauterne is a dry white wine. It is a sweet dessert wine, not dry. It can be used in making desserts, but spoils the taste of any entrée.

Wine in a Marinade: A good guideline is to use half wine and half water in the marinade, though the proportions may vary. If you use all wine, the flavor may be too strong.

Wine in Sauce or Gravy: As a guide, I would suggest one or two tablespoons per cup of the sauce or gravy.

Y

Yeast: Many devoted bakers (of the home variety) feel that fresh yeast (also known as "compressed" yeast) is the best kind. But sometimes, nowadays, it is hard to find, and one can get good results from dry yeast. When a recipe calls for one ounce of fresh yeast, the equivalent is two packages of dry yeast.

Yogurt: Yogurt is a custard-like food made by fermenting partly evaporated milk with Bulgarian bacillus. It has a slightly acid taste. In the Middle Eastern countries, where it is greatly used, yogurt is made from buffalo milk and is very rich, quite unlike our rather pallid counterparts.

Yogurt is a very good substitute to use in Indian curry recipes where "curd" is called for.

Z

Zabaglione: This is a mixture of eggs, sugar, and Marsala wine, beaten over hot water until thick and foamy. It is an Italian dessert which is served warm. It is also a dessert sauce.

Zest: The peel of an orange or lemon, carefully taken off the fruit so that the white part is not included.

Zucchini: This delicious vegetable is a variant of the common pumpkin, but to cooks it is variously known as Courgette, vegetable marrow, Italian squash, and Cocozelle. It is exceedingly popular in Greece and Italy and has become increasingly grown and appreciated here. If you buy small ones for most uses, it is unnecessary ever to peel them, and that's good because the color of the skin is most appetizing.

Cut into thin sticks, zucchini is excellent for a platter of *Crudités*. It can also be used raw in salad to good effect.

Zucchini is very good sautéed in olive oil or butter with garlic, onion, and sometimes Italian plum tomatoes. It is also good stir-fried in olive oil, well seasoned, and with other vegetables added, if so desired.

At the famous White Tower Restaurant in London (it's Greek), I got a recipe for their Courgettes Farcies à la Corfiote. To make it, you cut zucchini in half and remove the meat, leaving only a thin coating of it on the skin. The removed meat of the vegetable, chopped, is then mixed with chopped beef, onion, mint leaves, cooked rice, and seasonings, put back into the squashes and baked, with a bit of chicken stock in the bottom of the baking dish. The zucchini are removed to a serving dish and kept warm. With the remaining chicken stock (not more than half a cup), you make a sauce by adding cream, beaten egg yolk, butter, and lemon juice, cooked over low heat, stirring constantly, until slightly thickened. Serve poured over the squash.

I make my own variation of that dish by substituting well seasoned sausage meat for the beef, omitting the mint leaves and rice. I also sprinkle the stuffed squash with freshly grated Parmesan cheese before baking them. The sauce is the same—and it's good, if I do say so myself.

Zuppa Inglese: An Italian dessert (created for Lady Hamilton, Nelson's mistress) which is similar to an English trifle. It is made from ladyfingers, rum, and Crème Patissière, chilled in the refrigerator until set, and topped with whipped cream for serving.

EQUIVALENT WEIGHTS AND MEASURES

Familiar Designation	Equivalent	Weights in Ounces
Dash or pinch	A very small amount; vague—better to add ingredient "to taste"	
1½ teaspoons	½ tablespoon	¼ fluid ounce
1 tablespoon	3 teaspoons	½ fluid ounce
¼ cup	4 tablespoons	2 ounces
⅓ cup	5 tablespoons, plus 1 teaspoon	4½ ounces, plus a pinch or two more
⅜ cup	¼ cup, plus 1 tablespoon	2½ ounces
⅝ cup	½ cup, plus 2 tablespoons	5 ounces
⅞ cup	¾ cup, plus 2 tablespoons	7 ounces
1 cup	16 tablespoons or ½ pint	8 ounces (about)
1 pint	2 cups	1 pound (about)
1 quart	2 pints or 4 cups	2 pounds (about)
1 gallon	4 quarts	8 pounds (about)
1 liter (fluid)	1.057 liquid quarts	
1 ounce	28.35 grams	
1 pound	16 ounces or .454 kilograms	
1 gill	½ cup	4 fluid ounces
1 centiliter	2 teaspoons	.338 fluid ounces

EQUIVALENT WEIGHTS AND MEASURES
OF SPECIFIC FOODS

Food	Weight of One Cup in Ounces (about)	Measurement of One Pound in Cups (about)
Cottage or Cream Cheese	8	2
Liquid fats and oils	8	2
Solid fats (butter, margarine, lard)	8	2
Hydrogenated fats	6⅔	2½
Dry bread crumbs	3¼	5
Soft, fresh bread crumbs	1½	10
Cornmeal	5	3
Macaroni	4	4
Noodles	2⅔	6
Spaghetti	3⅓	4¾
Flour	4	4
Whole Wheat Flour	4¼	3¾
Cake flour	3⅓	4¾
Apples, peeled and diced	3⅓	3¾
Bananas, mashed	8	2
Bananas, sliced	7¼	2¼
Coconut, canned, moist	3	5⅓
Almonds (blanched, whole)	5½	3
Filberts	4¾	3⅓
Peanuts	5	3¼
Pecans, halved	3¾	4¼
Walnuts, halved	3½	4½
Seedless raisins, whole	5¾	2¾
Chocolate, melted	9	1¾

(continued on following page)

Food	Weight of One Cup in Ounces (about)	Measurement of One Pound in Cups (about)
Cocoa	4	4
Coffee	3	5⅓
Meat, ground, raw	8	2
Kidney and lima beans (dried)	6½	2½
Split peas (dried)	7	2¼
Sugar, brown and granulated	7	2¼
Sugar, superfine	7	2⅓
Sugar, confectioner's, sifted	4½	3½
Corn Syrup	11½	1⅓
Honey	12	1⅓
Maple Syrup	11	1½
Molasses	11½	1⅓
Cabbage, shredded, packed down	2½	6
Carrots, cut up	3¾	3¾
Mushrooms, cut up	3	5
Onions, sliced or diced	4	4
Potatoes, sliced or diced	4	4
Rice, raw	8	2

METRIC COOKING MEASURES—APPROXIMATIONS

Metric (millimeters)	Familiar Designation (cups)
250	1
200	¾, plus 1 tablespoon
190	¾
150	⅔
125	½
100	⅓, plus 1 tablespoon
75	⅓
50	¼
25	2 tablespoons
15	1 tablespoon
5	1 teaspoon
2	½ teaspoon
1	¼ teaspoon

To convert oven temperature from Celsius to Fahrenheit:

Celsius	Fahrenheit	Description of Oven Temperature
120–140	250–275	Very slow
150–160	300–350	Slow
180–190	350–375	Moderate
200–220	400–425	Hot
230–250	450–475	Very hot
260–270	500–525	Extremely hot

If recipe calls for the following pans:

Metric	Familiar Designation
33 x 23 x 55 cm oblong pan	13 x 9 x 2"
20 x .4 cm round pan	8 x 1½"
23 x .4 cm round pan	9 x 1½"
20 x 20 x .5 cm square pan	8 x 8 x 2"
23 x 23 x .5 cm square pan	9 x 9 x 2"
20 cm pie plate	8" pie plate
23 cm pie plate	9" pie plate
1 liter casserole	1 quart casserole
500 ml mold	2-cup mold

cm = centimeters   ml = millimeters

Index

N16